# BASIC
# FINANCIAL
# MANAGEMENT

# STUDY GUIDE

# BASIC FINANCIAL MANAGEMENT

**John D. Martin**
Texas A & M University

**J. William Petty**
Texas Tech University

**Arthur J. Keown**
Virginia Polytechnic Institute
and State University

**David F. Scott, Jr.**
Virginia Polytechnic Institute
and State University

PRENTICE-HALL, Inc., Englewood Cliffs, New Jersey 07632

Editorial/production supervision and
     interior design by Barbara Alexander

Manufacturing buyer:  Trudy Pisciotti

Printed in the United States of America

10  9  8  7  6  5  4  3  2  1

ISBN:  0-13-060558-1

Prentice-Hall International, Inc., London
Prentice-Hall of Australia Pty. Limited, Sydney
Prentice-Hall of Canada, Ltd., Toronto
Prentice-Hall of India Private Limited, New Delhi
Prentice-Hall of Japan, Inc., Tokyo
Prentice-Hall of Southeast Asia Pte. Ltd., Singapore
Whitehall Books Limited, Wellington, New Zealand

# Contents

# *Preface*

The objective of this Study Guide is to provide a student-oriented supplement to <u>Basic Financial Management</u>. There are two basic ways in which we have attempted to accomplish that end. The first involves providing a condensation of each chapter in the form of a detailed sentence outline. This overview of the key points of the chapter can serve both as a preview and quick survey of the chapter content and as a review. A second way in which we have attempted to accomplish our overall objective is through providing problems (with detailed solutions) and self-tests which can be used to aid in the preparation of outside assignments and in studying for examinations. The problems were keyed to the end-of-chapter problems in the text in order to provide a direct and meaningful student aid. Both multiple-choice and true-false questions are used to provide a self-test over the descriptive chapter material. The outline, problems and solutions, and self-tests combined provide what we believe is a valuable learning tool for the student of financial management.

# BASIC FINANCIAL MANAGEMENT

# The Role of Financial Management

Orientation: The role of the financial manager has undergone dramatic changes during this century. Currently the financial manager has a major voice in all aspects of both the raising and allocation of financial capital. This chapter focuses on the development of financial thought, the goal of the firm, the financial decision-making process and a brief preview of the book.

I. Development of financial thought

   A. To a large extent, the economic and business activity of the time determined what was of primary importance in the field of finance.

      1. During the early 1900's financial and economic news emphasized consolidations, mergers, and public regulation. Thus, these topics received the majority of attention in the field of finance.

      2. As the economy began to expand in the 1920's emphasis in finance shifted to methods and procedures for acquiring funds.

      3. The business failures of the 1930's caused an increased

emphasis to be placed on bankruptcy, liquidity management, and avoidance of financial problems.

    4. During the 1940's and early 1950's an increased emphasis was given to liquidity management and cash budgeting.

B. While the economic environment continued to affect financial thought, many factors together helped to bring about dramatic changes in the mid-1950's. During this time the field of finance evolved to one dealing with all aspects of acquiring and efficiently utilizing those funds.

C. The field of finance continues to develop, being reshaped by economic activity, primarily increased inflationary worries, and new theoretical developments.

II. Goal of the firm

A. In this book we will designate maximization of shareholder wealth, by which we mean maximization of the total market value of the firm's common stock, to be the goal of the firm. To understand this goal and its inclusive nature it is first necessary to understand the difficulties involved with the frequently suggested goal of profit maximization.

B. While the goal of profit maximization stresses the efficient use of capital resources, it assumes away many of the complexities of the real world and for this reason is unacceptable.

    1. One of the major criticisms of profit maximization is that it assumes away uncertainty of returns. That is, projects are compared by examining their expected values or weighted average profit.

    2. Profit maximization is also criticized because it assumes away timing differences of returns.

C. Profit maximization is unacceptable and a more realistic goal is needed.

III. Maximization of shareholder wealth

A. We have chosen the goal of shareholder wealth maximization because the effects of all financial decisions are included in this goal.

B. In order to employ this goal we need not consider every price change to be a market interpretation of the worth of our decisions. What we do focus on is the effect that our decision _should_ have on the stock price if everything were held constant.

IV. Financial decisions and risk-return relationships

   A. Almost all financial decisions involve some sort of risk-return tradeoff.

   B. In general, the more risk the firm is willing to assume, the higher will be the expected return from the given course of action.

## Self-Tests

TRUE-FALSE

_____   1. Profit maximization is considered to be a more appropriate goal than shareholder wealth maximization because it considers the timing of the expected returns of the firm.

_____   2. Shareholder wealth maximization considers the effects of the riskiness of a prospective earnings stream.

_____   3. Originally, the role of the financial manager of a firm was very extensive (covering many areas of the firm); recently, however, the manager's responsibilities have been narrowed so that he or she might devote more time to raising funds.

_____   4. Two major criticisms of the profit maximization goal are that it does not deal adequately with the uncertainty and the timing of returns.

_____   5. Historically, economic activity and business activity have strongly affected the development of financial thought.

_____   6. During the mid-1950's the point of view of finance shifted from that of an insider charged with the management and control of the firm's operations to that of an outsider assessing the condition and performance of a firm.

_____   7. In general, the less risk a firm is willing to assume, the higher the expected return will be from a given course of action.

_____   8. Business failures of the 1930's caused an increased emphasis to be placed on bankruptcy, liquidity management, and avoidance of financial problems.

_____   9. The business expansion of the 1920's caused a shift in the emphasis in finance from mergers and regulation to methods and procedures for acquiring funds.

_____  10. In order to employ the goal of shareholder wealth maximization, every stock price change should be considered to be a market interpretation of the worth of our financial decisions.

MULTIPLE CHOICE

1. The long-run goal of the firm is to:

   a. Hold large quantities of cash.
   b. Increase sales regularly.
   c. Maximize earnings per share.
   d. Maximize shareholder wealth.

2. Maximizing shareholder wealth means maximizing the:

   a. Value of the firm's assets.
   b. Value of the firm's cash.
   c. Value of the firm's investments.
   d. Value of the firm's profits.
   e. Market value of the firm's common stock.

3. The financial manager is concerned with which of the following:

   a. Determining the proper amount of funds to employ in the firm.
   b. Seeing that the financial statements of the firm are properly presented.
   c. Raising funds for the firm on the most favorable terms possible.
   d. a and b.
   e. a and c.

4. Important functions of financial management are:

   a. To provide for adequate financing.
   b. Long-range planning.
   c. To control costs.
   d. To identify desirable investment projects.
   e. All of the above.

5. Profit maximization is not the proper objective of a firm because:

   a. It is not as inclusive a goal as the maximization of shareholder wealth.
   b. It does not consider the uncertainty of the return.

    c. It does not consider the timing of the returns.
    d. All of the above.
    e. None of the above.

6. The market price of a share of stock is determined by:

    a. The New York Stock Exchange.
    b. The Federal Reserve.
    c. The company's management.
    d. Individuals buying and selling the stock.

7. The management of working capital deals with:

    a. The management of long-term assets.
    b. The management of long-term liabilities.
    c. The management of current assets.
    d. All of the above.
    e. None of the above.

# 2

# Legal Forms of Organization and the Tax Environment

Orientation:  The objective of this chapter is to afford the student a familiarity with the legal setting in which the firm operates.  In this regard, the basic forms of business organization are reviewed. Also, a highlight of the basic tax implications relating to financial decisions is given consideration.

I. Legal forms of business organization

A. Sole proprietorship: A business owned by a single person and that has a minimum amount of legal structure.

1. Advantages:

a. Easily established with few complications.

b. Minimal organizational costs.

c. Does not have to share profits or control with others.

2. Disadvantages:

a. Unlimited liability for the owner.

b. Owner must absorb all losses.

c. Equity capital limited to the owner's personal investment.

B. Partnership: Similar to proprietorship except that there is more than one owner.

   1. Two types of partnerships:

      a. General partnership: Relationship between partners is dictated by the partnership agreement.

         (1) Advantages:

            (a) Minimal organizational requirements.

            (b) Negligible government regulations.

         (2) Disadvantages:

            (a) All partners have unlimited liability.

            (b) Difficult to raise large amounts of capital.

      b. Limited partnership

         (1) There must be at least one general partner who has unlimited liability in the partnership.

         (2) Names of limited partners may not appear in the name of the firm.

         (3) Limited partners may not participate in the management of the business.

         (4) Advantages:

            (a) For the limited partners, liability is limited to the amount of capital invested in the company.

            (b) Withdrawal or death of a limited partner does not affect the continuity of the business.

            (c) Stronger inducement in raising capital.

C. The corporation: An "impersonal" legal entity having the power to purchase, sell, and own assets and to incur liabilities while existing separately and apart from its owners.

   1. Ownership is evidenced by shares of stock.

   2. Advantages:

      a. Limited liability of owners.

      b. Ease of transferability of ownership.

      c. The death of an owner does not result in the discontinuity of the firm's life.

      d. Ability to raise large amounts of capital is increased.

  3. Disadvantage: Most difficult and expensive to establish.

II. Federal income taxation

  A. Objectives of federal income taxation

    1. Provide government revenues.

    2. Achieve socially desirable goals.

    3. Stabilize the economy.

  B. Income taxes for individuals

    1. Measuring taxable income

      a. Gross income: Any wealth that flows to the taxpayer, except the principal part of an investment.

      b. Exclusions from gross income include gifts, inherited property, life insurance proceeds, disability benefits, dividend exclusions, interest on state and municipal securities, and others.

      c. Deductions to determine adjusted gross income: trade or business expenses, employee expenses, losses from sale or exchange of property, moving expenses, and others.

      d. Itemized deductions: medical expenses, contributions, taxes, interest, and others.

      e. Deductions (called exemptions) may be taken for the taxpayer (personal exemptions), for dependents within the family, for old-age, and for blindness.

    2. Individual capital gains and losses

      a. Short-term capital gains are taxed as ordinary income.

      b. One-half of long-term gains are taxed, with the maximum effective tax rate not to exceed 25%.

      c. Net short-term capital losses are deductible by the lesser of the actual loss, the amount of ordinary income or $2,000.

      d. Only 50% of net long-term capital losses are recog-

nized in reducing taxable income, with the limitations
being the same as those for short-term losses.

C. Income taxes for partnerships

   1. Partnership tax return reports every transaction that has
   a tax consequence and allocates the transactions as specified by the partnership agreement.

   2. The individual partners report their portions of the
   partnership income within their personal tax returns.

D. Income taxes for corporations

   1. Taxable income is determined in a similar manner as for
   the individual.

   2. Special deductions

      a. Dividend deductions: 85% of any dividends received
      from another corporation are tax exempt.

      b. A special deduction for income from foreign corpora-
      tions will exist until year-end 1979.

      c. Charitable contributions may be deducted if they do
      not exceed 5% of taxable income.  Contributions ex-
      ceeding this limitation may be carried forward into
      the 5 succeeding years.

   3. Corporate rate structure: The rates are 20% on the first
   $25,000 taxable income; 22% on income greater than
   $25,000 but not exceeding $50,000; and 48% on any additional profits.

   4. Capital gains and losses

      a. Short-term capital losses are subtracted from short-
      term capital gains, with any net gain being added to
      the corporation's ordinary income.

      b. Any net long-term capital gains in excess of net
      short-term capital losses are taxed at a rate not to
      exceed 30%.

      c. If after deducting all capital gains and capital loss-
      es the company has a net capital loss, such loss may
      be carried back for 3 years and forward for 5 years to
      offset any capital gains occurring during those
      periods.

5. Net operating loss: If a corporation has an operating loss in any year, the loss may be applied against the profits in the 3 prior years. If the loss has not been completely absorbed by the profits in these 3 years, the loss may be carried forward to each of the 7 following years.

6. Depreciation

   a. Three depreciation methods, among others, may be used for tax purposes:

      (1) Straight-line.

      (2) Double-declining balance.

      (3) Sum-of-the-years' digits.

   b. A long-term capital gain from the sale of a <u>depreciable</u> asset is treated as ordinary income to the extent of the accumulated depreciation. Any gain beyond this amount is considered to be a capital gain.

7. Investment tax credit is available to corporations and individuals who invest in certain types of qualified assets.

   a. Up to 10% of the total cost of a qualified asset may be used to offset taxes paid by the taxpayer.

   b. The credit is limited to the first $25,000 of the taxes plus one-half of the remaining taxes.

   c. The credit is restricted in terms of the useful life of the asset, with the entire dollar investment qualifying if the useful life is 7 years or more and less if the life is below 7 years.

8. Accumulated earnings tax is a penalty surtax assessed on the corporation on any accumulation of earnings by a corporation for the purpose of avoiding taxes by its shareholders.

9. Subchapter S corporation

   a. Subchapter S of the Internal Revenue Code permits the owners of a small corporation with 10 or fewer stockholders to use the corporate organizational form but be taxed as though the firm were a partnership.

      b. This treatment eliminates the double taxation normally associated with the corporate entity.

  D. Implications of taxes in financial decision making

    1. Taxes and capital investment decisions

      a. When a plant or equipment acquisition is being considered, the returns from the investment should be measured on an after-tax basis.

      b. The depreciation method will have an impact on the timing of taxes.

      c. The estimated salvage value also may have a tax impact; the greater the anticipated salvage value, the less the amount of annual depreciation charges.

    2. Taxes and the firm's capital structure: The tax deductibility of interest payments gives debt financing a definite cost advantage over preferred stock and common stock.

    3. Taxes and corporate dividend policies: The differential tax treatment for the firm's common investors might influence their preference between capital gains and dividends, which affects dividend policy.

## Study Problems

1. Bob James, who is single, had ordinary income of $150,000 in 1979. He also experienced a capital gain of $35,000 resulting from the sale of some common stock. What would he be required to pay in taxes?

  SOLUTION

  (1) Tax on ordinary income:

      $53,090 + 70% ($150,000 - $102,200) = $86,550

  (2) Tax on long-term capital gain:

      $35,000 X 25%                                              8,750

    Total tax liability                                          $95,300

2. Kenneth Moore had $35,000 of ordinary income in 1979.  He had a long-term capital loss on the sale of securities of $7,250 and a short-term capital loss of $900.

(a) What is his taxable income in 1979?

(b) What amounts of short-term and long-term capital losses will he carry forward?

SOLUTION

(a)

| | | |
|---|---|---|
| Ordinary income | | $35,000 |
| Capital loss reported in 1979: | | |
| Short-term loss | $ 900 | |
| Long-term loss to be reported (1/2 of $7,250) | 3,625 | |
| | $4,525 | |
| Maximum limit | $3,000 | |
| Deduction from ordinary income (lesser of $4,525 and $3,000) | | 3,000 |
| Taxable income for 1979 | | $32,000 |

(b)

Carry forward

| | |
|---|---|
| Loss that could be reported if no $3,000 limitation existed | $4,525 |
| Loss reported in 1979 | 3,000 |
| Loss carry forward | $1,525 |

3. John Gresham's salary this past year was $42,000.  He is married and has three children.  He contributed $1,500 during the year to a university; taxes and interest on his residence were $500 and $3,400, respectively.  His investment income this year amounted to $1,000 in dividends and $2,500 in interest.  These investments were owned jointly with his wife.  Compute Gresham's taxable income and tax liability.

SOLUTION

| | | |
|---|---|--:|
| Salary | | $42,000 |
| Dividends | | 1,000 |
| Interest | | 2,500 |
| Total income | | $45,500 |
| Dividend exclusion | | 200 |
| Gross income | | $45,300 |
| Deductions: | | |
| Contributions | $1,500 | |
| Taxes | 500 | |
| Interest | 3,400 | |
| Gross deductions | $5,400 | |
| Non-deductible amount | 3,200 | |
| Excess deductions | | 2,200 |
| Personal exemptions ($750 X 5) | | 3,750 |
| Taxable income | | $39,350 |
| Tax liability: | | |
| $10,340 + 45% ($39,350 - $39,200) = | | $10,407.50 |

4. A corporation had $145,000 in taxable earnings in 1979.  What is the tax liability?

SOLUTION

| Income | | Marginal Tax Rate | | Tax Liability |
|---|---|---|---|---|
| $ 25,000 | X | 20% | | $ 5,000 |
| 25,000 | X | 22% | | 5,500 |
| 95,000 | X | 48% | | 45,600 |
| $145,000 | | Total tax liability = | | $56,100 |

5. A corporation has earnings before interest and taxes of $86,000, dividend income of $8,000, and interest expenses of $9,000. Also, a contribution to a university was made in the amount of $1,000. What is the corporation's (a) taxable income and (b) tax liability?

SOLUTION

(a)

| | | |
|---|---:|---:|
| Operating income | | $86,000 |
| Dividend income | $8,000 | |
| Dividend exclusion 85% X $8,000 | 6,800 | |
| Taxable dividend income | | 1,200 |
| Interest expense | | (9,000) |
| Contribution | | (1,000) |
| Taxable income | | $77,200 |

(b)

| | | | | | |
|---|---|---:|---|---:|---|
| 20% | X | $25,000 | = | $ 5,000 | |
| 22% | X | 25,000 | = | 5,500 | |
| 48% | X | 27,200 | = | 13,056 | |
| | | $77,200 | | $23,556 | - Tax liability |

6. In 1972 the W-W Company purchased machinery for $60,000 that had a depreciable life of 12 years and a zero salvage value. Seven years later the firm sold the equipment for $75,000. The firm has a marginal tax rate of 48% and a capital gains rate of 30% and uses straight-line depreciation. What would be the tax liability resulting from the sale?

SOLUTION

| | | |
|---|---:|---:|
| Sale price | | $75,000 |
| Original cost | $60,000 | |
| Accumulated depreciation | 35,000 | |

Book value                                                              $25,000

Gain                                                                    50,000

Sale price over original
  cost                                     $15,000 (capital gain)

Recapture of depreciation                 $35,000 (ordinary income)

Taxes = (0.48) ($35,000) + (0.3) ($15,000) = $21,300

7. The taxable income of Broghm Corporation is as follows (losses are shown in parentheses):

|  |  |
|------|--------|
| 1970 | $ (125,000) |
| 1971 | 150,000 |
| 1972 | 300,000 |
| 1973 | (150,000) |
| 1974 | ( 20,000) |
| 1975 | 350,000 |
| 1976 | 400,000 |

What is Broghm's tax payment or tax refund in each year?

SOLUTION

| Year | Taxable Income Before Carry-Back or Carry-Forward | Tax Payment | Carry-Back | Carry-Forward | Tax Refunds |
|------|------|------|------|------|------|
| 1970 | $(125,000) | $ 0 | | | |
| 1971 | 150,000 | 5,000 | $ 25,000 from 1973 | $125,000 from 1970 | |
| 1972 | 300,000 | 130,500 | $125,000 from 1973 | | |
| | | | $ 20,000 from 1974 | | |
| 1973 | (150,000) | 0 | | | $65,000* |

*1973 refund = $5,000 (1971 taxes) + $60,000 (correction of 1972 taxes from $300,000 to $175,000).

| Year | Taxable Income Before Carry-Back or Carry-Forward | Tax Payment | Carry-Back | Carry-Forward | Tax Refunds |
|------|------|------|------|------|------|
| 1974 | $( 20,000) | $ 0 | | | $ 9,600[†] |
| 1975 | 350,000 | 154,500 | | | |
| 1976 | 400,000 | 178,500 | | | |

[†]1974 refund = $9,600 (correction of 1972 taxes from $175,000 to $155,000).

## Self-Tests

TRUE-FALSE

_____ 1. If a capital asset is held for more than 6 months and then sold for a gain, the gain is classified as a long-term capital gain.

_____ 2. Many businesses are formed as corporations because of the ease of establishment.

_____ 3. In a limited partnership there must be at least one general partner with unlimited liability.

_____ 4. The income from a partnership is reported by the partners in their personal tax returns.

_____ 5. Interest and dividend payments made by a corporation are tax deductible by the paying corporation.

_____ 6. For corporations, capital losses are not deductible against ordinary income.

_____ 7. When an acquisition of a plant or equipment is being considered, the returns from the investment should be measured on a before-tax basis.

_____ 8. A business that is formed as a Subchapter S corporation avoids the double taxation of income.

_____ 9. If the sum-of-the-years'-digits form of depreciation is used, the asset is never fully depreciated.

_____ 10. Charitable contributions of any amount may be deducted from ordinary income of a corporation.

   _____ 11. Long-term capital gains for individuals are always taxed at one-half of the individual's ordinary income tax rate up to a maximum rate of 25%.

   _____ 12. If a capital asset is sold for a price in excess of its depreciated book value but for less than its original cost, the gain is subject to a capital-gains tax.

MULTIPLE CHOICE

1. An individual's short-term capital gains are taxed:

   a. As ordinary income.
   b. At a rate not to exceed 25% of the gain.
   c. At one-half of the individual's ordinary tax rate.
   d. None of the above.

2. Advantages of the corporation include:

   a. Transferability of ownership.
   b. Unlimited liability.
   c. Ability of the corporation to raise capital.
   d. Double taxation of dividend income.
   e. a and c.
   f. a and b.

3. Disadvantages of the partnership are:

   a. Expense of formation.
   b. Lack of permanence.
   c. Double taxation on income.
   d. Unlimited liability.
   e. b and d.
   f. a and d.

4. A corporation owning stock in another corporation is taxed on what percentage of the dividends received from the owned corporation?

   a. 15%.
   b. 85%.
   c. 48%.
   c. 50%.

5. Which of the following is an advantage of the partnership?

   a. Limited liability.
   b. A voice in the management of the partnership.

   c. Limited life.
   d. a and b.
   e. a and c.

6. For corporations, net long-term capital gains are limited to a tax rate of:

   a. 50%.
   b. 48%.
   c. 30%.
   d. 22%.

7. Which of the following forms of business organization is the largest in number?

   a. Corporation.
   b. Partnership.
   c. Sole proprietorship.

8. If a corporation sustains a net operating loss, this loss may be:

   a. Deducted against long-term capital gains.
   b. Carried back 3 years and forward 5 years to offset taxable income.
   c. Carried back 5 years and forward 3 years to offset taxable income.

9. Advantages of the sole proprietorship are:

   a. Unlimited liability.
   b. Ease of formation.
   c. Double taxation.
   d. Nominal organizational costs.
   e. b and d.

10. The pair containing one advantage and one disadvantage of the corporation is:

   a. Costly to form and lack of secrecy.
   b. Unlimited liability and ease of transferability of ownership.
   c. Limited liability and more complex to form.
   d. Limited liability and perpetual life.
   e. a and c.
   f. b and c.

# Financial Analysis

Orientation:  Financial analysis can be defined as the process of assessing the financial condition of a firm.  The principal analytical tool of financial analysis is the financial ratio.  In Chapter 3 we provide an overview of a firm's basic financial statements followed by a survey of a set of key financial ratios and a discussion of their effective use.

I. Basic financial statements

   A. The <u>balance sheet</u> represents a statement of the financial position of the firm on a given date, its asset holdings, liabilities, and owner supplied equity.  This statement is considered to be the most important financial statement for judging the economic well-being of the firm.  The balance sheet consists of two basic components:  (1) assets and (2) liabilities plus owner's equity.

      1. On the asset side of the balance sheet we usually find two categories.

         a. <u>Current assets</u> are those assets that are expected to be realized in cash, sold, or consumed either in 1

       year or within the operating cycle of the firm, which-
       ever is longer.

   b. <u>Noncurrent assets</u> contain all those resources which
      are not expected to be converted into cash within the
      operating cycle of the firm.  Security investments,
      plant and equipment, and land are the most common non-
      current assets.

2. Liabilities represent the outstanding claims held against
   a firm's assets and are reported at their stated value.
   There are two basic categories of liabilities.

   a. <u>Current liabilities</u> represent obligations that are
      reasonably expected to be liquidated within 1 year.

   b. <u>Noncurrent liabilities</u> include permanent obligations
      of the firm that are not reasonably expected to be
      liquidated within the normal operating cycle of the
      firm but are payable at some later date.  Noncurrent
      liabilities are often referred to as long-term liabil-
      ities.

3. <u>Owner's equity</u> represents the book value of the owner's
   interest in the assets of the firm.  Owner's equity is
   comprised of capital stock and retained earnings (undis-
   tributed earnings).

B. The <u>income statement</u> represents an attempt to measure the
  net results of a firm's operations over a specified time
  interval.  Some of the more important components of the income statement are discussed below:

1. <u>Sales</u> represent the total net sale of products or services attributable to the period.  Under the accrual
   method of accounting, no distinction is made between
   cash and credit sales and only those sales directly
   attributable to normal operations are included under
   this sales category.

2. <u>Cost of goods sold</u> is simply the cost of the product sold
   or service provided.  There are two widely used methods
   for computing cost of goods sold.  The FIFO, or first-in,
   first-out method assigns to cost of goods sold the prices
   the firm paid on the oldest items in inventory. The LIFO,
   or last-in, first-out method, assigns cost to items sold
   based on the cost of the most recently purchased inventory item.  The method selected can have a very important

effect on net earnings for a period in which prices have risen or fallen significantly.  Cash flows under each of these methods differ according to the amount of income taxes paid by the firm.

3. Gross profit represents the amount by which sales exceed cost of goods sold.

4. Selling expense includes all those expenses incurred in the process of making the period's sales.

5. General and administrative expenses include all those operating expenses not directly attributed to the cost of merchandise sold or selling expenses.  These expenses usually include administrative salaries, utilities, non-income related taxes, insurance, and depreciation.  Depreciation is not a cash expense; it represents an attempt to allocate the cost of the firm's plant and equipment against the periods in which those assets are being used. The most commonly used methods are straight-line, sum-of-the-years' digits, and double-declining balance.  The latter two are referred to as accelerated methods because they provide for a more rapid rate of expensing the capitalized cost of the asset than does the straight-line method.

6. Net operating income reflects the net results of a firm's operations before considering financing costs and income taxes.

7. Net income after taxes represents net earnings for the period after income taxes.

8. Retained earnings for the period represent any earnings that remain after all dividends have been paid to stockholders.  This amount is then added to the existing retained earnings figure on the balance sheet.

C. The statement of changes in financial position, often referred to as a sources and uses statement, provides a specific period of time and the uses to which they were put. The information contained in this statement makes a very useful tool of financial analysis.  Two forms of source and use statements are currently acceptable.

1. The statement of sources and uses of working capital is designed to "explain" the change in the net working capital position of a firm for some stated period of time.

Sources and uses of net working capital can be summarized in terms of the following grid:

|                 | Sources | Uses |
|-----------------|---------|------|
| Fixed assets    | -       | +    |
| Long-term debt  | +       | -    |
| Common stock    | +       | -    |
| Net income      | +       | -    |

where the minus sign (-) indicates a decrease and the plus sign (+) an increase in the asset, liability, or owner's equity account. Thus, a decrease in fixed assets would be a source of net working capital whereas an increase in common stock would involve a use. The source and use of working capital statement does not detail the changes in current assets and current liabilities. To obtain this information, it is necessary to either add on a section to the working capital statement or prepare the more detailed source and use of funds (cash) statement.

2. The sources and uses of funds statement explains changes in cash for the period rather than net working capital whereby changes in current assets and liabilities are individually analyzed. In preparing this statement the analyst must consider the changes in the items in the above grid plus the following:

|                           | Sources | Uses |
|---------------------------|---------|------|
| Current asset account     | -       | +    |
| Current liability account | +       | -    |

II. Overview of financial ratios

A. Financial ratios provide the analysts with a means for making meaningful comparison of a firm's financial data over time and with other firms. Thus, financial ratios represent an attempt to standardize financial information in order to facilitate meaningful comparisons.

B. Financial ratios can be divided into three categories. These categories consist of liquidity ratios, leverage ratios, and profitability ratios.

III. Types of ratios

  A. Liquidity ratios are used to measure the ability of a firm to
     meet its short-term financial obligations. Within this cate-
     gory, there are ratios that measure overall liquidity and
     there are ratios that measure the liquidity of specific
     assets.

     1. The principle measures of overall liquidity follow:

        a. The current ratio is defined as

             current assets
             current liabilities

           with a higher ratio indicating increased liquidity.

        b. The acid-test ratio is computed as

             current assets - inventories
                 current liabilities

           Inventories are omitted because they are generally the
           least liquid of a firm's current assets.

     2. Measures of liquidity in specific assets seek to determine
        just how liquid a firm's specific assets are.

        a. The average collection period, defined as

             average accounts receivable
                 annual credit sales
                       360

           shows how rapidly a firm's accounts are being collect-
           ed. The average accounts receivable balance is usually
           computed by dividing the sum of the beginning and end-
           ing receivable balance by two.

        b. The inventory turnover ratio reflects the number of
           times that inventories are turned over (replaced)
           during the year. This ratio is defined as

             cost of goods sold
              average inventory

           where average inventory is an average of the beginning
           and year-end inventory balance.

B. <u>Leverage ratios</u> are used to measure the extent to which non-
owner supplied funds have been used to finance a firm's
assets.  Leverage ratios can be categorized as being either
balance-sheet ratios or coverage ratios.

   1. Balance-sheet leverage ratios measure the proportion of
the firm's assets financed with non-owner funds.

      a. The <u>debt ratio</u> is equal to

$$\frac{\text{total liabilities}}{\text{total assets}}$$

      b. The <u>long-term debt to total capitalization ratio</u>
measures the relative importance of long-term debt in
the firm's capitalization.

   2. <u>Coverage ratios</u> are used to measure a firm's ability to
cover the finance changes associated with its use of
financial leverage.

      a. The <u>times interest earned ratio</u> is defined as

$$\frac{\text{net operating income}}{\text{annual interest expense}}$$

and represents the most popular coverage ratio.

      b. The <u>cash flow overall coverage ratio</u> is computed as

$$\frac{\text{net operating income + lease expense + depreciation}}{\frac{\text{interest + lease expense + preferred dividends}}{(1 - T)} + \frac{\text{principal payments}}{(1 - T)}}$$

and reflects the total amount of earnings that are
available to meet interest and other finance related
charges.  It also improves on the times interest earned
ratio in that it considers lease payments, principal
payments, and preferred dividends, in addition to interest or finance charges that must be covered.

C. <u>Profitability ratios</u> serve as overall measures of the effectiveness of the firm's management.  These ratios can be
divided into those that measure profitability in relation to
sales and those that measure profitability in relation to
investment.

1. <u>Profitability in relation to sales ratios</u> reflects the ability of the firm's management to control the various expenses involved in generating sales.

   a. The <u>gross profit margin</u> is defined as

   $$\frac{gross\ profit}{net\ sales}$$

   and indicates both the efficiency of the firm's operations and the pricing policies of the firm.

   b. The <u>operating profit margin</u> serves as an overall measure of operating effectiveness and is computed as

   $$\frac{net\ operating\ income}{sales}$$

   c. The net profit margin is equal to

   $$\frac{net\ income}{sales}$$

   Net income in this ratio is after taxes.

2. <u>Profitability in relation to investment ratios</u> measures the firm's profitability in relation to invested funds used to generate those profits.

   a. <u>Operating income return on investment</u> is defined as

   $$\frac{operating\ income}{total\ tangible\ assets}$$

   and represents the before-tax return on invested capital.

   b. The rate of return earned on total invested capital after interest and taxes is indicated by the <u>return on total assets</u> ratio which is computed as follows:

   $$\frac{net\ income}{total\ tangible\ assets}$$

   c. The <u>reutrn on total assets ratio</u> is often broken down into the following components:

   $$\frac{net\ income}{sales} \times \frac{sales}{total\ tangible\ assets}$$

By breaking this ratio into two parts--net profit margin and sales to total invested capital--the analyst can easily determine the underlying reason for a particular return on assets produced by a firm. This formulation provides the basis for the Dupont system of financial analysis.

d. The return on common equity ratio is defined as

net income available to common
        common equity

and measures the net return on investment of the common shareholders.

IV. Using financial ratios

A. To fully understand a firm's strengths and weaknesses, the analyst should use one of the two following standards against which ratios can be compared:

1. Similar ratios can be computed for the same firm from its previous financial statements. This is commonly referred to as trend analysis and requires that the analyst look at each ratio over several statement periods.

2. A second type of standard for comparison comes from ratios generated from firms that have characteristics similar to the subject firm. These are referred to as industry average ratios and the two most common sources for such ratios are Dun and Bradstreet's Key Business Ratios in 125 Lines and Statement Studies published by Robert Morris and Associates.

Study Problems

1. Prepare a balance sheet for the A. R. Peterson Mfg. Co. from the scrambled list of items below. The owner's equity balance is not given but it can be determined as a balancing figure.

| Building | $49,100 | Office equipment | 4,100 |
| Accounts receivable | 21,600 | Land | 22,000 |
| Machinery | 2,950 | Notes payable | 14,000 |
| Cash | 9,200 | Owner's equity | |
| Accounts payable | 16,500 | | |

SOLUTION

A. R. Peterson Mfg. Co.
Balance Sheet

| Cash | $ 9,200 | Accounts payable | 16,500 |
|---|---|---|---|
| Accounts receivable | 21,600 | Notes payable | 14,000 |
| Land building | 22,000 | Owner's equity | 78,450 |
| Machinery | 49,100 | | |
| Office equipment | 2,950 | | |
| Total assets | 4,100 | Total liabilities | |
| | $108,950 | & owner's equity | $108,950 |

2. By studying the successive balance sheets for AMP, Inc. found below, determine what transactions have occurred. Prepare a list of the transactions and the corresponding balance-sheet dates. For example, on March 31, 1978 the firm's owners invested $200,000 in AMP, Inc. and started the business.

(a)
AMP, Inc.
Balance Sheet
March 31, 1979

| Assets | | Owner's Equity | |
|---|---|---|---|
| Cash | $200,000 | Owner's equity | $200,000 |

(b)
AMP, Inc.
Balance Sheet
April 2, 1978

| Assets | | Owner's Equity | |
|---|---|---|---|
| Cash | $100,000 | Owner's equity | $200,000 |
| Land | 100,000 | | |
| | $200,000 | | $200,000 |

(c)

AMP, Inc.
Balance Sheet
April 15, 1978

| Assets | | Owner's Equity | |
|---|---|---|---|
| Cash | $ 50,000 | Owner's equity | $200,000 |
| Building | 50,000 | | |
| Land | 100,000 | | |
| | $200,000 | | $200,000 |

(d)

AMP, Inc.
Balance Sheet
March 2, 1978

| Assets | | Liabilities and Owner's Equity | |
|---|---|---|---|
| Cash | $ 50,000 | Accounts payable | $ 25,000 |
| Inventories | 25,000 | Owner's equity | 200,000 |
| Building | 50,000 | | |
| Land | 100,000 | | |
| | $225,000 | | $225,000 |

(e)

AMP, Inc.
Balance Sheet
March 15, 1978

| Assets | | Liabilities and Owner's Equity | |
|---|---|---|---|
| Cash | $ 60,000 | Accounts payable | $ 25,000 |
| Inventories | 25,000 | Notes payable | 25,000 |
| Equipment | 15,000 | Owner's equity | 200,000 |
| Building | 50,000 | | |
| Land | 100,000 | | |
| | $250,000 | | $250,000 |

SOLUTION

(a) On March 31, 1978 the firm's owners invested $200,000 in AMP, Inc. and started the business.

(b) On April 2, 1978, $100,000 of the original investment by the owners was used to acquire land.

(c) On April 15, 1978, $54,000 of the original cash was used to acquire a building.

(d) On May 2, 1978, $25,000 of inventory was purchased on account (credit).

(e) On May 15, 1978, a $25,000 loan was obtained of which $15,000 of the proceeds were used to purchase equipment.

3. Balance sheets for Marion Mfg. Co. and the Sterlington Corp. are found below. Both firms are involved in the manufacture of electrical components used in small electronic calculators and digital wristwatches. Since both firms are less than 3 years old, their book values are reasonably close to actual market value.

Marion Mfg. Co.
Balance Sheet
November 30, 1978

| Assets | | | |
|---|---|---|---|
| Cash | $ 50,000 | Notes payable | |
| Accounts receivable | 90,000 | (due in 30 days) | $ 520,000 |
| Building | 225,000 | Accounts payable | 420,000 |
| Machinery | 320,000 | Owner's equity | 150,000 |
| Land | 375,000 | | |
| | $1,090,000 | | $1,090,000 |

```
                    Sterlington Corp.
                      Balance Sheet
                    November 30, 1978
─────────────────────────────────────────────────────────────────

           Assets
        ─────────────

Cash                    $ 50,000    Notes payable
Accounts receivable      200,000      (due in 30 days)    $120,000
Land                      10,000    Accounts payable       150,000
Machinery                350,000    Owner's equity         640,000
Building                 300,000                         ─────────
                        ─────────                         $910,000
                        $910,000
─────────────────────────────────────────────────────────────────
```

(a) Assume the role of a commercial banker who has been approached by both of the above firms with a request for a 90-day loan for $200,000. For which of the firms are you most likely to approve the loan? Why?

(b) If you were considering the purchase of one of these firms and assume the liabilities of each, which one would you be willing to pay the higher price for? (Obviously, you would want more information in order to make a complete analysis, but make your evaluation based on the balance sheets above).

SOLUTION

(a) Sterlington Corp: In reviewing requests for short-term loans, the commercial loan officer is most interested in the liquidity of the subject firm. The current ratio of Marion Mfg. Co. is a very weak 0.15 while Sterlington Corp.'s current ratio is 1.0. In addition, a quick glance at the balance sheet of Marion Mfg. shows that a very substantial note of $520,000 comes due in 30 days which the company may have difficulty paying.

(b) Sterlington Corp: If it is assumed that book values are reasonably close to actual market values, the difference between Sterlington's total assets and assumed debt is $640,000 as opposed to Marion's net difference of $150,000.

4. Burrus, Inc. had the following condensed balance sheet at the end of operations for 1977:

## Burrus, Inc.
## Balance Sheet
## December 31, 1978

| | | | |
|---|---|---|---|
| Cash | $ 24,000 | Current liabilities | $ 30,000 |
| Other current assets | 51,000 | Long-term notes payable | $ 33,000 |
| | 75,000 | Bonds payable | 50,000 |
| Investments | 40,000 | Capital stock | 150,000 |
| Fixed assets (net) | 125,000 | Retained earnings | 49,000 |
| Land | 62,000 | | |
| | $312,000 | | $312,000 |

During 1978 the following occurred:

(a) Burrus, Inc. sold some of its investments for $20,600 which resulted in a gain of $600.

(b) Additional land was purchased for $12,000.

(c) Bonds payable were paid in the amount of $10,000.

(d) An additional $20,000 in capital stock was issued.

(e) Dividends of $15,000 were paid to stockholders.

(f) Net income for 1978 was $42,000 after allowing for $18,000 in depreciation.

(g) Land was purchased through the issuance of $12,000 in bonds and $6,000 in long-term notes payable.

Required:

(a) Prepare a statement of changes in financial position for 1979.

(b) Prepare a condensed balance sheet for Burrus, Inc. at December 31, 1979.

Assume that current liabilities remained at $30,000 and other current assets did not change during the year.

SOLUTION

Burrus, Inc.
Statement of Changes in Financial Position
For the Year Ended December 31, 1979

| | |
|---|---:|
| Cash (12/31/78) | $ 24,000 |

Sources:

Increase (decrease) in working capital from operations:

| | |
|---|---:|
| Net income | $ 42,000 |
| Depreciation | 18,000 |
| Gain on sales of investments | (600) |
| | 59,400 |
| Sales of investments | 20,600 |
| Issuance of capital stock | 20,000 |
| Increase in bonds payable | 12,000 |
| Increase in long-term notes payable | 6,000 |
| Total sources of funds | $118,000 |

Uses:

| | |
|---|---:|
| Purchase of land | $30,000 |
| Payment of bond payable | 10,000 |
| Payment of dividends to stockholders | 15,000 |
| Total use of funds | $55,000 |
| Cash (12/31/79) | $87,000 |

Burrus, Inc.
Balance Sheet
December 31, 1978

| | | | |
|---|---:|---|---:|
| Cash | $ 87,000 | Current liabilities | $ 30,000 |
| Other current assets | 51,000 | Long-term notes payable | 39,000 |
| Total current assets | 138,000 | Bonds payable | 52,000 |
| Investments | 20,000 | Capital stock | 170,000 |
| Fixed assets (net) | 107,000 | Retained earnings | 66,000 |
| Land | 92,000 | | |
| | $357,000 | | $357,000 |

5. The financial manager of Sudhop, Inc. has hired you as a recent finance graduate. Now he wishes to test your familiarity with financial ratios and your overall ability to work with financial statements. He gives you the following incomplete year-end balance sheet:

Sudhop, Inc.
Balance Sheet
December 31, 1978

| Cash | $ | Accounts payable | $ |
|------|---|------------------|---|
| Accounts receivable | | Long-term debt | _____ |
| Inventory | | Total debt | |
| Total current assets | | Common stock | 125,000 |
| Fixed assets | 400,000 | Retained earnings | 225,000 |
| | $ | | $ |

He then gives you the following additional information and asks you to complete the above balance sheet.

| | |
|---|---|
| Average collection period (360-day year) | 30 |
| Interest paid on long-term debt (5% rate) | 5,000 |
| Debt-to-equity ratio | 0.75 |
| Sales to operating asset | 2.0 |
| Quick ratio | 1.0 |
| Current ratio | 1.2 |

SOLUTION

Sudhop, Inc.
Balance Sheet
December 31, 1978

| Cash | $225,000 | Accounts payable | $250,000 |
|------|----------|------------------|----------|
| Accounts receivable | 50,000 | Long-term debt | 50,000 |
| Inventory | 25,000 | Total debt | 300,000 |
| | 300,000 | Common stock | 125,000 |
| Fixed assets | 400,000 | Retained earnings | 275,000 |
| | $700,000 | | $700,000 |

6. The balance sheet and income statement for Miller Company are given for the year 1978 in addition to various financial ratios for the industry in which Miller operates.

Miller Company
Balance Sheet
December 31, 1978
(000's)

| | | | |
|---|---|---|---|
| Cash | $    230 | Notes payable | $ 1,015 |
| Accounts receivable | 9,380 | Accounts payable | 3,545 |
| Inventories | 7,515 | Accrued taxes | 225 |
| Current assets | 17,125 | Current liabilities | 4,784 |
| Fixed assets (net) | 34,125 | Long-term debt | 18,036 |
| Total assets | $51,250 | Deferred income taxes | 2,840 |
| | | | 20,876 |
| | | Common stock-par | 575 |
| | | Capital in excess of par | 7,945 |
| | | Retained earnings | 17,070 |
| | | Common equity | 25,590 |
| | | Total liabilities & | |
| | $51,250 | net worth | $51,250 |

Miller Company
Income Statement
Year Ended December 31, 1978

| | |
|---|---|
| Net sales (credit) | $46,235 |
| Cost of sales | 33,167 |
| Gross profit | 13,068 |
| General and administrative expense | 9,590 |
| Operating income | 3,478 |
| Interest changes | 1,120 |
| Net income before taxes | 2,358 |
| Income taxes | 1,130 |
| Net income | $ 1,228 |

Industry Ratios

|  | Industry |
|---|---|
| Current | 4.02 |
| Acid test | 3.00 |
| Inventory turnover | 7.50 |
| Average collection period |  |
| Operating income margin | 6.0% |
| Gross profit margin | 26.0% |
| Net profit margin | 5.0% |
| Return on total assets | 5.0% |
| Debt ratio | 5.01% |
| Times interest earned | 3.90 |

Required:

(a) Compute the various ratios indicated for Miller Company. The inventories were $6,800,000 and the receivables were $8,400,000, for Miller on December 31, 1978.

(b) Discuss the liquidity and leverage portion and profitability of Miller in relation to the industry norms.

SOLUTION

| (a) | Industry | Miller |
|---|---|---|
| Current ratio | 4.02 | 3.58 |
| Acid-test ratio | 3.00 | 2.01 |
| Inventory turnover | 7.50 | 4.63 |
| Average collection period | 63.1 | 70.2 |
| Gross profit | 26.0% | 28.3% |
| Operating income margin | 6.0% | 7.5% |
| Net profit margin | 5.0% | 2.7% |
| Return on total assets | 2.5% | 2.4% |
| Debt ratio | 38.0% | 50.1% |
| Times interest earned | 3.90 | 2.11 |

(b) Miller's <u>liquidity</u> position is well below the industry average. The most serious problem is with inventory turnover which is almost one-half the industry norm.

Miller's <u>leverage</u> position, based upon its debt ratio, is very unfavorable. It appears that any additional debt financing would be difficult to acquire at this point.

The <u>gross profit</u> and <u>operating profit</u> margins compare favorably with the industry average which could indicate that the operational and administrative operations of the firm are relatively efficient. However, the net profit margin is well below the industry average and appears to result from relatively high interest expense. This is also indicated by comparing the times interest earned ratio with the industry norm. This high degree of interest expense is undoubtedly directly related to the leverage portion of Miller discussed above.


## Self-Tests

TRUE-FALSE

_____ 1. The balance sheet is a statement of the firm's financial position over a specified time interval.

_____ 2. Noncurrent assets are those which are not expected to be converted into cash within the firm's operating cycle.

_____ 3. The income statement represents an attempt to measure the net results of the firm's operations on a given date.

_____ 4. The owner's equity represents the book value of the owner's interest in the assets of the firm.

_____ 5. A firm attempts to match revenues from the period's operations with the expenses incurred in generating those revenues by compiling the income statement on an accrual basis.

_____ 6. Reported revenues and expenses must represent actual cash flows for the period when the income statement is prepared on an accrual basis.

_____ 7. The LIFO method of inventory valuation assigns cost of the items sold based on the cost of the most recently purchased inventory items.

_____ 8. During a period of rising prices the FIFO method results in lower taxes being paid than would be the case if the LIFO method were used.

_____ 9. Accelerated methods of depreciation offer the advantage of

deferring the payment of taxes which increases the
present worth of the firm's operating cash flows.

_____ 10. The statement of changes in financial position is some-
times referred to as a sources and uses statement of
funds.

MULTIPLE CHOICE

1. Which of the following is generally considered to be the most
   important financial statement for judging the economic well-being
   of a firm?

   a. Income statement.
   b. Balance sheet.
   c. Statement of sources and uses of funds.
   d. All of the above.
   e. None of the above.

2. One of the limitations of the balance sheet is the fact that:

   a. Historical cost is used as the basis for valuation of assets
      and liabilities.
   b. Items which have financial value are omitted because of prob-
      lems of objective valuation.
   c. Appreciation in asset values is ignored.
   d. Estimates must be used in the valuation of several accounts.
   e. All of the above.

3. The _____ method of inventory valuation assigns to cost of goods
   sold the prices paid on the oldest items of inventory.

   a. FIFO.
   b. LIFO.
   c. All of the above.
   d. None of the above.

4. Use of the FIFO method in a period of rising prices will have the
   effect of _____ the true cost of goods sold and _____ the firm's
   gross profits.

   a. Overstating; overstating.
   b. Overstating; understating.
   c. Understating; understating.
   d. Understating; overstating.

5. Under conditions of rising inventory prices, the use of LIFO will
   _____ cost of goods sold and _____ gross profit.

a. Overstate; overstate.
b. Overstate; understate.
c. Understate; understate.
d. Understate; overstate.

6. The firm's cash flow from operations is largest when the method
   for determining cost of goods sold _____ the true cost and
   _____ the firm's earnings for the period.

   a. Overstates; overstates.
   b. Overstates; understates.
   c. Understates; understates.
   d. Understates; overstates.

7. A source of funds would be _____ in fixed assets or _____ in
   long-term debt.

   a. An increase; an increase.
   b. An increase; a decrease.
   c. A decrease; a decrease.
   d. A decrease; an increase.

8. A use of funds would be _____ in common stock or _____ in fixed
   assets.

   a. An increase; an increase.
   b. An increase; a decrease.
   c. A decrease; a decrease.
   d. A decrease; an increase.

9. The debt ratio is considered to be in the category of _____
   ratios.

   a. Liquidity.
   b. Profitability.
   c. Leverage.
   d. None of the above.

10. The average collection period is considered to be in tne category
    of _____ ratios.

    a. Leverage.
    b. Liquidity.
    c. Leverage.
    d. None of the above.

# Financial Forecasting, Planning, and Budgeting

Orientation:  This chapter is divided into two sections.  The first section includes an overview of the role played by forecasting in the firm's planning process.  The second section focuses on the construction of detailed financial plans.  This involves the preparation of budgets and pro forma financial statements for future periods of the firm's operations. A budget is a forecast of future events and provides the basis for taking corrective action in the event that budgeted figures do not reasonably match actual results.  Budgets can also be used for performance evaluation of individuals responsible for implementing budgeted plans.  The cash budget and pro forma financial statements provide the necessary information to determine estimates of future financing requirements of the firm.  These estimates are the key element in our discussion of financial planning and budgeting.

    I. Financial forecasting and planning

        A. The need for forecasting in financial management arises whenever the future financing needs of the firm are being estimated.  There are three basic steps involved in predicting financing requirements.

1. Project the firm's sales revenues and expenses over the planning period.

2. Estimate the levels of investment in current and fixed assets which are necessary to support the projected sales level.

3. Determine the financing needs of the firm throughout the planning period.

B. The key ingredient in the firm's planning process is the sales forecast. This forecast should reflect (1) any past trend in sales that is expected to continue and (2) the effects of any events which are expected to have a material effect on the firm's sales during the forecast period.

C. The traditional problem faced in financial forecasting begins with the sales forecast and involves making forecasts of the impact of predicted sales on the firm's various expenses, assets, and liabilities. There are a number of techniques that can be used to make these forecasts:

1. The percent of sales method involves projecting the financial variable as a percent of projected sales.

2. A slightly more refined technique involves the use of a scatter diagram in which the financial variable is plotted against corresponding levels of sales (or another predictor variable). A line is then visually fitted to the scatter plot and is used to predict the financial variable.

3. Regression analysis represents a method for mathematically "fitting" a line to a scatter plot. The resulting equation can then be used to predict the level of the subject financial variable. The regression method can be used whenever there is a single "predictor" variable (referred to as the independent variable, e.g., firm sales) and a single "predicted" variable (referred to as the dependent variable, e.g., firm inventories). Furthermore, a multiple regression analysis can be used whenever more than one predictor (independent) variable is used to predict a single financial variable.

II. Financial planning and budgeting

A. In general, a business will use four types of budgets: physical, cost, profit, and cash.

1. Physical budgets include budgets for unit sales, personnel or manpower, unit production, inventories, and actual physical facilities.  They are also used as a basis for generating cost and profit budgets.

2. Cost budgets are prepared for every major expense category of the firm, such as manufacturing or production cost, selling cost, and administrative cost.

3. The profit budget is prepared based upon information generated from the sales budget and cost budget.

4. The cash budget is generated by converting all budget information previously discussed into a cash basis.

B. The cash budget represents a detailed plan of future cash flows and can be broken down into four components: cash receipts, cash disbursement, net change in cash for the period, and new financing needed.  Cash budgets can also be either fixed or variable.

1. In a fixed cash budget, cash flow estimates are made for a single set of sales estimates.

2. The variable cash budget involves the preparation of several budgets with each budget corresponding to a different set of sales estimates.  This budget fulfills the two following basic needs:

   a. The variable budget gives management more information on the range of possible financing needs of the firm.

   b. Management is provided with a standard against which it can measure the performance of subordinates responsible for various cost and revenue items contained in the budget.

C. Although no strict rules exist, as a general rule, the budget period shall be long enough to show the effect of management policies, yet short enough so that estimates can be made with reasonable accuracy.  For instance, the capital expenditure budget may be properly developed for a 10-year period while a cash budget may only cover 12 months.

D. The development of pro forma financial statements represents the final stage of the budgeting process.

1. A pro forma income statement represents a statement of

planned profit or loss for the future period and is based
primarily on information generated in the cash budget.

2. The pro forma balance sheet for a future date is developed
by adjusting present balance-sheet figures for projected
information found primarily within the cash budget and pro
forma income statement.

## Study Problems

1. TAM Manufacturing Company is attempting to estimate its needs for
funds during each of the months covering the third quarter of 1978.
Pertinent information is given in the table.

(1) Past and estimated future sales:

| April | $100,000 | July | $100,000 |
|-------|----------|------|----------|
| May | 80,000 | August | 110,000 |
| June | 90,000 | September | 120,000 |
| | | October | 100,000 |

(2) Rent expense is $4,000 per month.
(3) A quarterly interest payment on $100,000 in 5% notes payable is
paid during September, 1978.
(4) Wages and salaries are estimated as follows:

| July | $10,000 |
|-----------|---------|
| August | 11,000 |
| September | 12,000 |

Payments are made within the month in which the wages are earned.
(5) Fifty percent of sales are for cash, with the remaining 50% collected in the month following the sale.  (Bad debts are negligible.)
(6) TAM pays 80% of the sales price for merchandise and makes payment
in the same month in which the sales occur, although purchases are
made in the month prior to the anticipated sales.
(7) TAM plans to pay $10,000 in cash for a new forklift truck in July,
1977.
(8) Short-term loans can be obtained at 12% annual interest with interest paid during each month for which the loan is outstanding.
(9) TAM's ending cash balance for June 30, 1977 is $55,000; the mini-
mum balance the firm wishes to have in any month is $45,000.

(a) Set up, in a logical and easy-to-follow format, a cash budget for TAM for the quarter ended September 30, 1978.

SOLUTION

### Worksheet

|  | June | July | August | September |
|---|---|---|---|---|
| Sales | $90,000 | $100,000 | $110,000 | $120,000 |
| Cash sales |  | 50,000 | 55,000 | 60,000 |
| Collections |  |  |  |  |
| (50% 1 month later) |  | 45,000 | 50,000 | 55,000 |
| Total cash collections |  | $ 95,000 | $105,000 | $115,000 |

### Cash Budget

|  | July | August | September |
|---|---|---|---|
| Cash receipts |  |  |  |
| From sales | $ 95,000 | $105,000 | $115,000 |
| Cash disbursements |  |  |  |
| Payments on purchases | (80,000) | (88,000) | (96,000) |
| Rent | ( 4,000) | ( 4,000) | ( 4,000) |
| Wages and salaries | (10,000) | (11,000) | (12,000) |
| Interest (0.05 X 100,000 X 1/4) |  |  | ( 1,250) |
| Purchase of forklift truck | (10,000) |  |  |
| Short-term-borrowing interest (0.12) |  |  |  |
| Total cash disbursement | (104,000) | (103,000) | (113,250) |
| Net | (9,000) | 2,000 | 1,750 |
| Beginning cash balance | 55,000 | 46,000 | 48,000 |
| Borrowing (repayment) | 0 | 0 | 0 |
| Ending balance | $ 46,000 | $ 48,000 | $ 49,750 |

(b) Prepare a pro forma income statement for TAM covering the quarter ended September 30, 1978. You may assume that TAM's marginal tax rate is 22%. Also, TAM has $110,000 in fixed assets with an average expected useful life of 10 years. (TAM uses straight-line depreciation.)

SOLUTION

TAM Mfg. Co.
Pro Forma Income Statement
for the Quarter Ended
September 30, 1978

| | |
|---|---:|
| Sales | $330,000 |
| Cost of goods sold | (264,000) |
| Gross profit | 66,000 |
| Operating expenses: | |
| Wages and salaries | (33,000) |
| Rent | (12,000) |
| Depreciation | ( 2,750) |
| Total operating expenses | (47,750) |
| Earnings before interest and taxes | 18,250 |
| Interest | (1,250) |
| Earnings before taxes | 17,000 |
| Taxes (22%) | (3,740) |
| Net profit after taxes | $ 13,260 |

(c) Given the following balance sheet for TAM (dated June 30, 1978) and the results of parts (a) and (b), construct a pro forma balance sheet as of September 30, 1978.

TAM Mfg. Co.
Balance Sheet
June 30, 1978

| | | | |
|---|---:|---|---:|
| Cash | $ 55,000 | Accounts payable | $100,000 |
| Accounts receivable | 45,000 | Accrued taxes | 0 |
| Inventories | 100,000 | Notes payable | 100,000 |
| Fixed assets, net | 100,000 | Common equity | 100,000 |
| | $300,000 | | $300,000 |

SOLUTION

## TAM Mfg. Co.
## Pro Forma Balance Sheet
## September 30, 1977

| | | | |
|---|---|---|---|
| Cash | $ 49,750 | Accounts payable | $100,000 [§] |
| Accounts receivable | 60,000* | Accrued taxes | 3,740 |
| Inventory | 100,000 [†] | Notes payable | 100,000 |
| Fixes assets, net | 107,250 [‡] | Common equity | 113,260 [η] |
| | $317,000 | | $317,000 |

| | |
|---|---|
| *Accounts receivable (beginning balance) | $ 45,000 |
| +credit sales | 165,000 |
| -collections | (150,000) |
| Ending balance | $ 60,000 |
| [†]Inventories (beginning balance) | $100,000 |
| +purchases | 264,000 |
| -cost of goods sold | (264,000) |
| Ending balance | $100,000 |
| [‡]Fixed Assets (beginning balance) | $100,000 |
| +purchases | 10,000 |
| -depreciation | ( 2,750) |
| Ending balance | $107,250 |
| [§]Accounts payable | $100,000 |
| +purchases | 264,000 |
| -payments | (264,000) |
| Ending balance | $100,000 |
| [η]Common equity (beginning balance) | $100,000 |
| +net income | 13,260 |
| -cash dividends | 0 |
| Ending balance | $113,260 |

2. The A&M Corporation's projected sales for the first 8 months of
1978 are as follows:

| | | | |
|---|---|---|---|
| January | $300,000 | May | $1,200,000 |
| February | 450,000 | June | 1,000,000 |
| March | 540,000 | July | 900,000 |
| April | 960,000 | August | 700,000 |

Twenty percent of A&M sales are for cash, another 40% is collected in the month following sale, and 40% is collected in the second month following sale.  November and December sales for 1977 were $800,000 and $650,000, respectively.

A&M purchases raw materials equal to 60% of sales and it makes its purchases 2 months in advance of sales.  The supplier is paid 1 month after the purchase.  For example, purchases for April sales are made in February and are paid for in March.

Furthermore, A&M pays $42,000 per month for rent and $90,000 per month for other expenditures.  Finally, tax deposits of $85,000 are made each quarter, beginning in March.

The company's cash balance at December 31, 1977 was $80,000 and a minimum balance of $50,000 must be maintained at all times.  Assume that any short-term financing needed to maintain the minimum cash balance would be paid off in the month following the month of financing with interest paid at a 12% annual rate.

Prepare a cash budget for A&M covering the first 6 months of 1978.

SOLUTION

| | January | February | March | April | May | June | July |
|---|---|---|---|---|---|---|---|
| Sales | $300,000 | $450,000 | $540,000 | $960,000 | $1,200,000 | $1,000,000 | $ 900,000 |
| Cash sales | 60,000 | 90,000 | 108,000 | 192,000 | 240,000 | 200,000 | 180,000 |
| Collections  1 month later | 260,000 | 120,000 | 180,000 | 216,000 | 384,000 | 480,000 | 400,000 |
| 2 months later | 320,000 | 260,000 | 120,000 | 180,000 | 216,000 | 384,000 | 480,000 |
| Total collections from sales | $640,000 | 470,000 | 408,000 | 588,000 | 840,000 | 1,064,000 | 1,060,000 |
| Purchases | 324,000 | 576,000 | 720,000 | 600,000 | 540,000 | 420,000 | 420,000 |
| Payments on purchases | 270,000 | 324,000 | 576,000 | 720,000 | 600,000 | 540,000 | 420,000 |
| **Cash receipts:** | | | | | | | |
| Collections from sales | 640,000 | 470,000 | 408,000 | 588,000 | 840,000 | 1,064,000 | 1,060,000 |
| **Cash disbursements:** | | | | | | | |
| Payments on purchases | 270,000 | 324,000 | 576,000 | 720,000 | 600,000 | 540,000 | 420,000 |
| Rent | 42,000 | 42,000 | 42,000 | 42,000 | 42,000 | 42,000 | 42,000 |
| Tax deposits | | | 85,000 | | | 85,000 | 85,000 |
| Total disbursements | 312,000 | 366,000 | 703,000 | 762,000 | 642,000 | 667,000 | 547,000 |
| Net change for the month | 328,000 | 104,000 | (295,000) | (174,000) | 198,000 | 397,000 | |
| Beginning cash balance | 80,000 | 408,000 | 512,000 | 217,000 | 50,000 | 240,930 | |
| Plus:  net change | 328,000 | 104,000 | (295,000) | (174,000) | 198,000 | | |
| Borrowing | | | | 7,000 | (7,000) | | |
| Interest for prior month's borrowing | | | | | (70)* | | |
| Ending cash balance | $408,000 | $512,000 | $217,000 | $ 50,000 | $240,930 | $241,327 | |
| Cumulative borrowing | | | | $ 7,000 | | | |

*0.12 X 7,000 X 1/12 = $70.00.

47

Self-Tests

TRUE-FALSE

_____  1. Budgets perform the basic functions of (1) providing the basis for taking corrective action and (2) providing the basis for performance evaluation.

_____  2. Physical budgets are used as the basis for generating cost and profit budgets.

_____  3. Depreciation expense is an essential element in the cash budget.

_____  4. Performance evaluation is a principal function that can be performed through the use of budgets.

_____  5. A budget of expected research and development costs for the coming year is an example of a physical budget.

_____  6. A fixed cash budget differs from a variable cash budget in that a fixed budget reflects cash flow estimates for only one set of sales estimates whereas a variable budget reflects cash flow estimates for several possible sales levels.

_____  7. As a general rule, all budgets of the firm should project no longer than 1 year in the future so that estimates can be made with reasonable accuracy.

_____  8. A pro forma income statement can be developed wholly from information found in the cash budget prepared for the same period.

_____  9. The cash budget is only as useful as the accuracy of the forecasts that are used in its preparation.

_____  10. Future net fixed assets are estimated for the pro forma balance sheet by adding planned expenditures to existing net fixed assets and adding to this sum depreciation for the period.

MULTIPLE CHOICE

1. The key(s) to the accuracy of most cash budgets is (are) the:

   a. Forecast of cash disbursements.
   b. Forecast of collection schedule.

c. Forecast of sales.
d. b and c only.
e. None of the above.

2. Pro forma statements embody:

a. Forecasts of prospective future cash positions of the firm.
b. Forecasts of all assets and liabilities.
c. Forecasts of the firm's long-range goals and objectives.
d. a and b only.
e. All of the above.

3. Which of the following items would be included in the cash budget?

a. Depreciation charges.
b. Goodwill.
c. Patent amortization.
d. All of the above.
e. None of the above.

4. The cash budget provides the following information:

a. The exact amount of borrowing needed for the budget interval.
b. The type of loan which should be obtained to meet the cash needs for the time interval.
c. A point estimate of the borrowing needs for the budget interval.
d. An estimate of the cash needed for depreciation expense.
e. A point estimate of the expected funds provided by operations.

5. In general, a firm will use the following type(s) of budgets:

a. Profit budgets.
b. Cash budgets.
c. Cost budgets.
d. Physical budgets.
e. All of the above.

6. Which of the following would not fall under the physical budget classification?

a. Unit sales budget.
b. Physical facilities budget.
c. Production cost budget.
d. Unit production budget.
e. None of the above.

# 5

# *Mathematics of Finance*

Orientation:  In this chapter the concept of a time value of money is introduced, that is, a dollar today is worth more than a dollar received a year from now.  Thus, if we are to logically compare projects and financial strategies, we must either move all dollar flows back to the present or out to some common future date.

I. Compound interest results when the interest paid on the investment during the first period is added to the principal and during the second period the interest is earned on the original principal plus the interest earned during the first period.

A. Mathematically, the future value of an investment if compounded annually at a rate of i for n years will be:

$$FV_n = P(1 + i)^n$$

where n = the number of years during which the compounding occurs,

i = the annual compound interest rate,

P = the principal or original amount invested at the beginning of the first period,

$$FV_n = \text{the future value of the investment at the end of } n \text{ years.}$$

1. The future value of an investment can be increased by either increasing the number of years we let it compound or by compounding it at a higher rate.

2. If the compounding period is less than 1 year, the future value of an investment can be determined as follows:

$$FV_n = P\left(1 + \frac{i}{m}\right)^{mn}$$

where m = the number of times compounding occurs during the year.

B. In the case of continuous compounding, the value of m in the above equation is allowed to approach infinity. As this happens, the value of

$$\left(1 + \frac{i}{m}\right)^{mn}$$

approaches $e^{in}$, with e being defined as follows and having a value of approximately 2.71828,

$$e = \lim_{m \to \infty} \left(1 + \frac{1}{m}\right)^{m}$$

where ∞ indicates infinity.

1. Thus, the future value of an [investment com]pounded continuously for n years can be [...]

$$FV_n = P \cdot e^{in}$$

where e = 2.71828,
      n = the number of year[s ...]
          occurs,
      i = the annual compoun[ding ...]
      P = the principal or o[...]
          the beginning of t[...]

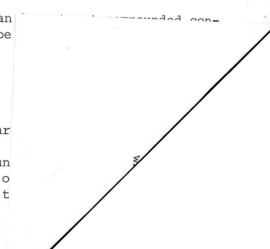

$FV_n$ = the future value of the investment at the end
of n years.

II. Determining the present value, that is, the value in today's
dollars, of a sum of money to be received in the future involves nothing other than inverse compounding. The differences
in these techniques come about merely from the investor's point
of view.

  A. Mathematically, the present value of a sum of money to be
  received in the future can be determined with the following
  equation:

$$P = FV_n \left( \frac{1}{(1 + i)^n} \right)$$

  where n = the number of years until payment will be received,
      i = the opportunity rate or discount rate,
      P = the present value of the future sum of money,
      $FV_n$ = the future value of the investment at the end of
          n years.

  1. The present value of a future sum of money is inversely
  related to both the number of years until the payment
  will be received and the opportunity rate.

III. An annuity is a series of equal dollar payments for a specified
number of years. Because annuities occur frequently in finance,
for example, bond interest payments, we treat them specially.

  A. A compound annuity involves depositing or investing an equal
  sum of money at the end of each year for a certain number of
  years and allowing it to grow.

  1. This can be done by using our compounding equation and
  compounding each one of the individual deposits to the
  future or by using the following compound annuity
  equation:

$$FV_n = A \sum_{t=0}^{n-1} (1 + i)^t$$

  where A = the annuity value deposited at the end of each
        year,
      i = the annual compound interest rate,

$$n = \text{the number of years for which the annuity will last,}$$

$$FV_n = \text{the future value of the annuity at the end of the nth year.}$$

B. Pension funds, insurance obligation, and interest received from bonds all involve annuities. To compare these financial instruments, we would like to know the present value of each of these annuities.

1. This can be done by using our present value equation and discounting each one of the individual cash flows back to the present or by using the following present value of an annuity equation:

$$P = A \left[ \sum_{t=1}^{n} \frac{1}{(1 + i)^t} \right]$$

where A = the annuity withdrawn at the end of each year,
       i = the annual interest or discount rate,
       P = the present value of the future annuity,
       n = the number of years for which the annuity will last.

IV. A perpetuity is an annuity that continues forever, that is, every year from now on this investment pays the same dollar amount.

A. An example of a perpetuity is preferred stock which yields a constant dollar dividend infinitely.

B. The following equation can be used to determine the present value of a perpetuity:

$$P = \frac{pp}{i}$$

where P = the present value of the perpetuity,
      pp = the constant dollar amount provided by the perpetuity,
       i = the annual interest or discount rate.

V. To aid in the calculations of present and future values, tables are provided at the back of <u>Basic Financial Management</u> (<u>BFM</u>).

1.  To aid in determining the value of $FV_n$ in the compounding
    formula

    $$FV_n = P(1 + i)^n$$

    tables have been compiled for values of $(1 + i)^n$ in Appendix
    A, "Compound Sum of $1," in _BFM_.

2.  Thus to determine the value of:

    $$FV_{10} = \$1,000(1 + 0.08)^{10}$$

    we need merely to look up the value of $(1 + 0.08)^{10}$ in
    Appendix A and substitute it in.  The table value given in
    the $n = 10$ row and 8% column of Appendix A is 2.159.  Substi-
    tuting this in the equation, we get

    $$FV_{10} = \$1,000(2.159)$$

    $$FV_{10} = \$2,159$$

3.  To aid in the computation of present values

    $$P = FV_n \frac{1}{(1 + i)^n}$$

    tables have been compiled for values of

    $$\frac{1}{(1 + i)^n}$$

    and appear in Appendix B in the back of _BFM_.

4.  Because of the time-consuming nature of compounding an
    annuity,

    $$FV_n = A \sum_{t=0}^{n-1} (1 + i)^t$$

    tables are provided in Appendix C of _BFM_ for

    $$\sum_{t=0}^{n-1} (1 + i)^t$$

for various combinations of n and i.

5. To simplify the process of determining the present value of an annuity

$$P = A\left(\sum_{t=1}^{n} \frac{1}{(1 + i)^t}\right)$$

tables are provided in Appendix D of <u>BFM</u> for various combinations of n and i for the value

$$\sum_{t=1}^{n} \frac{1}{(1 + i)^t}$$

## Study Problems

1. What will $1,000 invested for 10 years at 10% compounded annually accumulate to?

SOLUTION

Substituting into the compound value formula, we get:

$$FV_n = P(1 + i)^n$$

$$FV_{10} = \$1,000(1 + 0.10)^{10}$$

$$FV_{10} = \$1,000(2.594)$$

$$FV_{10} = \$2,594$$

2. How many years will it take $500 to grow to $1,586 if it is invested at 8% compounded annually?

SOLUTION

From the compound value formula we know:

$$FV_n = P(1 + i)^n$$

Substituting in the values that we know, we get:

$$\$1{,}586 = \$500(1 + 0.08)^n$$

or using table values, we get:

$$\$1{,}586 = \$500 \begin{bmatrix} \text{Table Value} \\ \text{Appendix A} \\ \text{n years} \\ 8\% \end{bmatrix}$$

Dividing both sides by $500, we get:

$$3.172 = \begin{bmatrix} \text{Table Value} \\ \text{Appendix A} \\ \text{n years} \\ 8\% \end{bmatrix}$$

Looking in the 8% column, we find a value of 3.172 in the 15-year row.  Thus, it will take 15 years.

3. At what annual rate would $1,000 have to be invested in order to grow to $4,046 in 10 years?

SOLUTION

From the compound value formula we know:

$$FV_n = P(1 + i)^n$$

Substituting the table value given in Appendix A of <u>BFM</u> for $(1 + i)^n$, we get:

$$FV_n = P \begin{bmatrix} \text{Table Value} \\ \text{Appendix A} \\ \text{n years} \\ i\% \end{bmatrix}$$

Substituting in the given values, we get:

$$\$4{,}046 = \$1{,}000 \begin{bmatrix} \text{Table Value} \\ \text{Appendix A} \\ \text{10 years} \\ i\% \end{bmatrix}$$

$$4.046 = \begin{bmatrix} \text{Table Value} \\ \text{Appendix A} \\ 10 \text{ years} \\ i\% \end{bmatrix}$$

Thus, we are looking for a table value of 4.046 in the 10-year row of Appendix A. This appears in the 15% column; thus, 15% is the annual rate we are looking for.

4. What is the present value of $1,000 to be received 8 years from now discounted back to present at 10%?

SOLUTION

Substituting into the present value formula, we get:

$$P = FV_n \left[ \frac{1}{(1 + i)^n} \right]$$

$$P = \$1,000 \left[ \frac{1}{(1 + 0.10)^8} \right]$$

$$P = \$1,000 \, [0.467]$$

$$P = \$467$$

5. What is the accumulated sum of the following streams of payments, $1,000 per year for 5 years compounded annually at 5%?

SOLUTION

Substituting into the compound annuity formula, we get:

$$FV_n = A \sum_{t=0}^{n-1} (1 + i)^t$$

$$FV_5 = \$1,000 \sum_{t=0}^{5-1} (1 + 0.05)^t$$

$$FV_5 = \$1,000 \, (5.526)$$

$$FV_5 = \$5,526$$

6. What is the present value of $100 a year for 15 years discounted back to the present at 15%?

SOLUTION

Substituting into the present value of an annuity formula:

$$P = A \left[ \sum_{t=1}^{n} \frac{1}{(1 + i)^t} \right]$$

$$P = \$100 \left[ \sum_{t=1}^{15} \frac{1}{(1 + 0.15)^t} \right]$$

$$P = \$100(5.847)$$

$$P = \$584.70$$

## Self-Tests

TRUE-FALSE

_____ 1. The fact that there is an opportunity cost to money brings on the concept of the time value of money.

_____ 2. The higher the rate used to compound a given sum, the larger it will be at some future date.

_____ 3. The future value of an investment can be increased by reducing the number of years we let it compound.

_____ 4. There is an inverse relationship between the effective annual interest rate and the length of the compounding period.

_____ 5. Continuous compounding takes on importance because it allows interest to be earned on interest more frequently than any other compounding period.

_____ 6. Determining present values is merely the inverse of compounding.

_____ 7. A compound annuity involves depositing or investing an equal sum of money at the end of each year for a certain number of years and allowing it to grow.

_____ 8. A perpetuity is an annuity that continues for 30 years or more.

MULTIPLE CHOICE

1. To determine the present value of a future sum we need only multiply it by:

a. $\dfrac{1}{(1 + i)^n}$

b. $\dfrac{1}{(1 + n)^i}$

c. $(1 + n)^i$

d. $(1 + i)^n$

2. The present value of a $100 perpetuity discounted back to present at 6% is:

a. $6,000.00.
b. $6,666.66.
c. $1,666.67.
d. $1,200.00.

3. If we place $100 in a savings account that yields 6% compounded semiannually, what will our investment grow to at the end of 5 years?

a. $133.80.
b. $130.00.
c. $125.00.
d. $134.40.

4. The future value of an investment compounded continuously for n years can be determined from the following formula (e = 2.71828):

a. $FV_n = e \cdot P^{in}$

b. $FV_n = P \cdot e^{in}$

c. $FV_n = P\left(\dfrac{1}{e^{in}}\right)$

d. $FV_n = P \cdot e \cdot i^n$

# Introduction to Working-Capital Management

Orientation: In this chapter we introduce working-capital management in terms of managing the firm's liquidity. Specifically, working capital is defined as the difference in current assets and current liabilities. The hedging principle is offered as one approach to working-capital decisions.

I. Managing current assets

    A. The firm's investment in current assets (like fixed assets) is determined by the marginal benefits derived from investing in them and their acquisition cost.

    B. However, the current fixed asset mix of the firm's investment in assets is an important determinant of the firm's liquidity. That is, the greater the firm's investment in current assets, other things remaining the same, the greater the firm's liquidity.

    C. The firm can invest in marketable securities to increase its liquidity. However, such a policy involves committing the firm's funds to a relatively low-yielding investment.

II. Managing the firm's use of current liabilities

    A. The greater the firm's use of current liabilities, other things being the same, the less will be the firm's liquidity.

    B. There are a number of advantages associated with the use of current liabilities for financing the firm's asset investments.

        1. Flexibility. Current liabilities can be used to match the timing of a firm's short-term financing needs exactly.

        2. Interest cost. Historically, the interest cost on short-term debt has been lower than that on long-term debt.

    C. Following are the disadvantages commonly associated with the use of short-term debt:

        1. Short-term debt exposes the firm to an increased risk of illiquidity because short-term debt matures sooner and in greater frequency, by definition, than does long-term debt.

        2. Since short-term debt agreements must be renegotiated from year to year, the interest cost of each year's financing is uncertain.

III. Determining the appropriate level of working capital

    A. Theoretically, it is impossible to derive the "optimal" level of working capital for the firm. Such a derivation would require estimation of the potential costs of illiquidity which, to date, have eluded precise measurement.

    B. Pragmatically, the "hedging principle" provides the basis for the firm's working-capital decisions.

        1. The "hedging principle" or "rule of self-liquidating debt" involves the following: Those asset needs of the firm not financed by spontaneous sources should be financed in accordance with the following rule: Permanent asset investments are financed with permanent sources and temporary investments are financed with temporary sources of financing.

        2. A <u>permanent investment in an asset</u> is one which the firm expects to hold for a period longer than 1 year. Such an investment may involve current or fixed assets.

        3. <u>Temporary asset investments</u> comprise the firm's investment

in current assets that will be liquidated and <u>not</u> replaced during the year.

4. <u>Spontaneous sources of financing</u> include all those sources which are available upon demand (e.g., trade credit-- Accounts Payable) or which arise naturally as a part of doing business (e.g., wages payable, interest payable, taxes payable, etc.).

5. <u>Temporary sources of financing</u> include all forms of current or short-term financing not categorized as spontaneous. Examples include bank loans, commercial paper, and finance company loans.

6. <u>Permanent sources of financing</u> include all long-term sources such as debt having a maturity longer than 1 year, preferred stock, and common stock.

C. Although the hedging principle provides a useful guide to the firm's working-capital decisions, no firm will follow its tenets strictly. At times a firm may find itself overly reliant on temporary financing but at other times it may have excess cash as a result of excessive use of permanent financing.

## Study Problem

1. The Harrison Mfg. Co. has projected its needs for both current and fixed assets over the next 5 years. At present Harrison has financed its assets using $75 million in common equity, $9 million in long-term debt, and the balance in payables. Payables generally equal 50% of current assets.

| Date | Current Assets | Fixed Assets |
|------|----------------|--------------|
| 1/ 1 /78 (now) | $18,000,000 | $75,000,000 |
| 6/30/78 | 26,000,000 | 77,000,000 |
| 1/ 1 /79 | 20,000,000 | 80,000,000 |
| 6/30/79 | 30,000,000 | 80,000,000 |
| 1/ 1 /80 | 22,000,000 | 81,000,000 |
| 6/30/80 | 32,000,000 | 83,000,000 |
| 1/ 1 /81 | 24,000,000 | 86,000,000 |
| 6/30/81 | 34,000,000 | 88,000,000 |
| 1/ 1 /82 | 26,000,000 | 90,000,000 |
| 6/30/82 | 36,000,000 | 93,000,000 |

Devise a financing plan for Harrison that is consistent with the hedging principle.

SOLUTION

| Date | Fixed Assets | Current Assets | Total Assets | Temporary Financing* | Permanent Financing[†] |
|---|---|---|---|---|---|
| 1/ 1 /78 | $75M | $18M | $ 93M | $ 0 | $ 93M |
| 6/30/78 | 77M | 26M | 103M | 3M | 100M |
| 1/ 1 /79 | 80M | 20M | 100M | 0 | 100M |
| 6/30/79 | 80M | 30M | 110M | 7M | 103M |
| 1/ 1 /80 | 81M | 22M | 103M | 0 | 103M |
| 6/30/80 | 83M | 32M | 115M | 0 | 115M |
| 1/ 1 /81 | 86M | 24M | 120M | 4M | 116M |
| 6/30/81 | 88M | 34M | 122M | 6M | 116M |
| 1/ 1 /82 | 90M | 26M | 116M | 0 | 116M |
| 6/30/82 | 93M | 36M | 129M | 13M | 116M |

| Date | Permanent Financing* | Spontaneous Financing[†] | Short-term Debt[‡] |
|---|---|---|---|
| 1/ 1 /78 | $84M | $ 9M | $ 0 |
| 6/30/78 | 87M | 13M | 3M |
| 1/ 1 /79 | 88M | 10M | 2M |
| 6/30/79 | 88M | 15M | 7M |
| 1/ 1 /80 | 92M | 11M | 0 |
| 6/30/80 | 98M | 16M | 0 |
| 1/ 1 /81 | 98M | 12M | 10M |
| 6/30/81 | 98M | 17M | 6M |
| 1/ 1 /82 | 98M | 13M | 5M |
| 6/30/82 | 98M | 18M | 13M |

*Permanent financing includes both common equity and long-term debt; ordinarily these sources of financing are issued for prolonged periods of time and thus do not fluctuate downward in the short run.

[†]Spontaneous financing (including payables) is estimated to be 50% of current assets.

[‡]Short-term debt equals the difference in total financing needs and that provided by permanent plus spontaneous sources.

COMMENTS:

(1) Note that since we are dealing with 6-month intervals and since assets are growing throughout the planning horizon, temporary financing or short-term debt does not periodically go to zero. This does not mean that short-term notes are not repaid. However, if Harrison is to avoid having to issue and then repay permanent funds or if the firm does not want excess cash due to over financing through permanent sources, then it appears that some short-term debt will be needed throughout most of the planning period.

(2) Note that we have not distinguished between debt and equity sources of permanent financing. This decision relates to the firm's choosing a financing mix and is discussed in Chapter 16.

## Self-Tests

TRUE-FALSE

_____  1. Working capital has traditionally been defined as the firm's investment in assets.

_____  2. Interest rates on short-term debt are higher than they are on long-term debt for a given borrower.

_____  3. The guiding principle for the firm's working-capital policies is referred to as the "principle of self-liquidating debt."

_____  4. The use of short-term sources of financing enhances the firm's liquidity and reduces the firm's rate of return on assets.

_____  5. There are two basic problems encountered in attempting to manage the firm's use of short-term financing: determining how much short-term debt to use and determining what sources to select.

_____  6. Investment decisions are undertaken in the expectation of receiving future benefits.

_____  7. In order to reduce the risk of illiquidity, a firm should decrease its investment in cash and marketable securities.

_____  8. Current liabilities provide a flexible source of financing.

_____ 9. The "hedging principle" is founded in valuation theory.

_____ 10. Spontaneous financing consists of trade credit and other accounts payable which arise "spontaneously" in the firm's day-to-day operations.


MULTIPLE CHOICE

1. Which of the following is an advantage associated with the use of current liabilities?

   a. The use of current liabilities subjects the firm to greater risk of illiquidity.
   b. The firm's interest costs can vary from year to year.
   c. All of the above.
   d. None of the above.

2. Spontaneous financing consists of:

   a. Accounts payable.
   b. Trade credit.
   c. Short-term notes payable.
   d. Common stock.
   e. All of the above.
   f. a and b.

3. Which of the following accounts would not be a prime consideration in working-capital management?

   a. Cash.
   b. Accounts payable.
   c. Bonds payable.
   d. Marketable securities.
   e. Accounts receivable.

4. The greatest margin of safety would be provided by:

   a. More current assets and less current liabilities.
   b. More current assets and more current liabilities.
   c. Less current assets and more current liabilities.
   d. Less current assets and less current liabilities.

5. Which asset-liability combination would result in the firm's having the greatest risk of technical insolvency?

   a. More current assets and less current liabilities.
   b. More current assets and more current liabilities.

    c. Less current assets and more current liabilities.
    d. Less current assets and less current liabilities.

6. Which of the following illustrates the use of the hedging approach?

    a. Temporary assets financed with long-term liabilities.
    b. Permanent assets financed with long-term liabilities.
    c. Temporary assets financed with short-term liabilities.
    d. All of the above.
    e. b and c.

# 7

# Cash and Marketable Securities Management-I

Orientation:  This chapter initiates our two-chapter study of cash
management.  Here, we focus on the cash flow process and the reasons
why a firm holds cash balances.  The objectives of a sound cash management system are identified.  The concept of float is defined.
Finally, several techniques that firms can use to favorably affect
their cash receipts and disbursements patterns are examined.

I. Why a company holds cash

   A. The firm's cash balance is constantly affected by a variety
      of influences.  Sound cash management techniques are based
      on a thorough understanding of the cash flow process.

      1. On an irregular basis cash holdings are increased from
         several external sources, such as from the sale of
         securities.

      2. In a similar fashion, irregular cash outflows reduce the
         firm's cash balance.  Typical examples include cash divi-
         dend payments and the interest requirements on debt
         agreements.

      3. Other major sources of cash arising from internal opera-

tions occur on a rather regular basis.  Accounts receivable collections are an example.

B. Three motives for holding cash balances have been identified by Keynes.[1]

   1. The transactions motive is the need for cash to meet payments that arise in the ordinary course of doing business.  Holding cash to meet a payroll or to acquire raw materials characterizes this motive.

   2. The precautionary motive describes the investment in liquid assets that are used to satisfy possible but as yet indefinite needs for cash.  Precautionary balances are a buffer against all kinds of things that might happen to drain the firm's cash resources.

   3. The speculative motive describes holding cash to take advantage of hoped-for, profit-making situations.

C. Many factors influence the firm's transactions and precautionary motives for holding cash and near-cash.  These include the following:

   1. Changing technology and plans for capital expenditures.

   2. Seasonality and the cash cycle.

   3. Cash commitments as required by debt contracts.

   4. Financial flexibility.

   5. The cash budget and cash flow predictability.

   6. The risk-bearing preferences of management with respect to the chances of running out of cash.

   7. The effectiveness of the company's cash management system.

II. Variations in liquid asset holdings

A. Considerable variation is present in the liquid asset holdings of major industry groups and individual firms.

   1. This is because (1) not all of the factors noted above affect every firm and (2) the executives in different firms who are ultimately responsible for cash management tasks have different risk-bearing preferences.

---

[1] John Maynard Keynes, The General Theory of Employment, Interest, and Money (New York:  Harcourt Brace Jovanovich, Inc., 1936).

    2. Some industries invest very heavily in liquid assets. For example, the total liquid assets to total assets ratio of the contract construction industry greatly exceeds that of the utility industry.

  B. Because assets are acquired, wasted, and sold every day, the management of liquid assets must be viewed as a dynamic process. The cash flow process is complex. In order to cut through this complexity, it is necessary that the firm's cash management system operate within clearly defined objectives.

III. Cash management objectives and decisions

  A. A properly designed cash management program forces the financial manager to come to grips with a big tradeoff.

    1. He or she must strike an acceptable balance between holding too much cash and holding too little cash.

    2. A large cash investment minimizes the chances of insolvency, but it penalizes company profitability.

    3. A small cash investment frees excess (cash) balances for investment in longer-lived and more profitable assets, which increases the firm's profitability.

    4. The big tradeoff, then, is a risk versus return choice.

  B. The firm's cash management system should strive to achieve two prime objectives:

    1. Enough cash must be on hand to dispense effectively with the disbursal needs that arise in the course of doing business.

    2. The firm's investment in idle cash balances must be reduced to a minimum.

  C. In the attempt to meet the two objectives noted above, certain decisions dominate the cash management process. These decision areas can be reduced to the three following questions:

    1. What can be done to speed up cash collections and slow down or better control cash outflows?

    2. How should the investment in liquid assets be split between actual cash holdings and marketable securities?

    3. What should be the composition of the marketable securities portfolio?

  D. Chapter 7 of the text deals with the first question and the other questions are treated in Chapter 8.

IV. Collection and disbursement procedures

  A. Cash acceleration and deceleration techniques revolve around the concept of _float_.  Float can be broken down into four elements:

    1. _Mail float_ refers to funds that are tied up as a result of the time that elapses from the moment a customer mails his or her remittance check until the firm begins to process the check.

    2. _Processing float_ refers to funds that are tied up as a result of the firm's recording and processing remittance checks prior to their deposit in the bank.

    3. _Transit float_ refers to funds that are tied up as a result of the time needed for a deposited check to clear through the commercial banking system and become "usable" funds to the firm.

    4. _Disbursing float_ refers to funds that are technically usable to the firm until its _payment_ check has cleared through the banking system and has been charged against its deposit account.

  B. Float reduction can result in considerable benefits in terms of (1) usable funds that are released for company use and (2) in the returns produced on these freed-up balances.  A study problem at the end of this chapter illustrates the calculation of such savings.

  C. Several techniques are available to improve the management of the firm's cash inflows.  These techniques may also provide for a reduction in float.

    1. The lock-box arrangement is a widely used commercial banking service for expediting cash gathering.

      a. The objective is to reduce _both_ mail and processing float.

      b. The procedure behind a lock-box system is very simple. The firm rents a local post office box and authorizes a local bank in which a deposit account is maintained to pick up remittances from the box.

   (1) Customers are instructed to mail their payments to the numbered post office box.

   (2) A deposit form is prepared by the <u>bank</u> for each batch of processed checks.

   (3) The bank may notify the firm daily as to the amount of funds deposited on the firm's behalf.

   (4) The firm that receives checks from all over the country establishes several lock boxes.

c. A lock-box arrangement provides for (1) increased working cash, (2) elimination of clerical functions, and (3) early knowledge of dishonored checks.

d. The firm must carefully evaluate whether this or any cash management service is worth the added costs. Usually, the bank levies a charge for each check processed through the system. The marginal income generated from released funds must exceed the added costs of the system to make it economically beneficial. A study problem at the end of this chapter illustrates this kind of calculation.

2. <u>Pre-authorized checks</u> (PAC's) are another method for speeding up the conversion of receipts into working cash.

   a. The objective of the PAC is to reduce mail and processing float.

   b. A PAC (1) is created with the individual's legal authorization, (2) resembles an ordinary check, and (3) does <u>not</u> contain the signature of the person on whose account it is being drawn.

   c. PAC systems are most useful to firms that (1) regularly receive a large volume of payments of a fixed amount (2) from the same customers. Insurance companies and savings and loan associations are prominent examples.

   d. The principle behind the PAC system is straightforward. The firm simply obtains an authorization from its customers to draw checks (at specified times and for specified amounts) on their (the customers') demand deposit accounts.

e. Figure 7.1 shows the operation of a PAC system.

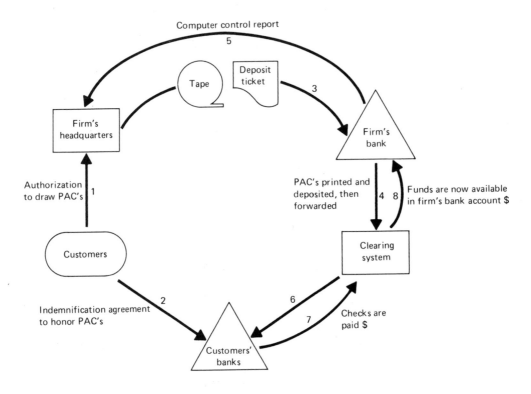

FIGURE 7.1

Pre-Authorized Check System (PAC)

     f. The benefits derived from a PAC system include (1)
       highly predictable cash flows, (2) reduced billing,
       postage, and clerical expenses, (3) customer prefer-
       ence, and (4) increased working cash stemming from
       reduced mail and processing float.

   3. Depository transfer checks are used in conjunction with
     concentration banking.  A concentration bank is one in
     which the firm maintains a major disbursing account.

     a. The major objective of using depository transfer checks
       (DTC's) is to eliminate excess cash balances held by
       the firm in its several regional banks.  A secondary
       objective, which is achieved through use of the
       automated depository transfer check (ADTC), is to

reduce float incurred by mailing (ordinary) DTC's from
a regional bank to a concentration bank.

b. The DTC provides a means for moving (transferring)
   funds from a local bank to a concentration bank.

   (1) The DTC is an unsigned, non-negotiable instrument.

   (2) The DTC is payable only to the bank of ultimate deposit.

   (3) DTC's can operate through the use of the U.S. mail
       system or an automated system (ADTC).

c. With the conventional DTC, a company employee deposits
   the day's cash receipts in a local bank, fills out a
   DTC for the amount of the deposit, and mails the DTC
   to the concentration bank.  When the DTC is received
   at the concentration bank, the transferred funds are
   credited to the firm's demand deposit account.

d. The ADTC eliminates the time required for the conventional DTC to travel through the mails and physically
   reach the concentration bank.  The deposit information
   is transmitted electronically to the concentration
   bank, which results in the saved time.  This system is
   shown in Figure 7.2.

4. Wire transfers offer the fastest method for moving funds
   between commercial banks.  Usable ("good") funds are
   transferred and thereby immediately become usable funds
   at the receiving bank.  There is no transit float with
   wire transfers.  Two major communication facilities are
   used to accommodate wire transfers:  (1) bank wire, which
   is privately operated by about 250 major commercial banks
   in the United States, and (2) Federal Reserve wire system,
   which is accessible to members of the Federal Reserve
   system.  The movement of small dollar amounts does not
   usually justify use of this system.

D. Techniques used by firms that hope to improve the management
   of their cash outflows include:  (1) zero balance accounts,
   (2) payable-through drafts, and (3) remote disbursing.

1. Zero balance accounts (ZBA's) permit centralized control
   (i.e., at the head office) over cash disbursements, but
   at the same time they allow the firm to maintain disbursing authority at the local or divisional level.

   a. The major objective of a ZBA system is to achieve

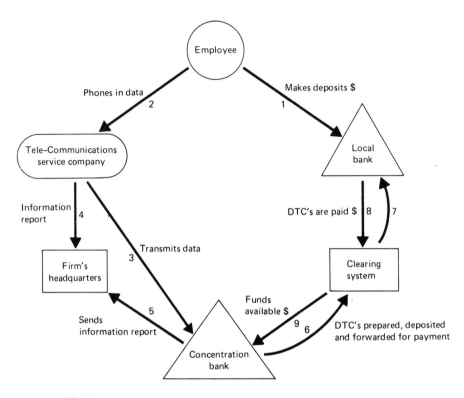

FIGURE 7.2

Automated Depository Transfer Check System (DTC)

better control over cash payments. A secondary benefit of this technique <u>might</u> be an increase in disbursement float.

b. Under a ZBA system, each profit center (division) has a disbursing account located in the <u>same</u> concentration bank.

(1) The firm's authorized employees write payment checks in the usual manner.

(2) These checks then clear through the banking system and are presented to the firm's concentration bank for payment.

(3) The checks are paid by the bank and negative

balances build up in the appropriate disbursing accounts.

(4) Daily the negative balances are restored to a zero level by means of credits to the various ZBA's and a corresponding reduction in the firm's master demand deposit account in the concentration bank.

c. For the firm that has several operating units, the benefits from using a ZBA system include:

(1) Centralized control over disbursements.

(2) Reduction of time spent on superficial cash management activities.

(3) Reduction of excess cash balances held in outlying accounts.

(4) An increase in disbursement float.

2. Payable-through drafts (PTD's) have the physical appearance of ordinary checks, but they are drawn on and paid by the issuing firm instead of the bank. The bank serves as a collection point for the documents and passes the documents on to the firm for inspection and authorization for payment.

a. The objective of a payable-through draft system is to provide for effective control of field-authorized payments. An example would be a claim settlement authorized by an insurance agent.

b. Stop payment orders can be initiated by the firm's headquarters on any drafts considered inappropriate.

c. Legal payment of individual drafts takes place after review and approval of the drafts by the company. Disbursing float, however, is usually not increased by the use of drafts. For purposes of measuring usable funds to the firm, drafts presented daily for payment are charged in total against the corporate master demand deposit account.

3. Remote disbursing, rather obviously, is intended to increase disbursing float.

a. To implement such a procedure, the firm only needs to open and use a deposit account located in a city distant from its customers' banks.

b. Since checks written on that account take longer to
   clear, the firm has use of its funds for a longer
   period of time.

c. The major constraint on this procedure is the possible
   alienation of important customers who must wait longer
   for their remittance checks to become usable funds.

V. Evaluating the costs of cash management services

A. Whether a particular cash management system will provide an
   economic benefit to the firm can be evaluated by use of this
   relationship:

   added costs = added benefits

B. Clearly, if the benefits exceed the costs of using the system,
   then the system is economically feasible.

C. On a per unit basis, this relationship can be expressed as
   follows:

   P = (D)    (S)    (i)

   where P = increase in per-check processing cost, if the new
             system is adopted,
         D = days saved in the collection process, i.e., float
             reduction,
         S = average check size in dollars,
         i = the daily, before-tax opportunity cost (rate of
             return) of carrying cash.

D. The sum of (D)    (S)    (i) must exceed P for the system to
   be beneficial to the firm.  A study problem at the end of
   this chapter provides an example of this logic.


Study Problems


1. Portland Energy Products is evaluating whether or not to use an
additional lock box.  If the lock box is used, check processing costs
will rise by $.20 a check.  The average check size that will be
mailed to the lock-box location is $1,000.  Funds that are freed by
using the lock box will be invested in marketable securities to yield
an annual before-tax return of 7%.  The firm uses a 365 day year in

its analysis procedures.  What reduction in check-collection time is required to justify use of the lock box?

SOLUTION

Solve the following relationship for D:

$$P = (D) \quad (S) \quad (i)$$

$$\$.20 = (D)(\$1,000)\left(\frac{0.07}{365}\right)$$

$$\$.20 = (D)(\$.192)$$

$$\frac{\$.20}{\$.192} = D = \underline{1.0417 \text{ days}}$$

Thus, the lock box is justified if it can speed up collections by more than 1.0417 days.

2. Annual sales for Austin Drilling Supply will total $250,000,000 next year.  What would be the annual value of 1-day's float reduction to this firm if it could invest the freed-up balances at 8% per year?

SOLUTION

Compute Austin's sales per day:

$$\frac{\text{annual revenues}}{\text{days in year}} = \frac{\$250,000,000}{365} = \$684,932$$

Compute the annual value of the 1-day float reduction:

$$(\$684,932)(0.08) = \underline{\$54,795}$$

Self-Tests

TRUE-FALSE

_____ 1. Accounts receivable are usually referred to as "near-cash assets."

_____ 2. Holding cash to pay for next week's labor bill (payroll) is an example of the precautionary motive for holding cash.

_____  3. Ready borrowing power enables the firm to reduce the cash
            balances actually held for precautionary purposes.

_____  4. Technical insolvency means that the firm is able to meet
            its short-term obligations on time but that its long-term
            obligations are in jeopardy.

_____  5. Cash flow forecasting is the initial step in any effec-
            tive cash management program.

_____  6. Wire transfers provide the fastest and least costly
            method of transferring funds among depository institu-
            tions.

_____  7. A possible benefit stemming from the use of pre-authorized
            checks is that cash flows can be more predictable.

_____  8. The major objective of using payable-through drafts is to
            extend disbursing float.

_____  9. The major reason for using lock boxes is to enjoy a reduc-
            tion in transit float.

_____ 10. Zero balance accounts are used to accelerate cash re-
            ceipts.


MULTIPLE CHOICE

1. Indicate the item that is not an advantage of the lock-box system.

    a. The cost is minimal.
    b. Speeds up the flow of cash to the firm.
    c. Remittances are collected sooner.
    d. All of the above are advantages.

2. Which of the following is not a cash acceleration technique?

    a. Lock boxes.
    b. Automated depository transfer checks.
    c. Pre-authorized checks.
    d. Payable-through drafts.
    e. All of the above are cash acceleration techniques.

3. Depository transfer checks mainly:

    a. Reduce mail and processing float.
    b. Extend disbursing float.
    c. Provide a method for moving funds from local banks to concen-
       tration banks.
    d. Centralize disbursing authority.

4. Zero balance accounts:

   a. Permit centralized control over disbursements.
   b. Provide for effective control over field payments.
   c. Are an integral part of a lock-box system.
   d. Are the same thing as pre-authorized checks.

5. A pre-authorized check system:

   a. Reduces mail float.
   b. Reduces processing float.
   c. Extends disbursing float.
   d. a and b.
   e. b and c.

# Cash and Marketable Securities Management – II

Orientation:  The intent of this chapter is (1) to determine the optimal division of the firm's liquid asset holdings between cash and marketable securities and (2) to determine the ultimate mix of marketable securities in the near-cash portfolio.

I. Dividing liquid assets between cash and marketable securities

    A. When the need for cash is certain, the financial manager may utilize the economic order quantity formula (inventory model).

        1. Objective: The purpose of this analysis is to balance the lost income that the firm suffers from holding cash rather than marketable securities against the transactions costs involved in converting securities into cash.

        2. Strategy:  The inventory model minimizes the total cost of maintaining the cash balance whenever the costs include:

            a. The carrying cost of holding cash.

            b. The fixed cost of converting marketable securities into cash.

3. Assumptions:

   a. Cash payments over the planning period are:
(1) a regular or constant amount; (2) continuous;
and (3) certain.

   b. No unanticipated cash receipts will be received during
the planning period.

   c. The interest rate on investments remains constant over
the analysis period.

   d. Transfers between cash and the securities portfolio
may take place at any time at a cost that is fixed,
regardless of the amount to be transferred.

4. Computation

   a. Notation:
     $C$ = the amount per order of marketable securities
to be converted into cash.
     $i$ = the interest rate per period available on invest-
ments in marketable securities.
     $b$ = the fixed cost per order of converting market-
able securities into cash.
     $T$ = the total cash requirements over the planning
period.
     $TC$ = the total costs associated with maintenance of a
particular average cash balance.

   b. Computation of costs:
     $T/C$ = the number of transfers during the period.
     $C/2$ = the average cash balance.
     Thus, the total costs (TC) of having cash on hand can
be expressed as:

$$TC = i\left(\frac{C}{2}\right) + b\left(\frac{T}{C}\right)$$

     total     total
     interest ordering
     income   costs
     forgone

   c. Minimization of total costs:  The optimal cash conversion size, $C^*$, can be found by using the following
equation:

$$C^* = \sqrt{\frac{2bT}{i}}$$

5. Example: Management estimates the total cash needs for the next 2 months to be $15,000. The cost of transferring marketable securities into cash is $30 for each trade, and the annual yield on securities is 12% (2% for 2 months). Find the optimal cash order size.

$$C^* = \sqrt{\frac{2bT}{i}} = \sqrt{\frac{2(30)(15,000)}{0.02}} = \$6,708.20$$

Further, the optimal average cash balance is $3,354.10 ($6,708.20/2).

6. Implications of the inventory model for cash management:

a. Notice that the optimal case order size, $C^*$, varies directly with the square root of the ordering costs, bT, and inversely with the yield, i, obtained on marketable securities.

b. Also notice that as T increases, $C^*$ does not rise proportionately. This implies the existence of economies of scale in cash management.

c. When the total cost of ordering and holding cash is minimized, the cash conversion cost and the interest income forgone are exactly equal.

d. The strict assumptions of the inventory model for cash management will not be completely satisfied in actual business practice.

B. When cash balances fluctuate randomly, the financial manager may use a stochastic (probabilistic) control-limit model to facilitate the decision process.

1. Objective: The control-limit model seeks to minimize the total costs of managing the firm's cash balance.

2. Strategy: Through the use of control theory, the model determines upper and lower limits beyond (out of) which the cash balance is not permitted to reach (or wander).

a. When the cash balance reaches the upper control limit (UL), a conversion of cash into marketable securities takes place. The amount converted is equal to UL-RP dollars, where RP is some calculated cash return point.

    b. When the cash balance reaches the lower control limit (LL), a conversion of marketable securities into cash is initiated by the financial officer. The amount converted is equal to RP-LL dollars.

3. Assumptions:

    a. The firm's cash balance changes in an irregular, unpredictable manner over time.

    b. The probability (chance) of a cash balance change being either positive or negative is 0.5 (i.e., equally likely).

4. Computation of UL and RP:

    a. Notation:
        b = the fixed cost per order of converting marketable securities into cash.
        i = the daily interest rate available on investments in marketable securities.
        $\sigma^2$ = the variance of daily changes in the firm's expected cash balances.

    b. The optimal cash return point, RP, can be determined by using the following equation:

$$RP = \sqrt[3]{\frac{3b\sigma^2}{4i}}$$

    c. The upper control limit (UL) can be calculated:

$$UL = 3RP$$

    d. The lower control limit (LL) is determined by management.

5. The average cash balance, CB*, that will be maintained by the firm during the analysis period can only be computed on an expected basis. It is approximated by

$$CB* = \frac{UL + RP}{3}$$

6. Example: Assume that the annual yield available on marketable securities is 11%. During a 365-day year, i

becomes 0.11/365 = 0.0003 per day.  Also assume that the
fixed cost of transacting a marketable securities trade
(b) is $40.  In addition, the firm has observed a variance
of $490,000 in past daily cash balance changes.  Manage-
ment has decided that $2,000 is an appropriate lower
control limit.

a. The optimal cash return point becomes

$$RP = \sqrt[3]{\frac{3(40)(490,000)}{4(0.0003)}} = \$3,659$$

b. The upper cash balance limit is

UL = 3($3,659) = $10,977

c. The expected average cash balance level is

$$CB^* = \frac{10,977 + 3,659}{3} = \$4,879$$

d. Once the cash balance reaches the upper limit of
$10,977, the financial manager would buy $7,318
(UL-RP) of marketable securities.  Should the cash
balance drop to the lower limit of $2,000, the finan-
cial manager would sell $1,659 (RP-LL) of marketable
securities.

7. Implications of the control-limit model for cash management:

a. The optimal cash return level, RP, will vary directly
with the cube root of both the transfer cost, b, and
the volatility of daily cash balance changes, $\sigma^2$.

b. The larger the transfer cost or cash balance volatility, the greater the absolute dollar spread between
the upper control limit and the cash return point.

c. The optimal cash return point varies inversely with
the cube root of the lost interest rate.

d. Like the inventory model, the control-limit model
implies the existence of economies of scale in cash
management.

C. Compensating balances.

1. The bank requires that the firm maintain deposits of a given minimum amount in its demand deposit account.

2. These balances are normally required of corporate customers in three situations:

   a. Whenever the firm has a loan commitment at the bank which is not entirely used, a compensating balance is required.

   b. If the firm has a loan outstanding at the bank, a compensating balance is required.

   c. Instead of paying directly for certain banking services (e.g., check clearing), a firm will be asked to maintain such a balance. The current trend, however, is toward unit pricing for these services.

3. Compensating balance policies vary among commercial banks and are influenced by general economic and financial market conditions. Several guidelines may, however, be offered.

   a. For the case of the unused portion of a loan commitment, the bank might require that the compensating balance range from 5% to 10% of the commitment.

   b. If a loan is outstanding with the bank, the requirement may be 10% to 20% of the unpaid balance.

   c. In order to compensate for various bank services, the firm may be asked to maintain a balance based on either an absolute amount or an average amount.

4. When determining the optimal split between cash and marketable securities, the financial officer must explicitly consider the compensating balance requirement.

   a. One approach is to ignore the requirement when performing the necessary calculations and then select the maximum of that suggested by the model or the bank's compensating balance requirement.

   b. A second approach is to include the compensating balance requirement in the requisite calculations.

      (1) The requirement could be treated as a safety stock in the inventory model.

(2) The requirement could be considered the lower control limit in the control-limit model.

II. Composition of the marketable securities portfolio

A. When selecting a proper marketable securities mix, five factors should be considered.

1. Financial risk is the uncertainty of expected returns from a security due to unforeseeable changes in the financial capacity of the security issuer to make future payments to the security owner.

2. Interest rate risk is the uncertainty in expected returns caused by possible changes in interest rates. This is particularly important for securities that have long, as opposed to short, terms to maturity. (See study problem 6 for an illustration of this point.)

3. Liquidity is the ability to transform a security into cash. Consideration should be given to (1) the time needed to sell the security and (2) the likelihood that the security can be sold at or near its prevailing market price.

4. The taxability of interest income and capital gains is seriously considered by some corporate treasurers.

a. The interest income from municipal obligations is tax-exempt.

b. The following equation may be used to determine an equivalent before-tax yield on a taxable security.
(1) Notation:
    $r$ = equivalent before-tax yield.
    $r^*$ = after-tax yield on tax-exempt security.
    $T$ = firm's marginal income tax rate.

(2) Computation

$$r = \frac{r^*}{(1 - T)}$$

(3) Example: Suppose a firm has a choice between investing in a 1-year tax-free debt issue yielding 6% on a $1,000 outlay or a 1-year taxable issue that yields 10% on a $1,000 outlay. The firm pays federal taxes at the rate of 48%. Which security

is more beneficial to the firm?

$$r = \frac{0.06}{(1 - 0.48)} = 11.54\%$$

    (4) Clearly, this firm should choose the tax-exempt security.

5. The <u>yield</u> criterion involves a weighing of the risks and benefits inherent in the four previously mentioned factors. The higher the risks associated with a particular security, the higher the expected yield (risk-return tradeoff).

B. Marketable security alternatives

1. A <u>Treasury bill</u> is a direct obligation of the U.S. government sold on a regular basis by the U.S. Treasury.

    a. These bills may be purchased in denominations of $10,000, $15,000, $50,000, $100,000, $500,000, and $1,000,000.

    b. The bills are currently offered with maturities of 91, 182, and 365 days. Nine-month bills are <u>not</u> presently sold.

    c. Since Treasury bills are sold on a discount basis, the investor does not receive an actual interest payment.

    d. The bills are marketed by the Treasury only in bearer form (without the name of the investor upon them) and are therefore easily transferable.

    e. Since Treasury bills are backed by the U.S. government, they are considered risk-free and consequently sell at lower yields than those obtainable on other marketable securities.

    f. The income from Treasury bills is only subject to federal income taxes and is always taxed as an ordinary gain.

2. <u>Federal agency securities</u> represent debt obligations of federal government agencies and were created to carry out lending programs of the U.S. government.

    a. The Federal National Mortgage Association (FNMA) renders supplementary assistance to the secondary market for mortgages.

b. The Federal Home Loan Banks (FHLB) function as a credit reserve system for member banks.

c. The Federal Land Banks grant loans to members of Federal Land Bank Associations who are engaged in agriculture, provide agricultural services, or own rural homes.

d. The Federal Intermediate Credit Banks grant loans to and purchase notes originating from loans made to farmers by other financial institutions.

e. The Banks for Cooperatives make loans to cooperative associations which are owned and controlled by individuals involved in general farm business.

f. Securities of these "big five" federally sponsored agencies are not directly backed by the U.S. government.

g. The maturities available range from 30 days to 15 years, with most (80%) maturing in 5 years or less.

h. The yields available always exceed those of Treasury bills of comparable maturity and are taxable at the federal, state, and local level.

3. Bankers' acceptances are largely concentrated in the financing of foreign transactions; this acceptance is a draft (order to pay) drawn on a specific bank by an exporter in order to obtain payment for goods shipped to a customer who maintains an account with that bank.

a. The maturities run mostly from 30 to 180 days, with the most common period being 90 days.

b. Like Treasury bills, the acceptances are sold on a discount basis.

c. Income generated from acceptances is fully taxable at all governmental levels.

d. Acceptances provide investors with a higher yield than do Treasury bills and agency obligations of comparable maturity.

4. A negotiable certificate of deposit (CD), is a marketable receipt for funds that have been deposited in a bank for a fixed time period at a fixed interest rate.

a. CD's are offered in denominations ranging from $25,000

to $10,000,000, with popular sizes of $100,000,
$500,000, and $1,000,000.

b. Original maturities on CD's range from 1 to 18 months.

c. Yields on CD's are higher than yields on Treasury
bills, and in recent years they have exceeded those
available on acceptances.

d. The income received from CD's is taxed at all governmental levels.

5. Commercial paper refers to short-term, unsecured promissory notes sold by large businesses in order to raise
cash.

a. Paper is usually sold in relatively large denominations, typically in excess of $25,000, and ranging up
to $1,000,000.

b. The notes are sold on a discount basis with maturities
ranging from 3 to 270 days.

c. It is the only investment instrument discussed here
that has no active trading in a secondary market.

d. The return on commercial paper is fully taxable at all
governmental levels.

6. Repurchase agreements are legal contracts that involve
the actual sale of securities by a borrower to the lender,
with a commitment on the part of the borrower to repurchase the securities at the contract price plus a stated
interest charge.

a. These agreements are usually executed in sizes of
$500,000 or more.

b. The maturity is either for a specified time period
(tailored to the needs of the investor) or there is no
fixed maturity date.

c. The yields are generally less than those of Treasury
bill rates of comparable maturities and are taxable
at all governmental levels.

7. Money market mutual funds usually invest in a diversified
portfolio of short-term, high-grade debt instruments like
those described in this section.

a. These funds sell their shares to a large number of

small investors in order to raise cash.

b. The funds offer the investing firm a high degree of liquidity and investment expertise.

c. The returns earned from owning shares in a money market fund are taxable at all governmental levels.

d. Table 8.1 summarizes the salient features of the major money market instruments.


## Study Problems

1. Using the inventory model, determine:  (a) the optimal cash conversion size; (b) the optimal level of cash the firm should hold; and (c) the total cost of having the optimal amount of cash on hand during the next 6 months.  The financial officer has developed the following information:

(1) The firm needs $5,000 in cash for transactions purposes during the next 6 months.

(2) The cost of transferring marketable securities into cash is $60 per order.

(3) The interest rate on marketable securities is 10% for the next year (5% for 6 months).


SOLUTION

(a)
$$C^* = \sqrt{\frac{2(60)(5,000)}{0.05}} = \underline{\$3,464}$$

(b) Optimal level of cash is

$$\frac{C^*}{2} = \frac{\$3,464}{2} = \underline{\$1,732}$$

(c)
$$TC = 0.05(\$1,732) + \$60\left(\frac{\$5,000}{\$3,464}\right) = \underline{\$173.20}$$

2. Using the inventory model, determine the optimal level of cash the firm should hold if:

(a) The available annual yield on marketable securities is 6%.

Table 8.1

Features of Selected Money Market Instruments

| Instrument | Denominations | Maturities | Basis | Form | Liquidity | Taxability |
|---|---|---|---|---|---|---|
| U.S. Treasury Bills: direct obligations of the U.S. government. | $ 10,000 15,000 50,000 100,000 500,000 1,000,000 | 91 days 182 days 365 days 9-month not presently issued | Discount | Bearer | Excellent secondary market | Exempt from state and local income; do not qualify for favorable capital gains rate |
| Federal Agency Securities: Obligations of corporations and agencies created to affect the federal government's lending programs. | Wide variation from $1,000 to $1,000,000 | 5 days* to more than 10 years (*Farm Credit consolidated system-wide discount notes) | Discount or coupon; usually on coupon | Bearer or registered | Good for issues of "Big Five" agencies | Generally exempt at local level; FNMA issues are not |
| Bankers' Acceptances: Drafts accepted for future payment by commercial banks. | No set size; typically range from $25,000 to $1,000,000 | Predominantly from 30 to 180 days | Discount | Bearer | Good for acceptances of large "money market" banks | Taxed at all levels of government |
| Negotiable Certificates of Deposit: Marketable receipts for funds deposited in a bank for a fixed time period. | $25,000 to $10,000,000 | 1 to 18 months | Accrued interest | Bearer or registered; bearer is preferable from liquidity standpoint | Fair to good | Taxed at all levels of government |
| Commercial Paper: Short-term, unsecured promissory notes. | $5,000 to $5,000,000; $1,000 and $5,000 multiples above the initial offering size are sometimes available | 3 to 270 days | Discount | Bearer | Poor; no active, secondary market in usual sense | Taxed at all levels of government |
| Repurchase Agreements: Legal contracts between a borrower (security seller) and lender (security buyer). The borrower will repurchase at the contract price plus an interest charge. | Typical sizes are $500,000 or more | According to terms of contract | Not applicable | Not applicable | Fixed by the agreement, i.e., borrower will repurchase | Taxed at all levels of government |
| Money Market Mutual Funds: Hold a diversified portfolio of short-term, high-grade debt instruments. | Some require an initial investment as small as $1,000 | Shares can be sold at any time | Net asset value | Registered | Good; provided by the fund itself | Taxed at all levels of government |

(b) The cost of converting from cash to marketable securities is $50 per transaction.

(c) The firm's transaction needs will total $1,000 over the next year.

SOLUTION

$$\text{transaction balance} = C^* = \sqrt{\frac{2(50)(1,000)}{0.06}} = \underline{\$1,291}$$

$$\text{optimal level of cash} = \text{transaction balance} \div 2 = \frac{C^*}{2} = \frac{\$1,291}{2}$$
$$= \underline{\$645.50}$$

3. Wolfpack industries is considering taking out a loan at the Piedmont National Bank. The firm is evaluating the option of a 10%, 1-year loan for $1,000, with interest and principal due at the end of the year. The alternative is a 9%, 1-year loan for $1,000 with the same repayment terms as the other loan, but a 13% compensating balance is required. Which loan do you recommend that Wolfpack take?

SOLUTION

The cost of the 10% loan is actually 10%. The cost of the 9% loan is

$$\frac{\$ \text{ interest}}{\text{funds available}} = \frac{\$90}{\$1,000 - \$130} = \frac{\$90}{\$870} = \underline{10.34\%}$$

Wolfpack should take the straight 10% loan option.

4. The cash balances of South Tampa Cigars fluctuate randomly, with a standard deviation of daily cash flows of $500. The current annual rate of interest on securities is 9%, with fixed conversion costs of $150. Also, management desires to have at least $3,000 in cash on hand at any point in time. The firm uses a 365-day year in its analysis procedures.

(a) Find the upper and lower control limits.

(b) In what lot sizes will marketable securities be purchased and sold?

SOLUTION

(a) The lower control limit (LL) is simply $\underline{\$3,000}$.

$$RP = \sqrt[3]{\frac{3(150)(500)^2}{4(0.000247}} = \$4,847$$

where $i = \dfrac{0.09}{365} = 0.000247$ and the optimal upper limit (UL) is

UL = 3RP = 3(4847) = $\underline{\$14,541}$.

(b) Marketable securities will be purchased in lot sizes equal to

$$UL - RP = \$14,541 - \$4,847 = \underline{\$9,694}$$

Securities will be sold in lot sizes equal to

$$RP - LL = \$4,847 - \$3,000 = \underline{\$1,847}.$$

5. The corporate treasurer of Buckeye Bottling is considering purchasing a municipal obligation with a 7% coupon and a $1,000 par value. Mr. Inside Info has telephoned the treasurer about another $1,000 par value offering which provides a 12% yield. This latter offering is, however, fully taxable. Buckeye is taxed at a 48% rate.

(a) Should the treasurer take Mr. Info's advice and purchase the 12% security?

(b) What is the equivalent before-tax yield on the municipal assuming Buckeye is in a 48% tax bracket?

SOLUTION

(a) The after-tax yield to Buckeye on the 12% offering is (0.12)(1 - 0.48) = 6.24%. Since the yield on the municipal is already stated on an after-tax basis, the treasurer should ignore Mr. Info's advice and purchase the municipal offering.

(b) The equivalent before-tax yield is:

$$r = \frac{0.07}{(1 - 0.48)} = \underline{13.46\%}$$

Thus, the taxable issue would have to yield in excess of 13.46% to be more attractive than the municipal to Buckeye.

6. Tech Electronics, manufacturers of fine calculators, has recently purchased 10-year bonds at their par value of $1,000 per security. Texas Parts, a close competitor, has just purchased 5-year bonds at their $1,000 par value. Both securities have a coupon rate set at 8%, are compounded annually, and have a maturity value of $1,000. Suppose the prevailing interest rate 1 year from now rises to 10%. What would the decline in market price be for each bond in 1 year?

SOLUTION

One year from now the 5-year issue has 4 years remaining to maturity. The market price in 1 year can be found by computing P according to the following:

$$P = \sum_{T=1}^{4} \frac{\$80}{(1 + 0.10)^T} + \frac{\$1,000}{(1 + 0.10)^4} = \$936.60$$

where $80 = (0.08)($1,000). Similarly, for the 10-year issue which now has 9 years to maturity,

$$P = \sum_{T=1}^{9} \frac{\$80}{(1 + 0.10)^T} + \frac{\$1,000}{(1 + 0.10)^9} = \$884.82$$

Thus, the 10-year security declines in price $115.18($1,000 − $884.82), while the 5-year security declines in price by only $63.40($1,000 − $936.60). This illustrates the concept of interest rate risk discussed in the text of Chapter 8.


Self-Tests

TRUE-FALSE

_____ 1. The firm's compensating balance requirement should be the primary consideration in the determination of its optimal average cash balance level.

_____ 2. Since no two commercial banks are exactly alike, there may be significant differences in their compensating balance requirements for a given level of account activity.

_____ 3. A construction firm would be more likely than a utility firm to find the control-limit cash management model useful.

_____ 4. Although they have a lower yield, agency securities are more readily marketable by the purchasing corporation than are Treasury bills.

_____ 5. Bankers' acceptances generally mature from 9 to 12 months after "sight."

_____ 6. Commercial paper is backed by specific assets of the firm.

_____ 7. The most common denomination for the negotiable CD is $10,000.

_____ 8. The longer the term of maturity, the less sensitive the price of a security to changes in interest rates.

_____ 9. Economies of scale reduce the cash balances needed by firms.

_____ 10. Long-term bonds may serve as a useful (comfortable) hedge against interest rate risk.

_____ 11. Compensating balances may have a direct impact on the effective rate of interest on a commercial loan.

_____ 12. Because of their higher financial risk, agency securities always yield more than Treasury securities of a comparable maturity do.

_____ 13. The higher the marginal tax bracket, the lower the after-tax rate of return on a taxable security.

_____ 14. Bankers' acceptances provide for a steady flow of interest payments to the investor in the form of coupon payments.

_____ 15. With respect to interest risk, Treasury securities are risk-free.

MULTIPLE CHOICE

1. The firm's optimal level of transactions and precautionary balances is influenced by:

a. The firm's debt maturity structure.
b. The anticipation of a short-term, general decline in the level of stock market prices over the near term.
c. Possible deviations from the firm's expected cash flows.
d. a and c.
e. All of the above.

2. Assumptions of the inventory model for cash management include:

   a. Cash payments are steady over the analysis period.
   b. Cash payments are completely predictable.
   c. The fixed cost of a transaction to buy or sell marketable securities is known with certainty.
   d. All of the above.
   e. None of the above.

3. The control-limit model for cash management considers:

   a. The variance of daily changes in the firm's expected cash balances.
   b. The fixed cost of a security transaction.
   c. The systematic risk of the firm's common stock returns.
   d. a and b.
   e. b and c.

4. You have decided to take out a $1,000 loan. Your bank gives you the following choices:
   (1) A 10%, 1-year loan with interest and principle due at the end of that time.
   (2) An 8%, 1-year loan with a 20% compensating balance, again with principle and interest due in 1 year.
   Which of the following would be your response?

   a. To take alternative (1) above.
   b. To take alternative (2) above.
   c. To flip a fair coin.

5. The Chance Co., a maker of dice, faces a stochastic demand for its products which affect its cash flows. The variance of these daily cash flows is $500,000. The interest rate available on marketable securities is 9%. The firm uses a 360-day year in its analysis procedures. Any time Chance buys or sells securities it incurs a fixed transaction cost of $300. At what level of cash will Chance buy marketable securities?

   a. $608,219.
   b. $7,663.
   c. $22,989.
   d. $202,740.

# Accounts Receivable and Inventory Management

Orientation: The investment of funds in accounts receivable and inventory involves a tradeoff between profitability and risk. In examining these investment problems, the analysis will center around the marginal benefits and costs associated with each investment. With respect to inventory management, a larger investment in inventory leads to more efficient production and speedier delivery, hence, increased sales. However, additional financing to support the increase in inventory and increased handling and carrying costs is required.

I. Accounts receivable

    A. Typically, accounts receivable accounts for about 24% of a firm's assets.

    B. The size of the investment in accounts receivable varies from industry to industry and is affected by several factors including the percentage of credit sales to total sales, the level of sales, and the credit and collection policies, more specifically the terms of sale, the quality of customer, and collection efforts.

    C. Although all these factors affect the size of the investment, only the credit and collection policies are decision variables under the control of the financial manager.

D. The terms of sale are generally stated in the form a/b net c, indicating that the customer can deduct a% if the account is paid within b days; otherwise, the account must be paid within c days.

E. If the customer decides to forego the discount and not pay until the final payment date, the annualized opportunity cost of passing up this a% discount and withholding payment until the cth day is determined as follows:

$$\text{annualized opportunity cost of foregoing the discount} = \frac{a}{1-a} \times \frac{360}{c-b}$$

Example:  Given the trade credit terms of 3/20 net 60, what is the annualized opportunity cost of passing up the 3% discount and withholding payment until the 60th day? Solution:  Substituting in the values from the example, we get:

$$27.8\% = \frac{0.03}{1-0.03} \times \frac{360}{60-20}$$

F. A second decision variable in determining the size of the investment in accounts receivable in addition to the trade credit terms is the type of customer.

1. The costs associated with extending credit to lower-quality customers include:

   a. Increased costs of credit investigation.

   b. Increased probability of customer default.

   c. Increased collection costs.

G. Analyzing the credit applicant is a major part of accounts receivable management.

1. Several avenues are open to the firm in considering the credit rating of an applicant.  Among these are financial statements, independent credit ratings and reports, bank checking, information from other companies, and past experiences.

2. Once the decision to extend credit has been made and if the decision is yes, a maximum credit line is established as a ceiling on the amount of credit to be extended.

H. The third and final decision variable in determining the size of the investment in accounts receivable is the firm's collection policies.

1. Collection policy is a combination of letter sending, telephone calls, personal visits, and legal actions.

2. The greater the amount spent on collecting, the lower the volume of bad debts.

   a. The relationship is not linear, however, and beyond a point is not helpful.

   b. If sales are independent of collection efforts, then methods of collection should be evaluated with respect to the reduction in bad debts against the cost of lowering those bad debts.

I. Credit should be extended to the point that marginal profitability on additional sales equals the required rate of return on the additional investment in receivables necessary to generate those sales.

II. Inventory

A. Typically, inventory accounts for about 6.87% of a firm's assets.

B. The purpose of carrying inventories is to uncouple the operations of the firm, that is, to make each function of the business independent of each other function.

C. As such, the decision with respect to the size of the investment in inventory involves a basic tradeoff between risk and return.

D. The risk comes from the possibility of running out of inventory if too little inventory is held, while the return aspect of this tradeoff results because increased inventory investment costs money.

E. There are several general types of inventory including:

1. Raw materials inventory consists of the basic materials that have been purchased from other firms to be used in the firm's productions operations. This type of inven-

tory uncouples the production function from the purchasing function.

2. Work in process inventory consists of partially finished goods that require additional work before they become finished goods. This type of inventory uncouples the various production operations.

3. Finished goods inventory consists of goods on which the production has been completed but the goods are not yet sold. This type of inventory uncouples the production and sales function.

4. Stock of cash inventory, already discussed in some detail in previous chapters, serves to make the payment of bills independent of the collection of accounts due.

F. In order to effectively manage the investment in inventory, two problems must be dealt with: the order quantity problem and the order point problem.

G. The order quantity problem involves the determination of the optimal order size for an inventory item given its expected usage, carrying, and ordering costs.

H. The economic order quantity (EOQ) model attempts to determine the order size that will minimize total inventory costs. The EOQ is given as:

$$Q* = \sqrt{\frac{2SO}{C}}$$

where C = carrying costs per unit,
     O = ordering costs per order,
     S = total demand in units over the planning period,
     Q* = the optimal order quantity in units.

I. The order point problem attempts to answer the following question: How low should inventory be depleted before it is reordered?

J. In answering this question two factors become important:

1. What is the usual procurement or delivery time and how much stock is needed to accommodate this time period?

2. How much safety stock does the management desire?

K. Modification for safety stocks is necessary since the usage rate of inventory is seldom stable over a given timetable.

L. This safety stock is used to safeguard the firm against changes in order time and receipt of shipped goods.

M. The greater the uncertainty associated with forecasted demand or order time, the larger the safety stock.

   1. The costs associated with running out of inventory will also determine the safety stock levels.

   2. A point is reached where it is too costly to carry a larger safety stock given the associated risk.


## Study Problems

1. Assume that a firm currently has annual sales, all credit, of $5,000,000 and a receivables turnover ratio of 3.5 times per year. The current level of bad debt losses is $100,000, and the firm's required rate of return on any new investment in receivables is 25%. Further assume that this firm produces only one product with variable costs equaling 80% of the selling price. The company is contemplating a change in its credit policy that would result in an increase in sales to $5,500,000, a decrease in the receivables turnover ratio to 3.1 times per year, and an increase in bad debt losses to $120,000. Should this credit policy change be made?

   SOLUTION

   Step 1: Determine what the marginal benefits would be from this change.

   | | |
   |---|---:|
   | Marginal increase in sales above the present policy ($5,500,000 − $5,000,000) | $500,000 |
   | Profit on increased sales (20%, since variable costs are 80%) | $100,000 |
   | Marginal loss from an increase in bad debts | $ 20,000 |
   | Profit on marginal increase in sales (less marginal increase in bad debt losses) | $ 80,000 |

Step 2: Determine the required return on the marginal investment in accounts receivable.

Marginal increase in receivables above the present policy

$$\text{(current average investment)} = \frac{\text{credit sales}}{\text{A/R turnover ratio}}$$

$$= \frac{\$5,000,000}{3.5} = \$1,428,571$$

and proposed·average investment $= \dfrac{\text{credit sales}}{\text{A/R turnover ratio}}$

$$= \frac{\$5,500,000}{3.1} = \$1,774,194;$$

thus, increased investment $= \$1,774,194 - \$1,428,571$

$\qquad = \$345,623$                                                        $\$345,623$

Marginal increase in investment in
   receivables (marginal increase in

$\qquad$ receivables X $\dfrac{\text{variable costs per unit}}{\text{selling price per unit}}$

$\qquad$ or \$345,623 X 0.80 = \$276,498)                    $\$276,498$
Required return (25%) on the marginal
   increase in receivables                                $\$\ 69,124.50$

Step 3: Compare the marginal benefits with the required return.

Profit on marginal increase in sales (less
   marginal increase in bad debt losses)
   less required return (25%) on the
   marginal increase in investment in
   receivables                                            $\$\ 10,875.50$

Since the benefits outweigh the costs, the change should be made.

2. The Swank Furniture Company is trying to determine the optimal order quantity for sofas. Annual sales for sofas are $800 at a retail price of $300. The cost of carrying sofas is $1 per month. It costs $35.00 to prepare and receive an order.

(a) Determine the EOQ.

(b) If the monthly sales rate for November-December is 100 and for June-July only 25, what is the EOQ for each period?

SOLUTION

(a) $EOQ = \sqrt{\dfrac{2(67)(35)}{1}} = \sqrt{4.690} = 68.48 = 69$ sofas

(b) $EOQ = \sqrt{\dfrac{2(100)(35)}{1}} = \sqrt{7,000} = 83.66$ (November-December)

$= \sqrt{\dfrac{2(25)(35)}{1}} = \sqrt{1,750} = 41.83$ (June-July)

Self-Tests

TRUE-FALSE

_____ 1. The objective in credit policy management is to minimize losses.

_____ 2. An increase in the time period over which credit must be repaid will increase demand.

_____ 3. Receivables arise from credit sales.

_____ 4. To speed up the turnover of receivables, a firm may either shorten the discount term or increase the discount offered.

_____ 5. The expression "5/10, net 30" means that the customers receive a 10% discount if they pay within 5 days; otherwise, they must pay within 30 days.

_____ 6. There is no one level of inventory that is efficient for all firms.

_____ 7. In determining the level of safety stock it is important to evauluate the tradeoff between the cost of carrying the additional inventory with the risk of running out of inventory.

_____ 8. Lead time in determining the reorder point refers to the time between the receipt of a customer's order and the shipment of that order.

_____ 9. Large safety stocks tend to reduce the possibility of stockouts.

_____ 10. The EOQ provides for an optimal safety stock determination.

MULTIPLE CHOICE

1. The major objective of a credit policy is to:

   a. Maximize sales.
   b. Minimize losses.
   c. Maximize profits.
   d. None of the above.

2. Which of the following is not part of the firm's credit and collection policy decisions?

   a. The credit period.
   b. The cash discount given.
   c. The dividend decision.
   d. The level of collection expenditures.
   e. The quality of account accepted.

3. Marginal analysis deals specifically with:

   a. Savings derived from varying receivables levels.
   b. Incremental benefits minus incremental costs.
   c. Excess production capacity.
   d. Reduction of carrying costs.

4. Which of the following would be a source of credit information?

   a. Firm's financial statement.
   b. Credit ratings from Dun & Bradstreet.
   c. A credit check through a bank.
   d. The company's past experience.
   e. All of the above.

5. Which of the following is a cost associated with relaxed credit standards?

   a. Enlarged credit department.
   b. Increased probability of bad debt.
   c. Additional investment in receivables.
   d. All of the above.
   e. None of the above.

6. All of the following are relationships that exist for safety stock except:

   a. The greater the risk of running out of stock, the larger the safety stock.
   b. The larger the opportunity cost of the funds invested in inventory, the smaller the safety stock.

c. The greater the uncertainty associated with future forecasts of use, the larger the safety stock.
d. The higher the profit margin per unit, the lower the safety stock necessary.

# Short-Term Financing

Orientation: This chapter is one of the four chapters dealing with the sources of financing. It deals with the sources of short-term financing that must be repaid within 1 year.

I. Determining the appropriate level of short-term financing

    A. In Chapter 6 the hedging concept was presented as one basis for determining the firms of short-term debt.

    B. Hedging involves attempting to match temporary needs for funds with short-term sources of financing and permanent needs with long-term sources.

II. Selecting a source of short-term financing

    A. In general, there are three basic factors that should be considered in selecting a source of short-term financing:

        1. The effective cost of the credit source.

        2. The availability of credit.

        3. The effect of the use of a particular source of credit on the cost and availability of other sources.

B. The basic procedure used in estimating the cost of short-term credit utilizes the basic interest equation, i.e., interest = principal X rate X time.

C. The problem faced in assessing the cost of a source of short-term financing involves estimating the annual effective rate (RATE) where the interest amount, the principal sum, and the time for which financing will be needed is known. Thus, the basic interest equation is "rearranged" as follows:

$$RATE = \frac{interest}{principal} \: X \: \frac{1}{time}$$

D. Compound interest was not considered in the simple RATE calculation. To consider compounding, the following relation is used:

$$RATE = \left(1 + \frac{R}{M}\right)^{M} - 1$$

where R is the nominal rate of interest per year and M is the number of compounding periods within 1 year. The effect of compounding is thus to raise the effective cost of short-term credit.

III. Sources of short-term credit

A. The two basic sources of short-term credit are unsecured and secured credit.

1. Unsecured credit consists of all those sources which have as their security only the lender's faith in the ability of the borrower to repay the funds when due.

2. Secured funds include additional security in the form of assets that are pledged as collateral in the event the borrower defaults in payment of principal or interest.

B. There are three major sources of unsecured short-term credit: trade credit, unsecured bank loans, and commercial paper.

1. Trade credit provides one of the most flexible sources of financing available to the firm. To arrange for credit, the firm need only place an order with one of its suppliers. The supplier then checks the firm's credit and if the credit is good, the supplier sends the merchandise.

2. Commercial banks provide unsecured short-term credit in two basic forms:  lines of credit and transaction loans (notes payable).  Maturities of both types of loans are usually 1 year or less with rates of interest depending on the credit worthiness of the borrower and the level of interest rates in the economy as a whole.

3. A line of credit is generally an informal agreement or understanding between the borrower and the bank as to the maximum amount of credit that the bank will provide the borrower at any one time.  There is no "legal" commitment on the part of the bank to provide the stated credit. There is another variant of this form of financing referred to as a <u>revolving credit agreement</u> whereby such a legal obligation is involved.  The line of credit generally covers a period of 1 year corresponding to the borrower's "fiscal" year.

4. Transaction loans are another form of unsecured short-term bank credit; the transaction loan, in contrast to lined credit, is made for a specific purpose.

5. Only the largest and most credit worthy companies are able to use commercial paper which consists of unsecured promissory notes in the money market.

   a. The maturities of commercial paper are generally 6 months or less with the interest rate slightly lower than the prime rate on commercial bank loans.  The new issues of commercial paper are either directly placed or dealer placed.

   b. There are a number of advantages that accrue to the user of commercial paper:  Interest rates are generally lower than rates on bank loans and comparable sources of short-term financing.  No minimum balance requirements are associated with commercial paper. Commercial paper offers the firm with very large credit needs a single source for all its short-term financing needs.  Since it is widely recognized that only the most credit worthy borrowers have access to the commercial paper market, its use signifies a firm's credit status.

   c. However, a very important "risk" is involved in using this source of short-term financing; the commercial paper market is highly impersonal and denies even the most credit worthy borrower any flexibility in terms of repayment.

B. Secured sources of short-term credit have certain assets of the firm, such as accounts receivable or inventories, pledged as collateral to secure a loan.  Upon default of the loan agreement, the lender has first claim to the pledged assets.

   1. Generally, a firm's receivables are among its most liquid assets.  Two secured loan arrangements are generally made with accounts receivable as collateral: (a) Under the arrangement of pledged accounts receivables, the amount of the loan is stated as a percent of the face value of the receivables pledged.  (b) Factoring accounts receivables involves the outright sale of a firm's accounts receivables to a factor.

   2. Four secured loan arrangements are generally made with inventory as collateral: (a) Under the floating lien agreement, the borrower gives the lender a lien against all his or her inventories.  (b) The chattel mortgage agreement involves having specific items of inventory identified in the security agreement.  (c) The field warehouse financing agreements means that the inventories used as collateral are physically separated from the firm's other inventories and are placed under the control of a third-party field warehousing firm.  (d) Terminal warehouse agreements involve tranporting the inventories pledged as collateral to a public warehouse which is physically removed from the borrower's premises.

## Study Problems

1. In order to meet a temporary need for working capital during an upcoming seasonal peak in sales, Gregory Sales Company will require $500,000.  Gregory's bank has agreed to loan the funds for the necessary 3-month interval at a rate of 12% with a 10% compensating balance.  Gregory Sales Company normally maintains a demand deposit account of $20,000.  Estimate the annual (effective) cost of the loan to Gregory.

   SOLUTION

To obtain the needed $500,000 and meet the compensating balance

requirement, Gregory must borrow X dollars, where X is found as
follows:

$$X - 0.20X - 20,000 = 500,000$$

$$0.80X = 480,000$$

$$X = \$600,000$$

Thus, Gregory borrows $600,000, for which it must maintain a
compensating balance of 0.20 X 600,000 = $120,000, of which
$20,000 will come from its normal demand deposit and $100,000
must be borrowed, which will leave the firm the use of $500,000.
The interest cost of the loan is computed as follows:

$$\text{interest} = 0.12 \times 600,000 \div 4 = \$18,000$$

Divide by 4 since the loan is for only 3 months or one-fourth of
a year. The effective annual cost of the loan is:

$$\text{annual rate} = \frac{\$ \text{ loan cost}}{\$ \text{ funds available}} \div \begin{array}{l} \text{loan maturity as a} \\ \text{fraction of 1 year} \end{array}$$

$$= \frac{18,000}{500,000} \div \frac{3}{12}$$

$$= \underline{0.144} \text{ or } \underline{14.4\%}$$

2. A factor has agreed to buy Thomas Brothers Company's receivables
($250,000 per month), which have an average collection period of 90
days. The factor will advance up to 80% of the face value of the
receivables for an annual charge of 10% of the funds advanced. The
factor also charges a handling fee of 5% of the face value of all
accounts purchased. What is the effective annual cost of the factoring arrangement to Thomas Brothers if the maximum advance is taken
every month?

SOLUTION

With an average collection period of 90 days and monthly credit
sales, Thomas Brothers could build up a loan advance over 3
months of 0.80 X 750,000 = $600,000. This loan would be constant-
ly rolling over as accounts were being collected and as new credit
sales were being made. The 90-day interest cost of the loan would
be computed:

$$\text{interest} = \$600,000 \text{ X } 0.10 \div 4 = \$15,000$$

The factor's fee would be as follows:

$$\text{fee} = 0.05 \text{ X } 750,000 = 37,500$$

Thus, the effective annual cost of the 90-day loan would be:

$$\text{annual rate} = \frac{\$15,000 + 37,500}{\$600,000} \div \frac{3}{12}$$

$$= \underline{0.35} \text{ or } \underline{35\%}$$

3. For the past 7 years Warden Company has been factoring its accounts receivables. The factor's fee is 3% and the factor will lend up to 90% of the volume of receivables purchased for an additional 1% per month. The firm typically has sales of $200,000 per month; 75% are on credit. Warden Company will save credit department costs of $3,500, since it will no longer need to operate a credit department. In addition, there will no longer be bad-debt losses which previously were 1¼% per month.

The firm's bank has recently offered to lend the firm up to 90% of the face value of the receivables shown on the schedule of accounts. The bank would charge 9% per annum interest plus a 2% processing charge per dollar of receivables loaned. The firm extends terms of net 30, and all customers who plan to pay will do so by the thirtieth of the month. Should the firm discontinue its factoring arrangement in favor of the bank's offer if the firm borrows, on the average, $100,000 per month on its receivables?

SOLUTION

The cost of factoring is:

| | |
|---|---|
| Fee (0.03 X $200,000 x 0.90) | $5,400 |
| Interest cost (0.01 X $100,000) | 1,000 |
| | $6,400 |

The cost of the bank loan is:

| | |
|---|---|
| Fee (0.02 X 100,000) | $2,000 |
| Interest (0.09 X $200,000 X 1/12) | 1,500 |
| | $3,500 |

Plus:

| | |
|---|---:|
| Credit department cost per month | $3,500 |
| Bad-debt losses ($200,000 X 90 X 0.0125) | 2,250 |
| Total cost | $5,750 |

Yes, go with the bank loan.

## Self-Tests

TRUE-FALSE

_____ 1. The amount of trade credit available to the firm varies inversely with the size of the cash discount.

_____ 2. Compensating balances are never required when a firm has a line of credit with a bank.

_____ 3. A transaction loan is made for a specific purpose or use for the funds involved.

_____ 4. An advantage of commercial paper to a credit worthy borrower is that repayment can be postponed if necessary.

_____ 5. Pledging involves selling accounts receivable to a factor.

_____ 6. The primary sources of collateral for secured short-term credit are accounts receivable and inventories.

_____ 7. Field warehouse financing agreements involve physically moving the pledged inventories to a public warehouse.

_____ 8. Commercial paper and trade credit are both forms of secured credit.

_____ 9. An advantage of trade credit is that the amount of credit extended expands and contracts with the needs of the firm.

_____ 10. The "prime rate of interest" represents the rate a bank charges its most credit worthy borrowers.

MULTIPLE CHOICE

1. Which of the following is not a form of security for short-term credit?
   a. General lien.
   b. Chattel mortgages.

   c. Commercial paper.
   d. Terminal warehouse receipt.
   e. Factoring.

2. Under which of the following agreements does the borrower retain physical possession of the inventory used as collateral for a loan?

   a. Field warehouse financing.
   b. Chattel mortgage.
   c. Terminal warehouse.
   d. All of the above.
   e. None of the above.

3. An informal agreement between a bank and its customer with respect to the maximum amount of unsecured credit the bank will permit the firm to owe at any one time is a:

   a. Line of credit.
   b. Revolving credit agreement.
   c. Transaction loan.
   d. None of the above.

4. When a firm needs short-term funds for only one purpose, it usually obtains _____.

   a. Line of credit.
   b. Revolving credit agreement.
   c. Transaction loan.
   d. Compensating balance.
   e. None of the above.

5. If a firm borrows $1 million at 8% and is required to maintain $100,000 in a compensating balance, the effective annual interest cost is:

   a. 8%.
   b. 8.88%.
   c. 7.27%.
   d. 9.5%.
   e. None of the above.

6. Inventory is in the possession of a third party under which of the following arrangements?

   a. Floating lien agreement.
   b. Terminal warehouse receipt loan.
   c. Chattel mortgage.
   d. Line of credit.
   e. None of the above.

# Capital Budgeting

Orientation:  Capital budgeting involves the decision-making process with respect to investment in fixed assets; specifically, it involves measuring the incremental cash flows associated with investment proposals and evaluating the attractiveness of these cash flows relative to the project's costs.  This chapter focuses on the estimation of those cash flows from investment proposals and the evaluation of those cash flows based on various decision criteria.


I.  What criteria should we use in the evaluation of alternative investment proposals?

   A. Use cash flows rather than accounting profits because cash flows allow us to correctly analyze the time element of the flows.

   B. Examine cash flows on an after-tax basis because they are the flows available to shareholders.

   C. Only include the incremental cash flows resulting from the investment decision.  Ignore all other flows.

II. Measuring cash flows: We are interested in measuring the incremental after-tax cash flows resulting from the investment proposal. In general, there will be three major sources of cash flows: initial outlays, differential cash flows over the project's life, and terminal cash flows.

A. Initial outlays include whatever cash flows are necessary to get the project in running order; for example:

1. The installed cost of the asset.

2. In the case of a replacement proposal, the selling price of the old machine plus (or minus) any tax gain (or loss) offsetting the initial outlay.

3. Any expense items (for example, training) necessary for the operation of the proposal.

4. Any other non-expense cash outlays required, even if not expenses such as increased working-capital needs.

5. The tax shield resulting from the investment tax credit.

B. Differential cash flows over the project's life include the incremental after-tax flows over the life of the project; for example:

1. Added revenue (less added selling expenses) for the proposal.

2. Any labor and/or material savings incurred.

3. Increases in overhead incurred.

4. These values are measured on an after-tax basis, thus allowing for the tax savings (or loss) from incremental increase (or decrease) in depreciation to be included.

5. A word of warning not to include financing charges (such as interest or preferred stock dividends), for they are implicitly taken care of in the discounting process.

C. Terminal cash flows include any incremental cash flows that result at the termination of the project; for example:

1. The project's salvage value plus (or minus) any taxable gains or losses associated with the project.

2. Any terminal cash flow needed, perhaps disposal of obsolete equipment.

3. Recovery of any non-expense cash outlays associated with the project, such as recovery of increased working-capital needs associated with the proposal.

III. Methods for evaluating projects

A. Average rate of return is

$$\begin{array}{c}\text{average rate} \\ \text{of return}\end{array} = \sum_{t=1}^{n} \frac{\dfrac{\text{annual profits after tax}_t}{n}}{\dfrac{\text{investment + salvage value}}{2}}$$

1. This formula assumes straight-line depreciation; thus, the average investment in the project is equal to the sum of the investment plus the salvage value divided by 2.

2. Although this measure has the advantages of being easy to calculate and of having familiar terms, it uses profits rather than cash flows in its calculations and does not consider the time value of money.

B. The payback method

1. The payback period of an investment tells the number of years required to recover the initial investment. The payback period is calculated by adding the cash flows up until they are equal to the initial fixed investment.

2. Although this measure does, in fact, deal with cash flows and is easy to calculate and understand, it ignores any cash flows that occur after the payback period and does not consider the time value of money within the payback period.

C. Present-value methods

1. The net present value of an investment project is the present value of the cash inflows less the present value of the cash outflows. By assigning negative values to cash outflows, it becomes:

$$NPV = \sum_{t=1}^{n} \frac{ACF_t}{(1 + k)^t} - IO$$

where $ACF_t$ = the annual after-tax cash flow in time period t (this can take on either positive or negative values),

$k$ = the required rate of return or appropriate discount rate or cost of capital[1],

$IO$ = the initial cash outlay,

$n$ = the project's expected life.

a. The acceptance criteria are:

accept if NPV > 0

reject if NPV < 0

b. The advantage of this approach is that it takes the time value of money into consideration in addition to dealing with cash flows.

2. The profitability index is the ratio of the present value of the expected future net cash flows to the initial cash outlay, or

$$\text{profitability index} = \frac{\sum\limits_{t=1}^{n} \dfrac{ACF_t}{(1 + k)^t}}{IO}$$

a. The acceptance criteria are:

accept if PI > 1.0

reject if PI < 1.0

b. The advantages of this method are the same as those for the net present value.

c. Either of these present-value methods will give the same accept-reject decisions to a project.

D. The internal rate of return is the discount rate that equates the present value of the project's future net cash flows with the project's initial outlay. Thus, the internal rate of return is represented by IRR in the equation below:

$$IO = \sum\limits_{t=1}^{n} \frac{ACF_t}{(1 + IRR)^t}$$

---

[1]The cost of capital is discussed in Chapter 14.

1. The acceptance-rejection criteria are:

accept if IRR > required rate of return

reject if IRR < required rate of return

The required rate of return is often taken to be the
firm's cost of capital, which will be discussed in
Chapter 14.

2. The advantages of this method are that it deal with cash
flows and recognizes the time value of money; however,
the procedure is rather complicated and time-consuming.

IV. Mutually exclusive projects: Although the IRR and the present-
value methods will, in general, give consistent accept-reject
decisions, they may not rank projects identically.  This
becomes important in the case of mutually exclusive projects.

A. A project is mutually exclusive if acceptance of it pre-
cludes the acceptance of one or more projects.  In this case,
the project's relative ranking becomes important.

B. Ranking conflicts come as a result of the different assumptions on the reinvestment rate on funds released from the
proposals.

C. Thus, when conflicting ranking of mutually exclusive projects results from the different reinvestment assumptions,
the decision boils down to which assumption is best.

D. In general, the net present value method is considered to be
theoretically superior.

V. Capital rationing is the situation in which a budget ceiling or
constraint is placed upon the amount of funds that can be invested during a time period.

A. Theoretically, a firm should never reject a project that
yields more than the required rate of return.  Although
there are circumstances that may create complicated
situations, in general, an investment policy limited by
capital rationing is less than optimal.


Study Problems

1. The cost of new machinery for a given investment project will be
$100,000.  Incremental cash flows after taxes will be $40,000 in

years 1 and 2 and will be $60,000 in year 3.  What is the payback period for this project, and if acceptable projects must recover the initial investment in 2.5 years, should this project be accepted or rejected?

SOLUTION

After 2 years they will have recovered $80,000 of the $100,000 outlay and they expect to recover an additional $60,000 in the third year.  Thus, the payback period becomes

$$2 \text{ years} + \frac{\$20,000}{\$60,000} = 2.33 \text{ years}$$

$$2.33 \text{ years} < 2.5 \text{ years}$$

Therefore, accept the project.

2. A given investment project will cost $50,000.  Incremental cash flows after taxes are expected to be $10,000 per year for the life of the investment, which is 7 years.  There will be no salvage value at the end of the 7 years.  The required rate of return is 14%.  On the basis of the profitability index method, should the investment be accepted?

SOLUTION

$$\text{PV of cash flow} = \$10,000(4.288) = \$42,880$$

$$\text{PV of cash outlay} = \$50,000$$

$$PI = \frac{\$42,880}{\$50,000} = 0.8576 < 1$$

Therefore, the project should be rejected.

3. Miller Electric Company is considering the replacement of an existing tool which has a current book value of $10,000 and can currently be sold for $4,000.  The salvage value of the old machine in 5 years will be zero, and the machine is being depreciated on a straight-line basis.  The new machine would perform the same function as the old machine and would yield annual savings before depreciation and taxes of $10,000 per year.  The new machine has a 5-year life, costs $34,000, and can be sold for an expected $4,000 at the end of the fifth year.  Assume straight-line depreciation, a 40% tax rate, and cost of capital of 12%.  Find the payback period and net present value.

SOLUTION

Initial outlay:

| | |
|---|---:|
| Purchase price | $-34,000 |
| Salvage value | 4,000 |
| Tax savings on loss ($10,000 - 4,000)0.4 | 2,400 |
| | $-27,600 |

Differential flows over the project's life (years 1 through 5):

| | Book Profit | Cash Flow |
|---|---|---|
| Savings: annual savings | $10,000 | $10,000 |
| Costs: increased depreciation ($6,000 - 2,000) | 4,000 | |
| Taxable income | $ 6,000 | |
| Taxes | $ 2,400 → → → → | 2,400 |
| Net cash flow after taxes | | $ 7,600 |

Terminal cash flow:

Salvage value = $4,000.

Cash-flow diagram:

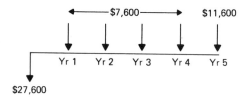

(a) Payback period: After 3 years they will have recovered
    $22,800 and during the fourth year they expect to recover
    $7,600. Thus, the payback period becomes

$$3 \text{ years} + \frac{\$4,800}{\$7,600} = 3.63 \text{ years}$$

(b) Net present value = $7,600(3.037) + $11,600(0.567) - $27,600
                      = $23,081 + $6,577 - $27,600
                      = $2,058

120

4. What is the project's internal rate of return?

    SOLUTION

    Try 14%:

$$\$27,600 = \$7,600(2.914) + \$11,600(0.519)$$
$$= \$22,146 + \$6,020$$
$$= \$28,166$$

    Try 15%:

$$\$27,600 = \$7,600(2.855) + \$11,600(0.497)$$
$$= \$21,698 + \$5,765$$
$$= \$27,463$$

Thus, the IRR is just a bit below 15%.


## Self-Tests

TRUE-FALSE

_____ 1. Cash flow, not income, is what is important in capital budgeting.

_____ 2. The net present value of a project decreases as the required rate of return increases.

_____ 3. The higher the discount rate, the more valued is the proposal with the early cash flows.

_____ 4. The net-present-value approach is preferred over the profitability index for mutually exclusive projects because it measures worth in absolute terms and the profitability index measures worth in relative terms.

_____ 5. Capital rationing occurs when profitable projects must be rejected because of shortage of capital.

_____ 6. The net present value of a project will equal zero whenever the average rate of return equals the required rate of return.

_____ 7. The net present value of a project will equal zero when-

ever the payback period of a project equals the required
payback period.

_____   8. The average rate of return will always equal the internal
rate of return.

_____   9. One difference in the net-present-value approach and the
internal-rate-of-return method is the reinvestment-rate
assumption.

_____  10. Capital rationing is not an optimal capital budgeting
strategy.

MULTIPLE CHOICE

1. Which of the following considers the time value of money?

   a. Payback method.
   b. Average rate of return.
   c. Profitability index.
   d. None of the above.

2. Which of the following is important to capital budgeting decisions?

   a. Depreciation method.
   b. Salvage value.
   c. Timing of cash flows.
   d. Taxes.
   e. All of the above.

3. Which of the following is an estimate approach?

   a. Average rate of return.
   b. Profitability index.
   c. Internal rate of return.
   d. Net present value.

4. The net-present-value approach and the internal-rate-of-return
   method may lead to discrepancies when:

   a. Projects are dependent.
   b. The discount rate equals zero.
   c. Projects are mutually exclusive.
   d. All of the above.

5. The average-rate-of-return method will always lead to the same
   accept or reject decision as will the:

   a. Profitability index.
   b. Net-present-value method.

c. Payback method.
d. Internal-rate-of-return method.
e. None of the above.

# Capital Budgeting under Uncertainty

Orientation:  The focus of this chapter will be on how to measure and adjust for the riskiness of a given project or combination of projects and on understanding how risk affects the value of a firm.

  I. Risk and the investment decision

   A. Up to this point we have treated the expected cash flows resulting from an investment proposal as being known with perfect certainty.  We will now introduce risk.

   B. The riskiness of an investment project is defined as the variability of its cash flows from the expected cash flow.

 II. Quantitative risk measures

   A. Probability distributions illustrate the complete set of probabilities for all possible outcomes for one particular event.

    1. A discrete probability distribution is one in which a probability is assigned to each possible outcome in the set of all possible outcomes.

    2. In a continuous probability distribution there are an

infinite number of possible outcomes, in which the probability of an event is related to a range of possible outcomes.

3. The expected value of a distribution is the arithmetic mean or average of all possible outcomes; those outcomes are weighted by the probability that each outcome will occur.

B. Risk, that is the dispersion of the distribution, can be measured in either relative or absolute terms.

1. The standard deviation provides a measure of the absolute spread of the probability distribution. Quantitatively, it is defined as:

$$\sigma = \sqrt{\sum_{i=1}^{n} \frac{(X_i - \overline{X})^2}{P(X_i)}}$$

where n = the number of possible outcomes,

$X_i$ = the value of the ith possible outcome,

$\overline{X}$ = the expected value,

$P(X_i)$ = the probability that the ith outcome will occur.

EXAMPLE 1

| State | Probability | Proposal A | Weighted Average | Proposal B | Weighted Average |
|-------|-------------|------------|------------------|------------|------------------|
| Deep recession | 0.2 | $20,000 | $ 4,000 | $10,000 | $ 2,000 |
| Normal | 0.6 | 25,000 | 15,000 | 25,000 | 15,000 |
| Major boom | 0.2 | 30,000 | 6,000 | 40,000 | 8,000 |
| | | Expected value = | $25,000 | | $25,000 |

$$\sigma_A = \sqrt{(\$20,000 - \$25,000)^2 (0.2) + (\$25,000 - \$25,000)^2 (0.6) + (\$30,000 - \$25,000)^2 (0.2)}$$

$$= \sqrt{\$5,000,000 + \$5,000,000} = \underline{\$3,162.28}$$

$$\sigma_B = \sqrt{(\$10,000 - \$25,000)^2 (0.2) + (\$25,000 - \$25,000)^2 (0.6) + (\$40,000 - \$25,000)^2 (0.2)}$$

$$= \sqrt{\$45,000,000 + \$45,000,000} = \underline{\$9,486.833}$$

  a. The standard deviation simply measures the tightness
     of a probability distribution.

  b. The lower the standard deviation of the cash flow,
     the lower the perceived risk.

2. The coefficient of variation is the measure of relative
   dispersion or risk in a project.

$$\gamma \quad \frac{\sigma}{\overline{X}}$$

  a. Whereas the standard deviation gives us a measure of
     absolute risk, the coefficient of variation gives us
     a measure of relative risk (i.e., risk per unit of
     return).

III. Methods for incorporating risk into capital budgeting

  A. The certainty equivalent approach involves a direct attempt
     to allow the decision maker to incorporate his or her
     utility function into the analysis.

     1. In effect, a riskless set of cash flows is substituted
        for the original set of cash flows between both of which
        the financial manager is indifferent.

     2. To simplify calculations, certainty equivalent coeffi-
        cients ($\alpha_t$'s) are defined as the ratio of the certain
        outcome to the risky outcome between which the financial
        manager is indifferent.

     3. Mathematically, certainty equivalent coefficients can be
        defined as follows:

$$\alpha_t = \frac{\text{certain cash flow}_t}{\text{risky cash flow}_t}$$

     4. The appropriate certainty equivalent coefficient is
        multiplied by the original cash flow (which is the risky
        cash flow) with this product being equal to the equiva-
        lent certain cash flow.

     5. Once risk is taken out of the cash flows, those cash
        flows are discounted back to present at the risk-free
        rate of interest and the project's net present value or
        profitability index is determined.

     6. If the internal rate of return is calculated, it is

then compared to the risk-free rate of interest rather than to the firm's required rate of return.

7. Mathematically, the certainty equivalent can be summarized as follows:

$$NPV = \sum_{t=1}^{n} \frac{\alpha_t ACF_t}{(1 + i_F)^t} - IO$$

where $\alpha_t$ = the certainty equivalent coefficient for time period t,

$ACF_t$ = the annual after-tax expected cash flow in time period t,

$IO$ = the initial cash outlay,

$n$ = the project's expected life,

$i_F$ = the risk-free interest rate.

B. The use of the risk-adjusted discount rate is based on the concept that investors demand higher returns for more risky projects.

1. If the risk associated with the investment is greater than the risk involved in a typical endeavor, then the discount rate is adjusted upward to compensate for this risk.

2. The expected cash flows are then discounted back to present at the risk-adjusted discount rate. Then the normal capital budgeting criteria are applied, except in the case of the internal rate of return, in which case the hurdle rate to which the project's internal rate of return is compared now becomes the risk-adjusted discount rate.

3. Expressed mathematically, the net present value using the risk-adjusted discount rate becomes

$$NPV = \sum_{t=1}^{n} \frac{ACF_t}{(1 + i^*)^t} - IO$$

where $ACF_t$ = the annual after-tax cash flow in time period t,

$IO$ = the initial outlay,

$i^*$ = the risk-adjusted discount rate,

$n$ = the project's expected life.

IV. **Additional approaches for dealing with risk in capital budgeting**

A. A simulation imitates the performance of the project being evaluated by randomly selecting observations from each of the distributions that affect the outcome of the project, combining those observations to determine the final output of the final project, and continuing with this process until a representative record of the project's probable outcome is assembled.

1. The firm's management then examines the resultant probability distribution, and if management considers enough of the distribution of possible net present values to be greater than zero, it will accept the project.

2. The use of a simulation approach to analyze investment proposals offers two major advantages:

a. The financial managers are able to examine and base their decisions on the whole range of possible outcomes rather than just point estimates.

b. They can undertake subsequent sensitivity analysis of the project.

B. A decision tree is a graphical exposition of the sequence of possible outcomes; it presents the decision maker with a schematic representation of the problem in which all possible outcomes are graphically displayed.

V. Other sources and measures of risk

A. Many times, especially with the introduction of a new product, the cash flows experienced in early years affect the size of the cash flows experienced in later years. This is called time dependence of cash flows, and it has the effect of increasing the riskiness of the project over time.

B. A distribution that is not symmetric is said to be skewed. When distributions are skewed, the expected value and standard deviation alone may not be enough to differentiate between two distributions.

C. The addition of some projects because of their particular cyclical patterns is able to lower the overall riskiness of the firm better than the addition of other projects. Risk in this context is called portfolio risk.

1. In order to measure the relationship between two projects, we use the concept of correlation.

2. If the correlation coefficient between two projects is close to -1.0, the projects move in opposite directions. If the correlation coefficient is close to 1.0, the projects move together linearly.

3. Since firm diversification can reduce the chance of bankruptcy, there is value to diversification.


## Study Problems

1. A firm with a 15% required rate of return is considering a project with an expected life of 5 years. The initial outlay associated with this project involves a certain cash outflow of $100,000. The expected cash inflows and certainty equivalent coefficients, $\alpha_t$'s, are as follows:

| Year | Expected Cash Flow | Certainty Equivalent Coefficient, $\alpha_t$ |
|------|--------------------|----------------------------------------------|
| 1 | $20,000 | 0.90 |
| 2 | 30,000 | 0.80 |
| 3 | 40,000 | 0.75 |
| 4 | 50,000 | 0.60 |
| 5 | 60,000 | 0.50 |

The risk-free rate of interest is 6%. What is the project's net present value?

SOLUTION

To determine the net present value of this project by using the certainty equivalent, we must first remove the risk from the future cash flows. We do so by multiplying each expected cash flow by the corresponding certainty equivalent coefficient:

| Year | Expected Cash Flow | Certainty Equivalent Coefficient, $\alpha_t$ | $\alpha_t$ X (Expected Cash Flow) = Equivalent Riskless Cash Flow |
|------|--------------------|----------------------------------------------|------------------------------------------------------------------|
| 1 | $20,000 | 0.90 | $18,000 |
| 2 | 30,000 | 0.80 | 24,000 |
| 3 | 40,000 | 0.75 | 30,000 |
| 4 | 50,000 | 0.60 | 30,000 |
| 5 | 60,000 | 0.50 | 30,000 |

The equivalent riskless cash flows are then discounted back to
the present at the riskless interest rate, not at the firm's
required rate of return:

| Year | Equivalent Riskless Cash Flow | Present Value Factor at 6% | Present Value |
|------|-------------------------------|----------------------------|---------------|
| 1 | $18,000 | 0.943 | $16,974 |
| 2 | 24,000 | 0.890 | 21,360 |
| 3 | 30,000 | 0.840 | 25,200 |
| 4 | 30,000 | 0.792 | 23,760 |
| 5 | 30,000 | 0.747 | 22,410 |

NPV = -$100,000 + $16,974 + $21,360 + $25,200 + $23,760 + $22,410

$\quad$ = $9,704.

Applying the normal capital budgeting decision criteria, we find
that the project should be accepted because its net present value
is greater than zero.

2. A firm is considering introducing a new product that has an expected life of 5 years. Since this product is much riskier than a
typical project for this firm, the management feels that the normal
required rate of return of 12% is not sufficient; instead, the mini-
mally acceptable rate of return on this project should be 20%. The
initial outlay would be $100,000, and the expected cash flows from
this project are as given below:

| Year | Expected Cash Flow |
|------|--------------------|
| 1 | $40,000 |
| 2 | 40,000 |
| 3 | 40,000 |
| 4 | 40,000 |
| 5 | 40,000 |

Should this project be accepted?

SOLUTION

Discounting this annuity back to present at 20% yields a present
value of the future cash flows of $119,640. Since the initial

outlay on this project is $100,000, the net present value becomes $19,640. The project should be accepted.

3. Project A is expected to net a present value of $24,000. Project A's standard deviation is expected to be $12,000. Project B is expected to net a present value of $60,000 with a standard deviation of $20,000. What are the coefficients of variation for these projects? Which project has the more relative risk?

SOLUTION

$$\gamma_A = \frac{\$12,000}{\$24,000} = 0.5$$

$$\gamma_B = \frac{\$20,000}{\$60,000} = 0.33$$

Project A has the largest coefficient of variation and therefore the most relative risk.

Self-Tests

TRUE-FALSE

_____ 1. The coefficient of variation is synonymous with the standard deviation.

_____ 2. Independent cash flows means that the outcome in period T is not dependent on the outcome of the T - 1 cash flow.

_____ 3. If two projects are mutually exclusive, the one with the highest expected value should always be chosen, even if it is riskier.

_____ 4. The coefficient of variation serves as a relative measure of risk.

_____ 5. The certainty equivalent coefficient is the ratio of the risky outcome to the certain outcome between which the financial manager is indifferent.

_____ 6. Projects which are negatively correlated move together.

_____ 7. The correlation among projects is an essential element in measuring the risk of a portfolio.

_____ 8. Standard deviation is a measure of dispersion from an expected value.

_____    9. A continuous distribution is one in which a probability
             is assigned to each possible outcome in the set of all
             possible outcomes.

_____   10. The standard deviation loses meaning if the distribution
             is skewed.

MULTIPLE CHOICE

1. If two projects are completely independent, the measure of correlation between them is:

   a. +1.
   b. 0.
   c. -1.

2. To reduce risk most effectively, projects would ideally be chosen
   with the following coefficient correlation:

   a. +1.
   b. 0
   c. -1.

3. Which of the following is not a method for adjusting for risk in
   capital budgeting?

   a. Certainty equivalent approach.
   b. Risk-adjusted discount rate.
   c. Skewed distributions.

4. The proposal with the greatest relative risk would have:

   a. The greatest standard deviation.
   b. The greatest coefficient of variation.
   c. The highest expected NPV.

# Valuation and Rates of Return

Orientation: This chapter introduces the concepts that underlie the valuation of securities. We are specifically concerned with common stock, preferred stock, and bonds. We also look at the concept of "required rate of return" and "expected rate of return."

I. The importance of valuation

   A. Understanding valuation concepts helps the financial manager to implement the overall objective of the firm--maximization of common stock value.

   B. Cost of capital used in capital budgeting decisions is computed from the required rates of return of the firm's investors.

II. Basic determinants of value

   A. Value is a function of three elements:

      1. The asset's expected cash flows.

      2. The riskiness of these cash flows.

      3. The investors' required rate of return for undertaking the investment.

B. The required rate of return is the minimum rate necessary to attract an investor to purchase or hold an asset.

C. The characteristics of an asset that are important in determining its value include:

1. The timing and amount of potential cash flows.

2. The level of risk associated with the asset's return.

D. The investor's attitude toward risk is reflected in his or her required rate of return.

E. Expected returns

1. Cash flows are the relevant variable to be measured in determining returns.

2. An expected cash flow in an uncertain world can be measured by

$$\overline{X} = \sum_{i=1}^{N} X_i P(X_i)$$

where $X_i$ = the ith possible outcome (cash flow).

$P(X_i)$ = the probability of the ith's event occurring.

F. Riskiness

1. Risk can be defined as the possible variation in cash flow about an expected value.

2. Statistically, risk may be measured by the standard deviation $\sigma$, computed as follows:

$$\sigma = \sqrt{\sum_{i=1}^{N} (X_i - \overline{X})^2 P(X_i)}$$

3. Example:

| State | Probability | Project A Outcome | Project B Outcome |
|-------|-------------|-------------------|-------------------|
| Recession | 0.2 | $10,000 | $ 5,000 |
| Normal | 0.6 | 15,000 | 15,000 |
| Boom | 0.2 | 20,000 | 25,000 |

Expected Value:  Project A

= 0.2($10,000) + 0.6($15,000) + 0.2($20,000)

= $15,000

Expected Value:  Project B

= 0.2($5,000) + 0.6($15,000) + 0.2($25,000)

= $15,000

Standard Deviation:  Project A

$$= [0.2(\$10,000 - \$15,000)^2 + 0.6(\$15,000 - \$15,000)^2$$
$$+ 0.2(\$20,000 - \$15,000)^2]^{\frac{1}{2}}$$

$$= [\$10,000,000]^{\frac{1}{2}}$$

= $3,162.28

Standard Deviation:  Project B

$$= [0.2(\$5,000 - \$15,000)^2 + 0.6(\$15,000 - \$15,000)^2$$
$$+ 0.2(\$25,000 - \$15,000)^2]^{\frac{1}{2}}$$

$$= [\$40,000,000]^{\frac{1}{2}}$$

= $6,324.55

We find that both investments have the same expected value, $15,000, but Project B has a much higher standard deviation than does Project A, which indicates a higher level of risk.  Given a risk averse investor, Project A is preferable to Project B.

G. Three factors determine the required rate of return for the investor:

1. The time value of money, which is measured by the risk-free interest.

2. The riskiness (variability in returns) of the asset.

3. The investor's attitude toward risk.

H. The security market line is:

1. The risk-return line that can be applied for <u>all investors</u>

who are actively involved in trading securities.

2. The investor opportunity set available to any investor interested in purchasing or selling securities.

I. Relevant risk

1. Total variability can be divided into:

a. The variability of returns unique to the security (diversifiable risk).

b. The risk related to market movements (nondiversifiable general or systematic risk).

2. By diversifying, the investor can eliminate the "unique" security risk. The systematic risk, however, cannot be diversified away.

3. Beta, a statistic that measures the systematic risk, is defined as the following ratio:

$$\frac{\text{covariance of the security returns with the market}}{\text{variance of market returns}}$$

4. If beta equals one, a 10% increase (decrease) in market returns will produce on average a 10% increase (decrease) in security returns.

5. A security having a higher beta is more volatile than a security having a lower beta value.

J. Capital asset pricing model. The required rate of return for a given security can be expressed as equal to:

risk-free rate + [security beta X (market return - risk-free rate)]

III. Bond valuation

A. Nature of a bond

1. A bond is a long-term promissory note.

2. A bond promises to pay the bondholder a predetermined, fixed amount of interest each year until maturity. At maturity, the principal will be paid to the bondholder.

3. A bond's par value is the amount that will be repaid by the firm when the bond matures, usually $1,000.

4. The bond has a maturity date, at which time the borrowing

firm is committed to repay the loan principal.

5. The contractual agreement of the bond specifies a coupon interest rate as a percent of the par value which the borrowing firm promises to pay the bondholder each year.

EXAMPLE:

9% coupon interest rate, $1000 par value.
Interest: 9% of $1,000 = $90 per year.

6. The only variable that can cause the value of a bond to increase or decrease is a change in the bondholders' required rate of return.

B. Procedure for valuing a bond

1. The value of a bond may be expressed as:

$$P_0 = \sum_{t=1}^{N} \frac{\$I_t}{(1 + R_b)^t} + \frac{\$M}{(1 + R_b)^N}$$

where I = the dollar interest to be received in each payment period,
M = the par value of the bond at maturity,
$R_b$ = the required rate of return for the bond-holder.
N = the number of periods to maturity.
In other words, we are discounting the expected future cash flows to the present at the appropriate discount rate (required rate of return).
(Note: The present-value tables may be used to acquire the interest factors).

2. If interest payments are received semiannually (most bonds pay interest semiannually), the valuation equation becomes:

$$P_0 = \sum_{t=1}^{2N} \frac{\dfrac{\$I_t}{2}}{\left(\dfrac{1 + R_b}{2}\right)^t} + \frac{\$M}{\left(\dfrac{1 + R_b}{2}\right)^{2n}}$$

EXAMPLE

The Hendricks Corporation has bonds outstanding with a face (par) value of $1,000, are due in 10 years, and have an 8% coupon rate. The required rate of return for the bondholder is 10%. What is the value of the bond today? Interest is paid semiannually.
The number of periods: 10 X 2 = 20.
Interest paid every 6 months: $80/2 = $40.
Required rate of return: 10%/2 = 5%.

$$P_0 = \sum_{t=1}^{20} \frac{\$40}{(1 + 0.05)^t} + \frac{\$1,000}{(1 + 0.05)^{20}}$$

$$= \$498.48 + \$377.00 = \$875.48$$

IV. Preferred stock valuation

    A. Owners of preferred stock receive dividends instead of interest.

    B. Most preferred stocks are perpetuities (nonmaturing).

    C. Value of preferred stock ($P_0$):

$$P_0 = \frac{\text{annual dividend}}{\text{required rate of return}}$$

V. Common stock valuation

    A. Although the bondholder and preferred stockholder are promised a specific amount each year, dividend for common stock is based on the profitability of the firm and the management's decision either to pay dividends or retain profits for reinvestment.

    B. The common dividend typically increases along with the growth in corporate earnings.

    C. The earnings growth of a firm should be reflected in a higher price for the firm's stock.

    D. In finding the value of a common stock ($P_0$), we should discount the expected dividends ($D_t$) to the present at the required rate of return for the stockholder ($R_c$). That is,

$$P_0 = \frac{D_1}{(1 + R_c)^1} + \frac{D_2}{(1 + R_c)^2} \cdot \cdot \cdot + \frac{D_\infty}{(1 + R_c)^\infty}$$

E. If we assume that the amount of dividend is increasing by a
constant growth rate each year,

$$D_t = D_0 (1 + g)^t$$

where g = the growth rate,
$\quad$ $D_0$ = the most recent dividend payment.
If the growth rate, g, is the same each year, the valuation
model becomes

$$P_0 = \frac{D_1}{R_C - g}$$

EXAMPLE

Find the value of a stock that paid a $3 dividend last year.
The stockholders' required rate of return is 15% and a 9%
growth rate in earnings is anticipated in the indefinite future.

$$P_0 = \frac{D_1}{R_C - g} = \frac{D_0(1 + g)}{R_C - g}$$

$$= \frac{\$3(1 + 0.09)}{(0.15 - 0.09)} = \frac{\$3.27}{0.06} = \$54.50$$

VI. Measuring the required rate of return

A. Valuation from a different perspective

1. If the value of a security and the cash flows are already
known, we can solve for the investor's required rate of
return.

2. The valuation equations studied earlier remain the same;
however, the unknown variable is the discount rate.
Thus, only our perspective has changed.

B. Bondholder's required rate of return

1. We solve for the bondholder's required rate of return,
$R_b$, by trial and error.

EXAMPLE

An investor is willing to pay only $754.70 for a 10-year bond
that has a 6% coupon interest rate and a face value of $1,000.

Interest is paid annually. What is the investor's required rate of return? We can find the required rate of return by solving for $R_b$ in the following equation:

$$\$754.70 = \frac{\$60}{(1 + R_b)^1} + \frac{\$60}{(1 + R_b)^2} \cdots + \frac{\$60}{(1 + R_b)^{10}} + \frac{\$1,000}{(1 + R_b)^{10}}$$

We can solve for an unknown "$R_b$" in the equation above by trial and error. A rate that exceeds the coupon interest rate should be selected because the investor is not willing to pay the full par value of the bond. At 10%, the present value of all cash flows is $754.70, computed as follows:

$60(6.145) + 1,000(0.386) = \$754.70$

Since the value obtained is precisely the amount that the investor is agreeable to pay, the required rate of return is 10%.

   C. Preferred stockholder's required rate of return

      1. If we know the amount an investor would pay for a preferred stock and the amount of the expected dividends, his or her required rate of return can be determined as follows:

$$\text{required rate of return} = \frac{\text{annual dividend}}{\text{market price of the stock}}$$

EXAMPLE

An investor is willing to pay $40 for a company's preferred stock that is paying a $4 annual dividend. The investor's required rate of return, $R_p$, is

$$R_p = \frac{\$4}{\$40} = 10\%$$

   D. Common stockholder's required rate of return

      1. The required rate of return for a common stockholder can be calculated from the valuation equations discussed earlier.

      2. Assuming that dividends are increasing at a constant annual growth rate (g), we can show that the required

rate of return for a common stockholder, $R_c$, is

$$\text{required rate} = \left(\frac{\text{dividend in year 1}}{\text{market price}}\right) + \text{growth rate} = \frac{P_1}{P_0} + g$$

EXAMPLE

The common stock of Narrow International Company has been valued by an investor at $40. If the expected dividend at the conclusion of this year is $2 and if dividends and earnings are growing at an annual rate of 6%, the investor's required rate of return would be

$$R_c = \frac{\$2}{\$40} + 6\% = 11\%$$

VII. Measuring the expected rate of return

   A. In actual calculation of the expected rate of return, the logic is very similar to that used in the measurement of the required rate of return. However, instead of the price at which a particular investor would prefer to purchase the security, the relevant figure is the price at which the security is actually selling in the market.

   B. The expected rate of return is found by determining the discount rate that sets the present value of the future cash flows equal to the current market price of the security.

   C. If the actual market price of a security is higher than the value assigned to the security by an individual investor, the expected rate is less than the required rate for this person.

   D. If the market price of a security is lower than the amount the investor is willing to pay, the expected rate is higher than the required rate.

   E. If the investor is willing to pay the market price for a security, the required rate of return is equivalent to the expected rate.

Study Problems

1. Phillips Inc., is considering an investment in one of two common

stocks.  Given the information below, which investment is better, based on risk and return.

| Common Stock A | | | Common Stock B | |
| --- | --- | --- | --- | --- |
| Probability | Return | | Probability | Return |
| 0.10 | -10% | | 0.30 | 5% |
| 0.20 | 6 | | 0.20 | 12 |
| 0.40 | 15 | | 0.40 | 10 |
| 0.30 | 9 | | 0.10 | 20 |

SOLUTION

Common Stock A:

Expected Return

$$0.1(-10\%) + 0.2(6\%) + 0.4(15\%) + 0.3(9\%) = -1\% + 1.2\% + 6\% + 2.7\% = 8.9\%$$

Standard Deviation

$$[(-10\% - 8.9\%)^2(0.10) + (6\% - 8.9\%)^2(0.2) + (15\% - 8.9\%)^2(0.4)$$
$$+ (9\% - 8.9\%)^2(0.03)]^{\frac{1}{2}} = [35.721\% + 1.682\% + 14.884\% + 0.003\%]^{\frac{1}{2}}$$
$$= 7.23\%$$

Common Stock B

Expected Return

$$0.3(5\%) + 0.2(12\%) + 0.4(10\%) + 0.10(20\%) = 1.5\% + 214\% + 4\% + 2\% = 9.9\%$$

Standard Deviation

$$[(5\% - 9.9\%)^2(0.3) + (12\% - 9.9\%)^2(0.2) + (10\% - 9.9\%)^2(0.4)$$
$$+ (20\% - 9.9\%)^2(0.1)]^{\frac{1}{2}} = [7.203\% + 0.882\% + 0.004\% + 10.201\%]^{\frac{1}{2}}$$
$$= 4.28\%$$

Common stock B has both a higher expected return and a smaller standard deviation (less risk).  Hence B is better.

2. Gents Clothiers, Inc. has bonds maturing in 6 years and pays 6% interest semiannually on a $1,000 face value.

(a) If your required rate of return is 10%, what is the value of the bond?

(b) How would your answer change if the interest were paid annually?

SOLUTION

(a) Value of bond if interest is paid semiannually:
    (1) Present value of interest payments:

$$= \$30 \begin{bmatrix} \text{TABLE VALUE} \\ \text{Appendix D} \\ \text{12 periods} \\ 5\% \end{bmatrix} = \$30(8.863)$$

$$= \$265.89$$

    (2) Present value of principal:

$$= \$1,000 \begin{bmatrix} \text{TABLE VALUE} \\ \text{Appendix B} \\ \text{12 periods} \\ 5\% \end{bmatrix} = \$1,000(0.557)$$

$$= \$557$$

| | |
|---|---:|
| Present value of the interest | $265.89 |
| Present value of the principal | 557.00 |
| Value of the bond | $822.89 |

(b) Value of bond if interest is paid annually:
    (1) Present value of the interest payments:

$$= \$60 \begin{bmatrix} \text{TABLE VALUE} \\ \text{Appendix D} \\ 10\% \\ \text{6 years} \end{bmatrix} = \$60(4.355)$$

$$= \$261.30$$

(2) Present value of the principal:

$$= \$1,000 \begin{bmatrix} \text{TABLE VALUE} \\ \text{Appendix B} \\ 10\% \\ 6 \text{ years} \end{bmatrix} = \$1,000(0.564)$$

$$= \$564$$

| | |
|---|---|
| Present value of the interest | $261.30 |
| Present value of the principal | 564.00 |
| Value of the bond | $825.30 |

3. Edge Manufacturing Corporation's bonds are selling in the market for $1,193.96.  These 15-year bonds pay 8% interest (annually) on a $1,000 par value.

(a) If they are purchased at the market price, what is the expected rate of return?

(b) What is your required rate of return?

SOLUTION

(a) <u>Expected Rate of Return</u>:

$$\$1,193.96 = \$80 \begin{bmatrix} \text{TABLE VALUE} \\ \text{Appendix D} \\ 15 \text{ years} \\ \text{at } R_b \end{bmatrix} + \$1,000 \begin{bmatrix} \text{TABLE VALUE} \\ \text{Appendix B} \\ 15 \text{ years} \\ \text{at } R_b \end{bmatrix}$$

where $R_b$ is the expected rate of return to be solved for by trial and error.  At 6%, the present value of the interest and principal is equal to

$$\$80(9.712) + \$1,000(0.417) = \$1,193.96$$

The expected rate of return is 6%.

(b) If the investor is willing to pay the market price, his required rate of return is the same as the expected rate of return.  Thus, the required rate of return is 6%.

4. You are willing to pay only $865.60 for a 5-year, 12% bond

($1,000 face value) that pays interest semiannually.  What is
your required rate of return?


SOLUTION

$$\$865.60 = \$60 \begin{bmatrix} \text{TABLE VALUE} \\ \text{Appendix D} \\ \text{10 periods} \\ \text{at } R_b \end{bmatrix} + \$1,000 \begin{bmatrix} \text{TABLE VALUE} \\ \text{Appendix B} \\ \text{10 periods} \\ \text{at } R_b \end{bmatrix}$$

where $R_b$ is the required rate of return (to be solved by trial
and error).   Try 8%:

$$\$60(6.710) + \$1,000(0.463) = \$865.60$$

The required rate of return is 8% (on a semiannual basis) or 16%
(on an annual basis).

5. The preferred stock of Craft Company pays a $3 dividend.  What is
the value of the stock if your required rate of return is 8%?


SOLUTION

$$\text{value of preferred stock} = \frac{\text{dividend}}{\text{required rate of return}}$$

$$\frac{\$3}{0.08} = \underline{\underline{\$37.50}}$$

6. Universal Machines' Common stock paid $1.50 in dividends last year
and is expected to grow indefinitely at an annual 6% rate.  What is
the value of the stock if you require a 12% return?


SOLUTION

$$\text{value } (P_0) = \frac{\text{dividend in year 1}}{\text{required rate - growth rate}} = \frac{D_1}{R_c - g}$$

where $D_1 = D_0(1 + g) = \$1.50(1 + 0.06)$
$$= \$1.59$$

$$R_c = 12\%$$

$$g = 6\%$$

$$P_0 = \frac{\$1.59}{0.12 - 0.06} = \$26.50$$

7. Texas Mining Company's common stock is selling for $35. The stock paid dividends of $2.50 last year and has a projected growth rate of 10%. If you buy the stock at the market price, what is your required rate of return?

SOLUTION

Required rate of return ($R_c$):

$$R_c = \frac{\text{dividend in year 1}}{\text{price}} + \text{growth} = \frac{D_1}{P_0} + g$$

where $D_1 = D_0(1 + g) = \$2.50(1 + 0.10) = \$2.75$

$P_0 = \$35$

$$R_c = \frac{\$2.75}{\$35.00} + 0.10 = 0.1785$$

$$= 17.85\%$$

8. Idalou Power Company's preferred stock is selling for $25 in the market and pays $2.50 in dividends.

(a) What is the expected rate of return on the stock?

(b) If an investor's required rate of return is 12%, what is the fair value of the stock for that investor?

(c) Should the investor acquire the stock?

SOLUTION

(a) Expected rate of return = $\dfrac{\$2.50}{\$25}$ = 10%

(b) Investor's value of the stock = $\dfrac{\$2.50}{0.12}$ = $20.83

(c) Since the investor's required rate of return is higher than the expected rate of return, the investor should not acquire it.

9. BC Incorporated, has a beta of 0.65. If the expected market return is 10% and the risk free rate is 5%, what is the appropriate expected return of BC Incorporated?

SOLUTION

Expected return of BC Incorporated

$$= \text{risk-free rate} + \text{Beta} \begin{pmatrix} \text{expected} & \text{risk-} \\ \text{market} & - & \text{free} \\ \text{return} & & \text{rate} \end{pmatrix}$$

$$= 5\% + 0.65(10\% - 5\%)$$

$$= 5\% + 3.25\% = 8.25\%$$

10. The market price of International Electric Corporation is $40. The price at the end of 1 year is expected to be $45. Dividends for next year should be $2.50. What is the capitalization rate (required rate of return)?

SOLUTION

$$\text{current price}(P_0) = \left(\frac{\text{dividend in year 1}}{1 + \text{required rate}} \atop \text{of return}\right) + \left(\frac{\text{price in year 1}}{1 + \text{required rate}} \atop \text{of return}\right)$$

$$\text{required rate} = \left(\frac{\text{dividend in year 1} + \text{price in year 1}}{\text{current price}}\right) - 1$$

$$\text{required rate} = \left(\frac{\$2.50 + \$45.00}{\$40.00}\right) - 1 = 18.75\%$$

## Self-Tests

TRUE-FALSE

_____ 1. The investor's required rate of return is the minimum rate necessary to attract an investor to purchase or hold a security.

_____ 2. Risk, as defined in this chapter, is the variation in returns about an expected value.

_____ 3. Time value of money can be represented by the risk-free rate of return.

_____ 4. A proxy for the risk-free rate is the Corporate AA Bond rate.

_____   5. An investor's required rate of return is always greater than the expected rate of return.

_____   6. By proper diversification, an investor can eliminate the market-related (systematic) risk.

_____   7. A security having a beta of 1 will move up (or down) on average with the market by the same percentage.

_____   8. The addition of a security with a beta of 0 provides no additional risk.

_____   9. The par value of a bond is essentially independent of the market value of the bond.

_____  10. The only variable that can cause the value of a bond to increase or decrease is a change in the bondholder's required rate of return

_____  11. An assumption necessary in the model for common stock valuation

$$P_0 = \frac{D_1}{R_C - g}$$

is that the amount of the dividend increases by a constant percent each year.

_____  12. If the market price of a security is larger than the value assigned to the security by an investor, then the expected rate is greater than the required rate of return.

MULTIPLE CHOICE

1. For a $1,000 par-value bond carrying an 8% coupon (interest paid quarterly) and having a 10% yield to maturity, the quarterly interest payments would be:

   a. $20.
   b. $30.
   c. $25.
   d. $50.
   e. $10.

2. The most recent dividend paid by Xeron on its common stock was $1.50 (annual). The required rate of return for the security is 6%. Growth is anticipated to be at 4% annually. The market

price of the stock should be:

a. $78.
b. $100.
c. $50.
d. $150.
e. $35.

3. Under the capital asset pricing model, the relevant risk is:

a. Diversifiable risk.
b. Systematic risk.
c. Financial risk.
d. Standard deviation.

4. The value of a security may be expressed as a function of:

a. Expected cash flows.
b. Riskiness of cash flows.
c. The investor's required rate of return.
d. a and b only.
e. a, b, and c.

5. If the market is in equilibrium, the expected rate of return and the required rate of return:

a. Will be the same.
b. Will be different.
c. Have no relationship to each other.

6. If the expected return for a security is 15% and the risk-free rate is 6%, the risk premium is:

a. 0%.
b. 6%.
c. 10%.
d. 9%.
e. 15%.

7. In terms of the security market line, a security with a beta of 1.5 should provide a risk premium _____ times the risk premium existing for the market as a whole.

a. 2.
b. 1.
c. 1.5.
d. 2.5.
e. 0.5

8. If everything is assumed to be constant, as the investor's required
   rate of return decreases, the value of a security:

   a. Stays the same.
   b. Increases.
   c. Decreases.
   d. Has no relationship to the investor's required rate of return.

# Cost of Capital

Orientation: In Chapter 13 we considered the valuation of debt and equity instruments. The concepts advanced there serve as a foundation for determining the required rate of return for the firm and for specific investment projects. The objective in this chapter is to determine the required rate of return to be used in evaluating invest- ment projects. This minimum required rate of return should result in acceptance of only those projects that will at worst leave the market value of the firm's stock unchanged and hopefully increase it.

    I. The concept of the cost of capital

        A. Two reasons for computing a firm's cost of capital:

            1. To determine the financial mix that has the lowest cost of capital.

            2. As a criterion for accepting or rejecting a capital ex- penditure.

        B. Defining the cost of capital:

            1. The rate that must be earned in order to satisfy the required rate of return of the firm's investors.

    2. The rate of return on investments at which the price of the firm's common stock will remain unchanged.

  C. Type of investors and the cost of capital:  Each type of capital (debt, preferred stock, and common stock) should be incorporated into the cost of capital, with the relative importance of a particular source being based on the percentage of the financing provided by each source of capital.

II. Factors determining the cost of capital

  A. General economic conditions determine the demand for and supply of capital within the economy, and the level of expected inflation, and are reflected in the riskless rate of return.

  B. As risk increases, the investor requires a higher rate of return.  An investor may be exposed to risk in several ways.

    1. The security may not be readily marketable when the investor wants to sell; or even if a continuous demand for the security does exist, the price may vary significantly.

    2. Risk also results from the decisions made within the company.  This risk is generally divided into two classes:

      a. Business risk is the variability in returns on assets and is affected by the company's investment decisions.

      b. Financial risk is the increased variability in returns to the common stockholders as a result of using debt and preferred stock.

  C. Amount of financing required.  The last factor determining the corporation's cost of funds is the amount of financing required, where the cost of capital increases as the financing requirements become larger.  This increase may be attributable to one of several factors.

    1. As increasingly larger security issues are floated in the market, additional flotation costs (costs of issuing the security) and underpricing will affect the percentage cost of the funds to the firm.

    2. As management approaches the market for large amounts of capital relative to the firm's size, the investors' required rate of return may rise.

3. Suppliers of capital become hesitant to grant relatively large amounts of funds without evidence of management's capability to absorb this capital into the business.

III. Assumptions of the cost of capital model

A. Constant business risk. We assume that any investment being considered will not significantly change the firm's business risk.

B. Constant financial risk. Management is assumed to use the same financial mix as it used in the past.

C. Constant dividend policy.

1. For ease of computation, it is generally assumed that the firm's dividends are increasing at a constant annual growth rate. Also, this growth is assumed to be a function of the firm's earning capabilities and not merely the result of paying out a larger percentage of the company's earnings.

2. We also implicitly assume that the dividend payout ratio (dividend/net income) is constant.

IV. Computing the weighted cost of capital. A firm's weighted cost of capital is a function of (1) the individual costs of capital, (2) the make up of the capital structure mix, and (3) the level of financing necessary to make the investment.

A. Determining individual costs of capital.

1. The before-tax cost of debt is found by solving for $r_d$ in

$$NP_0 = \sum_{t=1}^{N} \frac{\$I_t}{(1 + r_d)^t} + \frac{\$M}{(1 + r_d)^N}$$

where $NP_0$ = the market price of the debt, less flotation costs,

$\$I_t$ = the annual dollar interest paid to the investor each year,

$\$M$ = the maturity value of the debt,

$r_d$ = cost of the debt,

$N$ = the number of years to maturity.

The after-tax cost of debt is

$$K_d = r_d(1 - t)$$

where t = the corporation's marginal tax rate.

2. Cost of preferred stock, $K_p$, equals the dividend yield, or

$$K_p = \frac{\text{dividend}}{\text{net price}} = \frac{D}{NP_0}$$

3. Cost of common stock

  a. Cost of internally generated common equity.

$$K_c = \frac{\text{dividend in year 1}}{\text{market price}} + \left(\begin{array}{c}\text{annual growth}\\ \text{in dividends}\end{array}\right)$$

$$K_c = \frac{D_1}{P_0} + g$$

  b. Cost of new common stock

$$K_{nc} = \frac{D_1}{NP_0} + g$$

where $NP_0$ = the market price of the common stock less flotation costs incurred in issuing new shares.

B. Selection of weights. The individual costs of capital will be different for each source of capital in the firm's capital structure. To use the cost of capital in investment analyses, we must compute a composite or overall cost of capital.

1. It will be assumed that the company's current financial mix is relatively stable and that these weights will closely approximate future financing patterns.

2. Market value weights, as opposed to book value weights, will be used in measuring a composite cost of capital.

V. Level of financing and the weighted cost of capital. The weighted marginal cost of capital specifies the composite cost for each additional dollar of financing. The firm should continue to invest up to the point where the marginal internal rate of return earned on a new investment (IRR) equals the marginal cost of new capital.

A. Impact of a new common stock issue. Issuing new common stock will increase the firm's weighted cost of capital because external equity capital has a higher cost than internally generated common equity.

B. General effect of new financing on marginal cost of capital. Increases in the marginal cost of capital curve will occur at the dollar financing level where

$$\text{financing level from all sources} = \frac{\text{maximum amount of a cheaper source of capital}}{\text{percentage financing provided by the source}}$$

## Study Problems

1. A $1,000 par value bond will sell in the market for $1,072 and carries a coupon interest rate of 9%. Issuance costs will be 7.5%. The number of years to maturity is 15 and the firm's tax rate is 52%. What is the cost of this security ($K_d$)?

SOLUTION

$$\$1,072(1 - 0.075) \text{ or } \$991.60 = \sum_{t=1}^{15} \frac{\$90}{(1 + r_d)^t} + \frac{\$1,000}{(1 + r_d)^{15}}$$

Try 10%: $923.54 = $90(7.606) + $1,000(0.239).
Try  9%: $1,000 = $90(8.061) + $1,000(0.275).

$$
\begin{array}{ll}
9\% & \left.\begin{array}{l}\$1,000.00 \\ \$\ \ 991.60\end{array}\right\} \$8.40 \\
10\% & \$\ \ 923.54
\end{array}
\left.\begin{array}{l} \\ \\ \end{array}\right\} \$76.46
$$

$$r_d = 0.09 + \left(\frac{\$8.40}{\$76.46}\right) 0.01 = 9.11\%$$

$$K_d = 9.11\%(1 - 0.52) = 4.37\%$$

2. The current market price of ABC Company's common stock is $32.50. The firm expects to pay a dividend of $1.90, and the growth rate is projected to be 7% annually. The company is in a 50% tax bracket. Flotation costs would be 6% if new stock were issued. What is the cost of (a) internal and (b) external common equity?

SOLUTION

Let $K_c$ = cost of internal common.
   $K_{nc}$ = cost of external (new) common.
   $D_1$ = next dividend to be paid.
   $P_0$ = market price.

   $g$ = growth rate.
   $NP_0$ = market price less flotation costs

(a)
$$K_c = \frac{D_1}{P_0} + g$$

$$K_c = \frac{\$1.90}{\$32.50} + 0.07 = 12.85\%$$

(b)
$$K_{nc} = \frac{D_1}{NP_0} + g$$

$$K_{nc} = \frac{\$1.90}{\$32.50(1 - 0.06)} + 0.07 = 13.22\%$$

3. Pharr, Inc.'s preferred stock pays a 6% dividend.  The stock is selling for \$62.75, and its par value is \$40.  Issuance costs are 5% and the firm's tax rate is 48%.  What is the cost of this source of financing?

SOLUTION

$$K_p = \frac{D}{NP_0}$$

$$K_p = \frac{\$40(0.06)}{\$62.75(1 - 0.05)} = \frac{\$2.40}{\$59.61} = 4.03\%$$

4. The current capital structure of Smithhart, Inc., is as follows:

| | | |
|---|---|---|
| Bonds (7%, \$1,000 par, 15 years) | | \$  750,000 |
| Preferred stock (\$100 par, 2.5% dividend) | | 1,000,000 |
| | | |
| Common stock: | | |
|   Par value (\$5 par) | \$500,000 | |
|   Retained earnings | 350,000 | 850,000 |
|       Total | | \$2,600,000 |

The market price is $975 for the bonds, $60 for the preferred stock, and $42 for common stock. Flotation costs are 9% for bonds and 5% for preferred stock. The firm's tax rate is 48%. Common stock will pay a $2.80 dividend which is not expected to grow. What is the weighted cost of capital using only internal common equity?

### SOLUTION

| Source of Financing | Market Value | Weight |
|---|---|---|
| Bonds | $ 731,250 | 13.22% |
| Preferred stock | 600,000 | 10.85 |
| Common stock | 4,200,000 | 75.93 |
| | $5,531,250 | 100.00% |

### Cost of debt

$$\$975(1 - 0.09) \text{ or } \$887.25 = \sum_{t=1}^{15} \frac{\$70}{(1 + r_d)^t} \quad \frac{\$1,000}{(1 + r_d)^{15}}$$

From a trial-and-error-method and interpolation, $r_d$ equals 8.36%

$$K_d = 8.36\%(1 - 0.38)$$
$$K_d = 4.35\%$$

### Cost of preferred stock

$$K_p = \frac{\$2.50}{\$60(1 - 0.05)} = 4.39\%$$

### Cost of internal common equity

$$K_c = \frac{\$2.80}{\$42} + 0 = 6.67\%$$

### Weighted Cost of Capital

| Source of Financing | Cost | Weight | Weighted Costs |
|---|---|---|---|
| Bonds | 4.35% | 13.22% | 0.575 |
| Preferred stock | 4.39 | 10.85 | 0.476 |
| Common stock | 6.67 | 75.93 | 5.065 |
| | | | 6.12% |

5. Croweger Freight, Inc. maintains a capital mix consisting of 35% debt, 15% preferred stock, and 50% common equity. The company is considering several investments and needs a weighted marginal cost of capital curve. Retained earnings of $600,000 will be available for these investments. The company's financial analysts have computed the costs of capital for the various sources of financing as follows:

| Source | Amount of Capital | Cost |
|---|---|---|
| Debt (after-tax) | $ 0 to $500,000 | 6.5% |
| | Over $500,000 | 7.75% |
| Preferred stock | 0 to $100,000 | 8.0% |
| | Over $100,000 | 8.5% |
| Common stock | 0 to $600,000 | 13.0% |
| | 600,000 to $800,000 | 15.0% |
| | Over $800,000 | 17.0% |

Construct the weighted marginal cost of capital curve. (Note: The first level of common ($600,000) represents the internally generated common.)

SOLUTION

First compute the breaks in the curve.
Debt

$$\frac{\$500,000}{0.35} = \$1,428,571.40$$

Preferred stock

$$\frac{\$100,000}{0.15} = \$666,666.67$$

Common equity

$$\frac{\$600,000}{0.50} = \$1,200,000$$

$$\frac{\$800,000}{0.50} = \$1,600,000$$

## Weighted Cost of Capital

### $0 to $666,666

| Source | Amount of Financing | Weight | Cost | Weighted Cost |
|---|---|---|---|---|
| Bonds | $233,333.33 | 35% | 6.5% | 2.275% |
| Preferred stock | 100,000.00 | 15 | 8.0 | 1.200 |
| Common equity | 333,333.34 | 50 | 13.0 | 6.500 |
| | $666,666.67 | | | 9.975% |

### $666,666 to $1,200,000

| Source | Amount of Financing | Weight | Cost | Weighted Cost |
|---|---|---|---|---|
| Bonds | $420,000.00 | 35% | 6.5% | 2.275% |
| Preferred stock | 180,000.00 | 15 | 8.5 | 1.275 |
| Common equity | 600,000.00 | 50 | 13.0 | 6.500 |
| | $1,200,000.00 | | | 10.05% |

### $1,200,001 to $1,428,571

| Source | Amount of Financing | Weight | Cost | Weighted Cost |
|---|---|---|---|---|
| Bonds | $500,000.00 | 35% | 6.5% | 2.275% |
| Preferred stock | 214,285.70 | 15 | 8.5 | 1.275 |
| Common equity | 714,285.70 | 50 | 15.0 | 7.500 |
| | $1,428,571.40 | | | 11.05% |

### $1,428,572 to $1,600,000

| Source | Amount of Financing | Weight | Cost | Weighted Cost |
|---|---|---|---|---|
| Bonds | $560,000.00 | 35% | 7.75% | 2.7125% |
| Preferred stock | 240,000.00 | 15 | 8.5 | 1.2750 |
| Common equity | 800,000.00 | 50 | 15.0 | 7.5000 |
| | $1,600,000.00 | | | 11.4875% |

### Over $1,600,000

| Source | Amount of Financing | Weight | Cost | Weighted Cost |
|---|---|---|---|---|
| Bonds | $560,000.35 | 35% | 7.75% | 2.7125% |
| Preferred stock | 240,000.15 | 15 | 8.5 | 1.2750 |
| Common equity | 800,000.50 | 50 | 17.0 | 8.5000 |
| | $1,600,001.00 | | | 12.4875% |

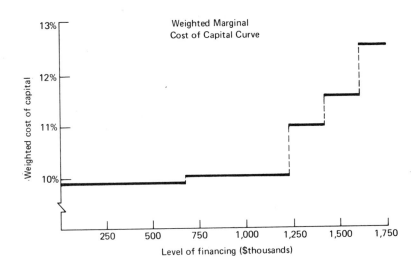

**Weighted Marginal
Cost of Capital Curve**

Level of financing ($thousands)

6. If Croweger's weighted marginal cost of capital curve is the same as the one constructed in problem 5, which of the following investments should Croweger accept?

| Investment | | Cost | Internal Rate of Returns |
|---|---|---|---|
| A | | $ 300,000 | 15.0% |
| B | | 925,000 | 17.0 |
| C | | 600,000 | 10.0 |
| D | | 500,000 | 12.5 |
| E | | 750,000 | 19.0 |
| | Total | $3,075,000 | |

SOLUTION

First, rank the investments in order of the internal rate of return and then compare the cost of capital at that level of financing.

| Investment | | Cost | Internal Rate of Return | Weighted Cost of Capital |
|---|---|---|---|---|
| E | | $ 750,000 | 19.0% | 10.05% |
| B | | 925,000 | 17.0 | |
| | Total | $1,675,000 | | 12.4875 |
| A | | 300,000 | 15.0 | |
| | Total | $1,975,000 | | 12.4875 |
| D | | 500,000 | 12.5 | |
| | Total | $2,475,000 | | 12.4875 |
| C | | 600,000 | 10.0 | |
| | Total | $3,075,000 | | 12.4875 |

160

Investments E, B, A, and D would be accepted because the IRR of D is higher than the cost of capital at the level of financing required by the total cost of all the investments.

## Self-Tests

### TRUE-FALSE

_____ 1. The cost of capital may be defined as the rate of return on investments which causes the price of the firm's common stock to increase.

_____ 2. The level of expected inflation is reflected in the risk premium.

_____ 3. The cost of capital is an appropriate investment criterion only for investments of similar risk level to the existing assets.

_____ 4. Financial risk is the risk that the price of the security may vary significantly.

_____ 5. The cost of preferred stock must be adjusted for taxes.

_____ 6. In computing a weighted cost of capital, it is assumed that the company's current capital structure is stable.

_____ 7. Issuance of any new security will cause the firm's weighted cost of capital to increase.

_____ 8. If the cost of capital rises as the level of financing increases, the weighted marginal cost of capital is the appropriate criterion for making investment decisions.

_____ 9. New common stock would be issued only if internal common equity does not provide sufficient equity capital for the amount of investments under consideration.

_____ 10. The only difference in the calculation of internal and external common equity is the market price.

### MULTIPLE CHOICE

1. What is/are the reason(s) for computing a firm's cost of capital?

   a. To determine the capital sturcture that has the lowest cost.
   b. To assure the investors that their required rate of return

is being met.

c. To use the cost of capital as an investment criterion.

d. b and c.

e. a and c.

f. a, b, and c.

2. The cost of capital may be defined as:

a. The rate that must be earned in order to satisfy the required rate of return of the firm's investors.

b. The rate of return on investments at which the price of the firm's common stock remains unchanged.

c. The rate of return on investments which will increase the price of the firm's common stock.

d. a and b.

e. a and c.

3. What combination of the factors listed below is reflected in the risk premium?

     I. Inflation
    II. Business risk
   III. Financial risk
    IV. Financing level
     V. Marketability of securities

a. I, II, III, and V.

b. II, III, IV, and V.

c. II, III, and V.

d. I, II, and III.

e. All of the factors.

4. All of the following variables are needed in the computation of the cost of debt except:

a. Market price of debt.

b. Issuance cost.

c. Tax rate for the firm.

d. Growth rate.

e. Maturity value.

5. Adjustment for taxes is required for which cost?

a. Cost of preferred stock.

b. Cost of debt.

c. Cost of internal common equity.

d. Cost of external common equity.

<u>Appendix 14A</u>

THE REQUIRED RATE OF RETURN FOR INDIVIDUAL PROJECTS

I. Required rate of return for individual projects

  A. The weighted marginal cost of capital, $K_0$, does not allow for varying levels of project risk.  A return-risk line specifies the appropriate required rates of return for investments having different amounts of risk.

  B. The return-risk line is defined as:

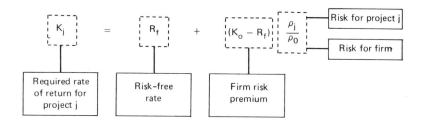

II. The effect of diversification

  A. Diversification can be used to reduce risk relative to the expected return of a portfolio of assets or to increase the expected return relative to the riskiness of the portfolio of investments.

  B. The ability to diversify occurs at two levels.

    1. The firm can diversify its holdings in capital investments.

    2. The firm's investors can diversify their own investments.

  C. Perfect markets are assumed to exist whenever (1) information is readily available to all investors at no cost, (2) there are no transaction costs, (3) investment opportunities are readily accessible to all prospective investors, and (4) financial distress and bankruptcy costs are nonexistent.

  D. Under these assumptions, the appropriate criterion for accepting or rejecting the jth project would be:

    1. Accept project j if the expected return exceeds the required rate of return, $K_j$.

163

$$K_j = R_f + (R_m - R_f) \beta_j$$

where $R_f$ = the risk-free rate.

$R_m$ = the return on the market portfolio.

$\beta_j$ = the volatility of the jth project returns relative to the investor's widely diversified portfolio.

This equation is the <u>capital asset pricing model</u> (CAPM).

E. Limitations of the capital asset pricing model.

1. The difficulty of the determination of $r_{jm}$, the relationship between the market returns and the project returns.

2. Bankruptcy costs are assumed to equal zero.


## Study Problems

1. Hanoverian Manufacturing is evaluating several investments. Hanoverian's overall cost of capital is 12.75% and its average project's standard deviation is 6.5%. If the current risk-free rate is 10.5%, which projects should be accepted?

| Project | Expected Return | Standard Deviation |
|---------|-----------------|--------------------|
| I       | 19.00%          | 10.1%              |
| II      | 17.50           | 9.8                |
| III     | 10.88           | 3.9                |
| IV      | 12.30           | 5.7                |
| V       | 15:60           | 8.2                |

SOLUTION

The required rate of return for each project would be:

I. $K_j = 10.5\% + (12.75\% - 10.5\%) \left( \dfrac{10.1\%}{6.5\%} \right)$
  $K_j = 14\%$

II. $K_j = 10.5\% + (12.75\% - 10.5\%) \left( \dfrac{9.8\%}{6.5} \right)$
  $K_j = 13.89\%$

III. $K_j = 10.5\% + (12.75\% - 10.5\%) \left( \dfrac{3.9\%}{6.5\%} \right)$
  $K_j = 11.85\%$

IV. $K_j = 10.5\% + (12.75\% - 10.5) \left(\dfrac{5.7\%}{6.5}\right)$

$K_j = 12.47\%$

V. $K_j = 10.5\% + (12.75\% - 10.5\%) \left(\dfrac{8.2\%}{6.5\%}\right)$

$K_j = 13.34\%$

| Project | Expected Return | Required Rate of Return | Decision |
|---------|-----------------|-------------------------|----------|
| I | 19.00% | 14.00% | Accept |
| II | 17.50 | 13.89 | Accept |
| III | 10.88 | 11.85 | Reject |
| IV | 12.30 | 12.47 | Reject |
| V | 15.60 | 13.34 | Accept |

2. The management of Capp Corporation is concerned about the effect of a new project on the riskiness of a diversified portfolio. Capp is currently considering the three investments shown below. The risk-free rate is 9%. If the expected return for the market is 12% and its standard deviation is 4%, which investments should be accepted?

| Project | Expected Return | Standard Deviation | Correlation with Market Returns |
|---------|-----------------|--------------------|---------------------------------|
| A | 19% | 9.8% | 0.730 |
| B | 12 | 6.7 | 0.870 |
| C | 14 | 8.0 | 0.785 |

SOLUTION

Using the following equation, we get:

$$\begin{bmatrix} \text{required} \\ \text{rate for} \\ \text{project j} \end{bmatrix} = \begin{bmatrix} \text{risk-free} \\ \text{rate} \end{bmatrix} + \begin{bmatrix} \dfrac{\text{risk premium for a widely diversified portfolio}}{\text{standard deviation of the returns for a widely diversified portfolio}} \end{bmatrix} \begin{bmatrix} \text{correlation of project returns with portfolio returns} \end{bmatrix} \begin{bmatrix} \text{standard deviation of the jth project} \end{bmatrix}$$

The required rate for each project would be

A. $K_j = 9\% + \left(\dfrac{12\% - 9\%}{4\%}\right)(0.73)(9.8\%)$

$K_j = 14.37\%$

B. $K_j = 9\% + \left(\dfrac{12\% - 9\%}{4\%}\right)(0.87)(6.7\%)$

$K_j = 13.37\%$

C. $K_j = 9\% + \left(\dfrac{12\% - 9\%}{4\%}\right)(0.785)(8.0\%)$

$K_j = 13.71\%$

| Project | Expected Return | Required Return | Decision |
|---------|-----------------|-----------------|----------|
| A | 19% | 14.37% | Accept |
| B | 12 | 13.37 | Reject |
| C | 14 | 13.71 | Accept |

3. Wells Mining is considering the investments shown below. A diversified portfolio has an expected return of 10% and a standard deviation of 7%. The rate on government securities is 6.5%. If the capital asset pricing model is used, which projects should management accept?

| Investment | Expected Return | Standard Deviation | Beta |
|------------|-----------------|--------------------|------|
| A | 13% | 5.0% | 1.35 |
| B | 17 | 8.0 | 1.78 |
| C | 18 | 8.5 | 1.83 |

SOLUTION

$$K_j = R_f + (R_m - R_f)\beta_j$$

where $K_j$ = the required rate of return for investment j,

$R_f$ = the risk-free rate,

$R_m$ = the return on the diversified portfolio,

$\beta_j$ = the beta for the jth investment.

A. $K_j = 6.5\% + (10\% - 6.5\%)(1.35)$

$K_j = 11.23\%$

B. $K_j$ = 6.5% + (10% - 6.5)(1.78)

   $K_j$ = 12.73%

C. $K_j$ = 6.5% + (10% - 6.5%)(1.83)

   $K_j$ = 12.91%

| Project | Expected Return | Required Return | Decision |
|---------|-----------------|-----------------|----------|
| A | 13% | 11.23% | Accept |
| B | 17 | 12.73 | Accept |
| C | 18 | 12.91 | Accept |

## Self-Tests

### TRUE-FALSE

_____ 1. One limitation of the weighted cost of capital is that it does not allow for varying levels of project risk.

_____ 2. The return risk line takes into account the risk of the project, but not the risk for the firm.

_____ 3. The capital asset pricing model (CAPM) includes the excess return-risk relationship of an individual firm.

_____ 4. Beta measures the volatility of the project returns relative to the investor's widely diversified portfolio.

_____ 5. If a project increases the probability of firm bankruptcy, the CAPM is the appropriate investment criterion.

### MULTIPLE CHOICE

1. Which of the following is a limitation of the return-risk equation?

   a. The assumption of no bankruptcy risk.
   b. The requirement that the existing financial mix remains constant.
   c. The standardization of the risk premium relative to the riskiness of the firm's average project.

2. Which of the following is not an assumption of a perfect market?

   a. No transaction costs.
   b. No bankruptcy costs.

   c. No inflation premiums.

   d. Free, readily available information.

3. An investment with a beta of 0.80 means that the returns of the investment:

   a. Are more volatile than the market returns.

   b. Are less volatile than the market returns.

   c. Have no correlation with the market returns.

   d. Are perfectly correlated with the market returns.

4. If the capital asset pricing model is used in investment decision making, what risk measure should be used?

   a. Total variability in returns.

   b. Beta.

   c. Standard deviation.

   d. Diversifiable risk.

# *Analysis and Impact of Leverage*

Orientation: This chapter focuses on useful aids to the financial
manager in his or her determination of the firm's proper financial
structure.  It includes the definitions of the different kinds of
risk, a review of break-even analysis, the concepts of operating
leverage, financial leverage, the combination of both leverages, and
their effect on EPS (earnings per share).

  I. Business risk and financial risk

     A. Risk has been defined as the likely variability associated
        with expected revenue streams.

        1. Focusing on the financing decision, the variations in the
           income stream can be attributed to:

           a. The firm's exposure to business risk.

           b. The firm's decision to incur financial risk.

     B. Business risk can be defined as the variability of the firm's
        expected earnings before interest and taxes (EBIT).

        1. Business risk is measured by the firm's corresponding
           expected coefficient of variation (i.e., the larger the

ratio, the more risk a firm is exposed to).

   2. Dispersion in operating income does not cause business
      risk.  It is the result of several influences, for
      example, the company's cost structure, product demand
      characteristics, and intra-industry competition.  These
      influences are a direct result of the firm's investment
      decision.

  C. Financial risk is a direct result of the firm's financing
     decision.  When the firm is selecting different financial
     alternatives, financial risk refers to the additional vari-
     ability in earnings available to the firm's common share-
     holders and the additional chance of insolvency borne by the
     common shareholder caused by the use of financial leverage.

   1. Financial leverage is simply the financing of a portion
      of the firm's assets with securities bearing a fixed
      (limited) rate of return in hopes of increasing the
      ultimate return to the common shareholders.

   2. Financial risk is to a large extent passed on to the
      common shareholders who must bear almost all of the
      potential inconsistencies of returns to the firm after
      the deduction of fixed payments.

II. Break-even analysis

  A. The objective of break-even analysis is to determine the break-
     even quantity of output by studying the relationships among the
     firm's cost structure, volume of output, and operating profit.

   1. The break-even quantity of output is the quantity of output
      (in units) that results in an EBIT level equal to zero.

  B. Use of the model enables the financial officer to:

   1. Determine the quantity of output that must be sold to
      cover all operating costs.

   2. Calculate the EBIT that will be achieved at various
      output levels.

  C. Some actual and potential applications of break-even analysis
     include:

   1. Capital expenditure analysis as a complementary technique
      to discounted cash flow evaluation models.

   2. Pricing policy.

   3. Labor contract negotiations.

    4. Evaluation of cost structure.

    5. The making of financial decisions.

D. Essential elements of the break-even model are:

  1. Fixed costs are costs that do not vary in total amount as the sales volume or the quantity of output changes over some relevant range of output.  For example, administrative salaries are considered fixed because these salaries are generally the same month after month.  Other examples are:

    a. Depreciation.

    b. Insurance premiums.

    c. Property taxes.

    d. Rent.

  The total fixed cost is unchanged regardless of the quantity of product production or sales, although, over some relevant range, these costs may be higher or lower (i.e., in the long run).

  2. Variable costs are costs that tend to vary in total as output changes.  Variable costs are fixed per unit of output.  For example, direct materials are considered a variable cost because they vary with the amount of products produced.  Other variable costs are:

    a. Direct labor.

    b. Energy cost associated with the production area.

    c. Packaging.

    d. Freight-out.

    e. Sales commissions.

  3. To implement the behavior of the break-even model, it is necessary for the financial manager to:

    a. Identify the most relevant output range for his or her planning purposes.

    b. Approximate all costs in the semifixed, semivariable range and allocate them to the fixed and variable cost categories.

  4. Total revenue and volume of output

    a. Total revenue from sales is equal to the price per
       unit multiplied by the quantity sold.

    b. The volume of output is the firm's level from opera-
       tions and is expressed as sales dollars or a unit
       quantity.

E. Finding the break-even point

  1. The break-even model is just a simple adaptation of the
     firm's income statement expressed in the following format:

     sales - (total variable costs + total fixed costs) = profit

    a. Trial and error

       1. Select an arbitrary output level.

       2. Calculate the corresponding EBIT amount.

       3. When EBIT equals zero, the break-even point has
          been found.

    b. Contribution margin analysis

       1. The difference between the unit selling price and
          the unit variable cost equals the contribution
          margin.

       2. Then, the fixed cost divided by the contribution
          margin equals the break-even quantity in units.

    c. Algebraic analysis

       1. $Q_B$ = the break-even level of units sold,

          P = the unit sales price,
          F = total fixed cost for the period,
          V = unit variable cost.

       2. Then,

$$Q_B = \frac{F}{P - V}$$

F. The break-even point in sales dollars:

  1. Computing a break-even point in terms of sales dollars
     rather then units of output is convenient, especially if
     the firm deals with more than one product.  Also, if the
     analyst cannot get unit cost data, he or she can compute

a general break-even point in sales dollars by using the firm's annual report.

2. Since variable cost per unit and the selling price per unit are assumed constant, the ratio of total sales to total variable costs (VC/S) is a constant for any level of sales. So, if the break-even level of sales is denoted $S^*$, the corresponding equation is:

$$S^* = \frac{F}{1 - \frac{VC}{S}}$$

C. Limitations of break-even analysis:

1. The cost-volume-profit relationship is assumed to be linear.

2. The total revenue curve is presumed to increase linearly with the volume of output.

3. A constant production and sales mix is assumed.

4. The break-even computation is a static form of analysis.

III. Operating leverage

A. Operating leverage is the responsiveness of a firm's EBIT to fluctuations in sales. Operating leverage results when fixed operating costs are present in the firm's cost structure. It should be noted here that fixed operating costs do not include interest charges incurred from the firm's use of debt financing.

B. The responsiveness of a firm's EBIT to fluctuating sales levels can be measured as follows:

$$\begin{array}{l} \text{degree of operating} \\ \text{leverage from the} \\ \text{base sales level} \end{array} = DOL_s = \frac{\% \text{ change in EBIT}}{\% \text{ change in sales}}$$

for example, if $DOL_s$ equals five times, a 10% rise in sales over the coming period will result in a 50% rise in EBIT. (This means of measure also holds true for the negative direction.)

C. If unit costs are available, the $DOL_s$ can be measured by the following formula:

$$DOL_s = \frac{Q(P - V)}{Q(P - V) - F}$$

D. If an analytical income statement is the only thing available, the following formula can be used to produce the same results:

$$DOL_s = \frac{\text{revenue before fixed costs}}{EBIT} = \frac{S - VC}{S - VC - F}$$

E. It should be noted here that the three formulas stated above all produce the same results. But, more important is the understanding that in this example a 1% change in sales will result in a 5% change in EBIT.

F. Implications of operating leverage

1. At each point above the break-even level the degree of operating leverage decreases (i.e., the greater the sales level, the lower the $DOL_s$).

2. At the break-even level of sales the degree of operating leverage is undefined.

3. Operating leverage is present anytime the percentage change in EBIT divided by the percentage change in sales is greater than one.

4. The degree of operating leverage can be attributed to the business risk that a firm faces.

IV. Financial leverage

A. Financial leverage, as defined earlier, is the practice of financing a portion of the firm's assets with securities bearing a fixed rate of return in hopes of increasing the ultimate return to the common stockholders. To see if financial leverage has been used to benefit the common shareholders, the discussion here will focus on the responsiveness of the company's earning per share (EPS) to changes in its EBIT. It should be noted here that not all analysts rely exclusively on this type of relationship. In fact, the weakness of such a contention will be examined in the following chapter.

B. The firm is using financial leverage and is exposing its owners to financial risk when:

$$\frac{\text{\% change in EPS}}{\text{\% change in EBIT}} \text{ is greater than 1.00}$$

C. A precise measure of the firm's use of financial leverage can be expressed in the following relationship:

$$\begin{array}{l}\text{degree of financial} \\ \quad \text{leverage from the} \\ \quad \text{base EBIT level}\end{array} = \text{DFL}_{\text{EBIT}} = \frac{\text{\% change in EPS}}{\text{\% change in EBIT}}$$

1. As was the case with operating leverage, the degree of financial leverage concept can be in the negative direction as well as in the positive direction.

2. You should also note that the greater the degree of financial leverage, the greater the fluctuations (positive or negative) in EPS.

D. An easier way of measuring the degree of financial leverage that produces the same results without computing percentage changes in EBIT and EPS is:

$$\text{DFL}_{\text{EBIT}} = \frac{\text{EBIT}}{\text{EBIT} - 1}$$

where I is the sum of all fixed financing costs.

V. Combining operating and financial leverage

A. Since changes in sales revenues cause greater changes in EBIT, and if the firm chooses to use financial leverage, changes in EBIT turn into larger variations in both EPS and EAC (earnings available to common shareholders). Then, combining operating and financial leverage causes rather large variations in EPS.

B. One way to measure the combined leverage can be expressed as:

$$\begin{array}{l}\text{degree of combined} \\ \quad \text{leverage from the} \\ \quad \text{base sales level}\end{array} = \text{DCL}_{\text{s}} = \frac{\text{\% change in EPS}}{\text{\% change in sales}}$$

If the $\text{DCL}_{\text{s}}$ is equal to 5.0 times, then it is important to understand that a 1% change in sales will result in a 5% change in EPS.

C. The degree of combined leverage is actually the product of the two independent leverage measures.  Thus, we have:

$$DCL_S = (DOL_S) \ X \ (DFL_{EBIT})$$

D. As you might have guessed, there is still another way to compute $DCL_S$.  It is a more direct way in that no percentage fluctuations or separate leverage values have to be determined.  You need only substitute the appropriate values into the following equation:

$$DCL_S = \frac{Q(P - V)}{Q(P - V) - F - I}$$

All variables have previously been defined.

E. Implications of combining operating and financial leverage

1. The total risk exposure that the firm assumes can be managed by combining operating and financial leverage in different degrees.

2. Knowledge of the various leverage measures that have been examined here aids the financial officer in his or her determination of the proper level of overall risk that should be accepted.


Study Problems

1. Gilbert's Stop and Go party store expects to earn $10,000 next year before interest and taxes.  Sales will be $150,000.  The store is located near the fraternity-row district of Cambridge Springs State University and sells only kegs of beer for $30 a keg.  The variable cost per keg is $20.  The store experiences a 40% tax rate.

(a) What are the party store's fixed costs expected to be next year?

(b) Calculate the store's break-even point in units and dollars.

SOLUTION

(a) To compute fixed cost:

$$S - (VC + FC) = EBIT$$

$$\frac{\$150,000}{\$30} = 5,000 \text{ units sold}$$

$$\$150,000 - [(5,000)(\$20) + X] = \$10,000$$
$$\$150,000 - \$100,000 - X = \$10,000$$
$$X = \$40,000$$

(b) First, the break-even point in units:

$$Q_B = \frac{F}{P - V} = \frac{\$40,000}{\$30 - \$20} = 4,000 \text{ units}$$

Then, the break-even point in dollars:

$$S^* = \frac{F}{1 - \dfrac{VC}{S}} = \frac{\$40,000}{1 - \dfrac{\$100,000}{\$150,000}} = \$120,000$$

2. The Redstone Corporation projects that next year its fixed costs will total $80,000. Its only product sells for $10 per unit, of which $5 is a variable cost. The management of Redstone is considering the purchase of a new machine that will lower the variable cost per unit to $4. The new machine, however, will add to fixed costs through an increase in depreciation expense. How large can the addition to fixed costs be in order to keep the firm's break-even point in units produced and sold unchanged?

SOLUTION

Compute the present level of break-even output:

$$X = \frac{F}{P - V}$$

$$= \frac{\$80,000}{10 - 5} = \frac{\$80,000}{5} = 16,000 \text{ units}$$

Compute the new level of fixed costs at the break-even output:

$$F + (4)(16,000) = (10)(16,000)$$
$$F + 64,000 = 160,000$$
$$F = \$96,000$$

Compute the addition to fixed costs:

$$\$96,000 - \$80,000 = \underline{\$16,000 \text{ addition}}$$

3. The management of Redstone Corporation decided not to purchase the new piece of equipment. Using the existing cost structure, calculate the degree of operating leverage at 20,000 units of output.

SOLUTION

$$\text{DOL at 20,000 units} = \frac{20,000(\$10 - \$5)}{20,000(\$10 - \$5) - \$80,000}$$

$$= \frac{\$100,000}{\$20,000} = 5 \text{ times}$$

This indicates, for example, that a 10% increase in sales for the Redstone Corporation will result in a 50% increase in EBIT, provided the assumptions of cost-volume-profit analysis hold.

4. The Durham Recreation Company manufactures a full line of lawn furniture. The average selling price of a finished unit is $30. The associated variable cost is $20 per unit. Fixed costs for Durham average $60,000 per year.

(a) What would be the company's profit or loss at the following units of production sold? 6,000 units; 7,000 units; 9,000 units.

(b) Find the degree of operating leverage for the production and sales given in part (a) above.

SOLUTION

(a) The company's profit or loss:

|  | @ 6,000 units | @ 7,000 units | @ 9,000 units |
|---|---|---|---|
| Sales (P X Q) | $180,000 | $210,000 | $270,000 |
| -VC (VC/unit X Q) | 120,000 | 140,000 | 180,000 |
| -FC | 60,000 | 60,000 | 60,000 |
| Profit | $ -0- | $ 10,000 | $ 30,000 |

(b) The degree of operating leverage at the different levels of output:

$$\text{DOL}_S = \frac{Q(P - V)}{Q(P - V) - F}$$

$$\text{DOL at 6,000 units} = \frac{6,000(\$30 - \$20)}{6,000(\$30 - \$20) - \$60,000} = \frac{\$60,000}{0} = \text{undefined}$$

$$\text{DOL at 7,000 units} = \frac{7,000(\$30 - \$20)}{7,000(\$30 - \$20) - \$60,000} = \frac{\$70,000}{\$10,000} = 7 \text{ times}$$

DOL at 9,000 units = 3 times

5. An analytical income statement for the Redstone Corporation is shown below. It is based on an output level of 32,000 units.

| | |
|---|---:|
| Sales | $320,000 |
| Variable costs | 160,000 |
| Revenue before fixed costs | $160,000 |
| Fixed costs | 80,000 |
| EBIT | $ 80,000 |
| Interest expense | 20,000 |
| Earnings before taxes | $ 60,000 |
| Taxes | 30,000 |
| Net income | $ 30,000 |

(a) Calculate the degree of operating leverage at this output level.

(b) Calculate the degree of financial leverage at this level of EBIT.

(c) Determine the combined leverage effect at this output level.

SOLUTION

(a) DOL at 32,000 units = $\dfrac{32,000(\$10 - \$5)}{32,000(\$10 - \$5) - \$80,000}$ = 2 times

(b) DFL at EBIT of $80,000 = $\dfrac{\$80,000}{\$80,000 - \$20,000}$ = 1.333 times

(c) Combined leverage effect = $\dfrac{32,000(\$10 - \$5)}{32,000(\$10 - \$5) - \$80,000 - \$20,000}$

= 2.667 times

Notice that the combined leverage effect is the product of the degrees of operating and financial leverage. A 1% increase in sales for Redstone would be magnified into a 2.667% increase in net income because of the combined leverage effect.

6. You are supplied with the following analytical income statement for your firm. It reflects last year's operations.

| | |
|---|---:|
| Sales | $20,000 |
| Variable costs | 12,000 |
| Revenue before fixed cost | $ 8,000 |
| Fixed costs | 4,000 |
| EBIT | $ 4,000 |
| Interest expense | 1,500 |
| Earnings before taxes | $ 2,500 |
| Taxes | 1,250 |
| Net income | $ 1,250 |

(a) What is the degree of operating leverage at this level of output?

(b) What is the degree of financial leverage?

(c) What is the degree of combined leverage?

(d) If sales should increase by 20%, by what percent would earnings before interest and taxes increase?

(e) What is your firm's break-even point in sales dollars?


SOLUTION

(a) The degree of operating leverage:

$$\text{DOL at } \$20,000 = \frac{\text{revenue before fixed costs}}{\text{EBIT}} = \frac{S - VC}{S - VC - F}$$

$$= \frac{\$8,000}{\$4,000} = 2 \text{ times}$$

(b) The degree of financial leverage:

$$\text{DFL at } \$4,000 \text{ EBIT} = \frac{\text{EBIT}}{\text{EBIT} - I} = \frac{\$4,000}{\$4,000 - \$1,500} = 1.6 \text{ times}$$

(c) The degree of combined leverage:

$$\text{DCL}_S = (\text{DOL}_S)(\text{DFL}_{EBIT}) = (2)(1.6) = 3.2 \text{ times}$$

(d) An increase in sales of 20% would result in a 40% increase in EBIT.

(e) Break-even level in sales dollars:

$$S^* \frac{F}{1 - \frac{VC}{S}} = \frac{\$4,000}{1 - \frac{\$12,000}{\$20,000}} = \$10,000$$

## Self-Tests

TRUE-FALSE

_____ 1. Dispersion in operating income causes business risk.

_____ 2. Your firm adds to its facilities a completely automated product line. This will have no effect on the break-even point (in units of output).

_____ 3. The concept of cost-volume-profit analysis dwells upon the "short run."

_____ 4. Your firm expects a 7% increase in sales for the next year. The degree of financial leverage will decrease for your firm.

_____ 5. The degree of financial leverage for firm A has just increased. Selling common stock could have caused the increase.

_____ 6. When the firm uses more financial leverage, its stock-holders expect a greater return.

_____ 7. A firm cannot lower financial leverage by increasing its sales.

_____ 8. If EBIT were to remain constant while the firm incurred additional interest expense, the degree of financial leverage would increase.

_____ 9. If future sales are expected to increase, then decreasing the degree of operating leverage would be a wise decision.

_____ 10. In actual practice, the separating of costs to either fixed costs or variable costs is not an easy task.

MULTIPLE CHOICE

1. Which of the following is <u>not</u> a limitation of break-even analysis?

a. The price of the product is assumed to be constant.
b. In multiple product firms, the product mix is assumed to be constant.
c. It provides a method for analyzing operating leverage.
d. Variable costs per unit are assumed to be constant.

2. Which of the following is not considered a fixed cost?

a. Depreciation.
b. Rent.
c. Electricity.
d. Administrative salaries.

3. If the degree of operating leverage increases and if all else stays the same, the degree of combined leverage will:

a. Increase.
b. Decrease.
c. Stay the same.
d. Either a or c.

4. The degree of financial leverage will be increased with all of the following financing methods except:

a. Retained earnings.
b. Common stock.
c. First mortgage bonds.
d. Preferred stock.
e. Second mortgage bonds.

5. The degree of operating leverage a firm has can be attributed to:

a. Its financial risk.
b. Its break-even level of sales.
c. Luck.
d. Its business risk exposure.

6. An operating leverage factor of 8.00 indicates that if sales increase by:

a. 1%, EBIT will increase by 1%.
b. 1%, EBIT will increase by 8%.
c. 8%, EBIT will fall by 1%.
d. 8%, EBIT will rise by 8%.

7. In the context of cost-volume-profit analysis, if the selling price per unit rises and if all other variables remain constant, the break-even point in units will:

   a. Fall.
   b. Rise.
   c. Stay the same.
   d. Either a or c.

8. The combined effect of financial and operating leverage is:

   a. The sum of the degree of financial leverage and the degree of
      operating leverage.
   b. The product of the two degrees.
   c. The product of the degrees minus the sum of the degrees.
   d. None of the above.

# Planning the Firm's Financing Mix

Orientation: This chapter concentrates on the way the firm arranges its sources of funds. The cost of capital-capital structure argument is highlighted. A moderate view on the effect of financial leverage use on the composite cost of capital is adopted. Later, techniques useful to the financial officer faced with the determination of an appropriate financing mix are described.

I. Introduction

    A. A distinction can be made between the terms financial structure and capital structure.

        1. Financial structure is the mix of all items that appear on the right-hand side of the firm's balance sheet.

        2. Capital structure is the mix of the long-term sources of funds used by the firm.

        3. In this chapter we do <u>not</u> dwell on the question of dealing with an appropriate maturity composition of the firm's sources of funds. Our main focus is on capital structure management, i.e., determining the proper proportions relative to the total in which the permanent forms of

financing should be used.

B. The <u>objective</u> of capital structure management is to mix the permanent sources of funds in a manner that will maximize the company's common stock price.  This will minimize the firm's composite cost of capital.  This proper mix of funds sources is referred to as the <u>optimal capital structure</u>.

II. Capital structure theory

A. The cost of capital-capital structure argument may be characterized by this question:

1. Can the firm affect its overall cost of funds, either favorably or unfavorably, by varying the mixture of financing sources used?

B. The argument deals with the postulated effect of the use of financial leverage on the overall cost of capital of the company.

C. If the firm's cost of capital can be affected by the degree to which it uses financial leverage, then capital structure management is an important subset of business financial management.

D. The analytical discussion in Chapter 16 revolves around a simplified version of the basic dividend valuation model. Recall that the basic dividend valuation model can be expressed as:

$$P_0 = \sum_{t=1}^{\infty} \frac{D_t}{(1 + K_c)^t}$$

where $P_0$ = the current price of the firm's common stock,

$D_t$ = the cash dividend per share expected by investors during period t,

$K_c$ = the cost of common equity capital.

1. If it is assumed that (1) cash dividends will <u>not</u> change over the infinite holding period and that (2) the firm retains none of its current earnings, then the cash dividend flowing to investors can be viewed as a level payment over an infinite holding period.

2. Under these conditions, the basic dividend valuation

model reduces to the equation noted below, where $E_t$ represents earnings per share during the time period t:

$$P_0 = \frac{D_t}{K_c} = \frac{E_t}{K_c}$$

3. The various capital structure theories discussed in Chapter 16 use the above equation in the context of a partial equilibrium analysis in order to assess the impact of leverage use on common stock price.

III. Capital structure theory:  The independence hypothesis

A. According to this position, made famous by professors Franco Modigliani and Merton H. Miller, in a setting in which business income is not subject to taxation (and, thus, the deductibility of interest expense is irrelevant for valuation purposes) the firm's composite cost of capital, $K_0$, and common stock price, $P_0$, are both <u>independent</u> of the degree to which the firm chooses to use (or avoid) financial leverage.

B. This means that the total market value of the firm's outstanding securities (taken to be the market value of debt plus the market value of common stock) is <u>unaffected</u> by the manner in which the right-hand side of the balance sheet is arranged.

C. The independence hypothesis rests upon what is called the <u>net operating income</u> (NOI) <u>approach to valuation</u>. When corporate income is not taxed, this methodology arrives at the market value of the firm by capitalizing (discounting) the firm's expected net operating income stream. The division of that income stream to investors (either debt or equity) is a mere detail that does not affect enterprise value.

D. In this framework, the use of a greater degree of financial leverage may result in greater earnings and dividends, but the firm's cost of common equity will rise at precisely the same rate as the earnings and dividends. This means that the firm's common stock price is unaffected by the use of financial leverage over all degrees of leverage use.

E. This viewpoint is illustrated in Figures 16.1 and 16.2. Figure 16.1 shows that the weighted cost of capital, $K_0$, is independent of the degree of financial leverage used. The

use of more debt would cause the cost of common equity to
rise, resulting in exactly the same overall cost of capital
that persisted before more debt was, in fact used.  Figure
16.2 shows that stock price, $P_0$, is not influenced by the
degree of financial leverage used.

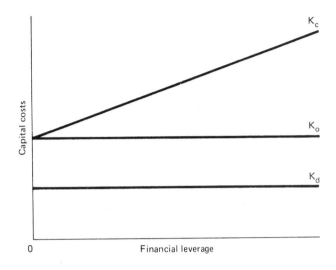

Figure 16.1

Capital Costs and Financial Leverage:  No Taxes
The Independence Hypothesis (NOI Theory)

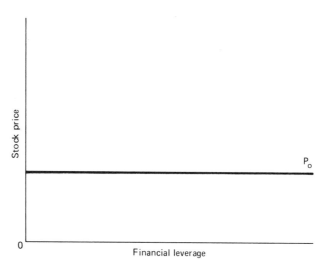

Figure 16. 2

Stock Price and Financial Leverage:  No Taxes
The Independence Hypothesis (NOI Theory)


IV. Capital structure theory:  The dependence hypothesis

   A. This position is at the opposite pole from the previously out-
      lined independence hypothesis.  The dependence hypothesis sug-
      gests that both the weighted cost of capital, $K_0$, and the
      firm's common stock price, $P_0$, are affected by the firm's use
      of financial leverage.

   B. At this extreme, no matter how modest or excessive the firm's
      use of debt financing, both its cost of debt capital, $K_d$, and
      cost of equity capital, $K_c$, will not be affected by capital
      structure adjustments.

   C. So, the cost of debt is less than the cost of common equity,
      which implies that greater financial leverage use will lower
      the firm's weighted cost of capital, $K_0$, indefinitely.  Fur-
      ther, greater use of debt financing will have a favorable
      effect on the firm's stock price.

   D. The dependence hypothesis rests upon what is called the net
      income (NI) approach to valuation.  Both the NOI model and
      the NI model are illustrated at the end of this Study Guide

188

chapter in the first study problem.  You should be familiar
with their structure, assumptions, and implications.

E. The dependence hypothesis viewpoint is shown in Figures
   16.3 and 16.4  Notice in Figure 16.3 that the firm's cost of
   capital, $K_0$, decreases as the debt-to-equity ratio increases.

   Figure 16.4 shows that according to this position, the common
   stock price rises with increased leverage use.  The implica-
   tion is that the firm should use as much financial leverage
   as is possible.

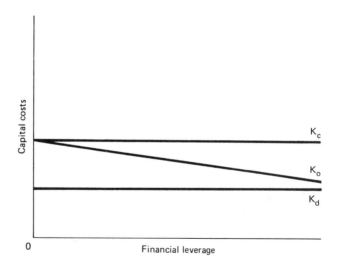

Figure 16.3

Capital Costs and Financial Leverage:    No Taxes
The Dependence Hypothesis (NI Theory)

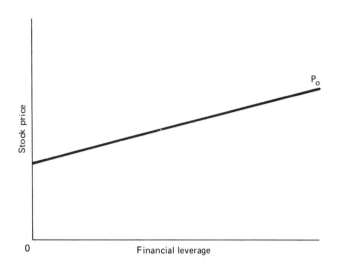

Figure 16.4

Stock Price and Financial Leverage:   No Taxes
The Dependence Hypothesis (NI Theory)


V. Capital structure theory:   A moderate position

   A. The moderate position on capital structure importance admits
      to the facts that (1) interest expense is tax deductible in
      the world of corporate activity and (2) the probability of the
      firm's suffering bankruptcy costs is directly related to the
      company's use of financial leverage.

   B. When interest expense is tax deductible, the sum of the cash
      flows that the firm could pay to all contributors of corporate
      capital (debt investors and equity investors) is affected by
      its financing mix.   This is not the case when an environment
      of corporate taxation is presumed.

      1. A dollar amount labeled the tax shield on interest may be
         calculated as:

         Tax shield = $r_d$(M)(t)

         where $r_d$ = the interest rate paid on outstanding debt,
               M  = the principal amount of the debt,
               t  = the firm's tax rate.

2. The moderate position presents the view that the tax shield must have value in the marketplace. After all, the government's take is decreased and the investor's take is increased because of the deductibility of interest expense.

3. Therefore, according to this position, financial leverage affects firm value and it must also affect the cost of corporate capital.

C. To use too much financial leverage, however, would be imprudent. It seems reasonable to offer that the probability that the firm will be unable to meet the financial obligations contained in its debt contracts will increase the more the firm uses leverage-inducing instruments in its capital structure (debt). The likelihood of firm failure, then, carries with it certain costs (bankruptcy costs) that rise as leverage use increases. There will be some point at which the expected cost of default will be large enough to outweigh the tax shield advantage of debt financing. At that point the firm will turn to common equity financing.

D. Figure 16.5 depicts the moderate view on capital structure importance. This view of the cost of capital-capital structure argument produces a saucer-shaped or U-shaped average cost of capital curve. In Figure 16.5 the firm's optimal range of financial leverage use lies between points A and B. It would be imprudent for the firm to use additional financial leverage beyond point B because (1) the average cost of capital would be higher than it has to be and (2) the firm's common stock price would be lower than it has to be. Therefore, we can say that the degree of financial leverage use signified by point B represents the firm's debt capacity.

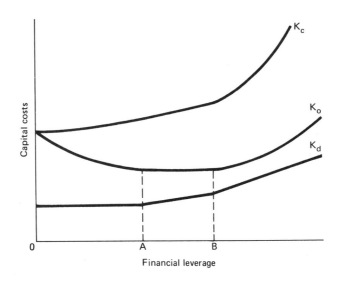

Figure 16.5

Capital Costs and Financial Leverage:  The Moderate
View Which Considers Taxes and Financial Distress

E. We conclude that the determination of the firm's financing mix
   is centrally important to both the financial manager and the
   firm's owners.

VI. Basic tools of capital structure management

A. Recall that the use of financial leverage has two effects on
   the earnings stream flowing to the firm's common stockholders:
   (1) the added variability in the earnings per share (EPS)
   stream that accompanies the use of fixed-charge securities
   and (2) the level of EPS at a given earnings before interest
   and taxes level (EPIT) associated with a specific capital
   structure.  The first effect is quantified by the degree of
   financial leverage measure discussed in Chapter 15.  The
   second effect is analyzed by means of what is generally referred to as EBIT-EPS analysis.

B. The objective of EBIT-EPS analysis is to find the EBIT level
   that will equate EPS regardless of the financing plan chosen
   (from among two plans) by the financial manager.

   1. A graphic analysis or an algebraic analysis can be used.

2. By allowing for sinking fund payments, the analysis can focus upon uncommitted earnings per share (UEPS).

3. Study problems 2 and 3 at the end of this chapter illustrate the nature of EBIT-EPS analysis.

4. EBIT-EPS analysis considers only the level of the earnings stream and ignores the variability (riskiness) in it. In other words, this tool of capital structure management disregards the implicit costs of debt financing. Therefore, it must be used with caution and in conjunction with other basic tools of capital structure management.

C. Comparative leverage ratios provide another tool of capital structure management. This involves the computation of various balance sheet leverage ratios and coverage ratios. Information for the latter comes essentially from the income statement. The ratios that would exist under alternative financing plans can then be computed and examined for their suitableness to management.

D. The use of industry norms in conjunction with comparative leverage ratios can aid the financial manager in arriving at an appropriate financing mix. Industry norms can be thought of as standards for comparison. We recognize that industry groupings contain firms whose basic business risk may differ widely. Nevertheless, corporate financial analysts, investment bankers, commercial loan officers, and bond rating agencies rely on industry classes in order to compute such "normal" ratios. Since so many observers are interested in industry standards, the financial officer must be too.

E. Finally, the financial officer can study the projected impact of capital structure decisions on corporate cash flows. This is often called cash flow analysis or the study of company-wide cash flows. This involves the preparation of a series of cash budgets under (1) different economic conditions and (2) different capital structures. The net cash flows under these different situations can be examined to determine if the financing requirements expose the firm to such a high degree of default risk that it is unbearable. According to this tool, the appropriate level of financial leverage use is reached when the chance of running out of cash is exactly equal to that which management will assume. An underlying assumption is that management's riskbearing preferences are conditioned by the investing marketplace.

Study Problems

1. The Montana Fertilizer Company has $8,000,000 of net operating earnings. In its capital structure, $12,500,000 worth of debt is outstanding, with an interest rate of 8%. The debt is selling in the marketplace at its book value. Parts (a) and (b) assume that there is no tax on corporate income.

(a) According to the NOI valuation method, compute the total value of the firm and the implied equity-capitalization rate. Assume an implied overall capitalization rate, $k_0$, of 16%.

(b) Compute the total value of the firm and the implied overall capitalization rate, $k_0$, according to the dependence hypothesis, (NI theory) capitalization model. Assume an equity-capitalization rate, $k_c$, of 20%.

(c) Now, allow for the existence of a federal tax on corporate income at a 50% rate. Calculate the value of the firm's tax shield.

SOLUTION

(a)

| | | | |
|---|---|---|---|
| O | Net operating earnings | | $ 8,000,000 |
| $k_0$ | Overall capitalization rate | | 0.16 |
| V | Total value of the firm | | $50,000,000 |
| B | Market value of debt | | -12,500,000 |
| S | Market value of stock | | $37,500,000 |

$$k_c = \frac{O - I}{S} = \frac{\$8,000,000 - \$1,000,000}{\$37,500,000} = 18.67\%$$

where I = interest expense.

(b) 
O = $ 8,000,000
I = 1,000,000
E = $ 7,000,000
$k_c$ = 0.20
S = $35,000,000
B = 12,500,000
V = $47,500,000

$$k_0 = \frac{O}{V} = \frac{\$8,000,000}{\$47,000,000} = 16.84\%$$

(c) Tax shield $= r_d(M)(t)$

$$= (0.08)(\$12,500,000)(0.5)$$
$$= \underline{\$500,000}$$

2. Gilbert and Associates, Inc., are planning to open a small manufacturing corporation. The company will manufacture a full line of water beds. Two financing plans have been proposed by the investors. Plan A is an all common equity alternative. Under this plan, 100,000 common shares will be sold to net the firm $10 per share. Plan B involves the use of financial leverage. A debt issue with a 20-year maturity period will be privately placed. The debt issue will carry an interest rate of 8% and the principal borrowed will amount to $400,000. The corporate tax rate is 50%.

(a) Find the EBIT indifference level associated with the two financing proposals.

(b) Prepare an analytical income statement that proves EPS will be the same regardless of the plan chosen at the EBIT level found in part (a).

(c) If a detailed financial analysis projects that long-term EBIT will always be close to $100,000 annually, which plan would be chosen? Why?

SOLUTION

(a) In the following equations, E = EBIT.

$$\frac{(E - \$0)(1 - 0.5) - 0}{100,000} = \frac{(E - \$40,000)(1 - 0.5) - 0}{50,000}$$

$$\frac{0.5E}{100,000} = \frac{0.5E - \$20,000}{50,000}$$

$$25,000E = 50,000E - \$2,000,000,000$$

$$E = \underline{\$80,000}$$

(b)                    Analytical Income Statement

|                               | With C/S Financing | Financing with C/S and Debt |
|-------------------------------|--------------------|------------------------------|
| EBIT                          | $ 80,000           | $80,000                      |
| Less: Interest expense        | -0-                | 40,000                       |
| Earnings before taxes         | $ 80,000           | $40,000                      |
| Less:  Taxes @ 50%            | 40,000             | 20,000                       |
| Earnings available to common  | $ 40,000           | $20,000                      |
| C/S outstanding               | 100,000            | 50,000                       |
| EPS                           | $.40               | $.40                         |

(c) Plan b, because at any level above the indifference point, the more heavily levered financing plan will generate a higher EPS.

3. Alabama Leather Outlets, Inc., ended this past year of operations with the capital structure shown below:

| | |
|---|---|
| First mortgage bonds at 8% | $ 2,000,000 |
| Debentures at 9% | 1,000,000 |
| Common stock (1,000,000 shares) | 6,000,000 |
| Retained earnings | 1,000,000 |
| Total | $10,000,000 |

The federal income tax rate is 50%.  The firm wants to raise an additional $1,000,000 to open new facilities in Louisiana and Tennessee. Two approaches are open to the firm.  It can sell a new issue of 20-year debentures with a 10% interest rate.  Alternatively, 20,000 new shares of common stock can be sold to the public to net the company $50 per share.  A recent study performed by an outside consulting organization projected Alabama Leather's long-term EBIT level at approximately $4,750,000.

(a) Find the indifference level of EBIT (with regard to earnings per share) between the suggested financing plans.

(b) Which alternative do you recommend that Alabama Leather pursue?

SOLUTION

(a) In the following equations, E = EBIT.

196

$$\frac{(E - \$250,000)(0.5)}{1,020,000} = \frac{(E - \$350,000)(0.5)}{1,000,000}$$

$$\frac{0.5E - \$125,000}{102} = \frac{0.5E - \$175,000}{100}$$

$$50E - \$12,500,000 = 51E - \$17,850,000$$

$$E = \underline{\$5,350,000} \text{ indifference level of EBIT}$$

(b) The consulting firm projected Alabama Leather's long-term EBIT at \$4,750,000. Since this projected level of EBIT is less than the indifference level of \$5,350,000, the earnings per share of the firm will be greater if the common stock is issued.


Self-Tests

TRUE-FALSE

_____ 1. The mix of all items appearing on the right-hand side of a company's balance sheet is said to be that firm's financial structure.

_____ 2. The major influence on the maturity structure of the financing plan is the nature of the assets owned by the firm.

_____ 3. In computing the firm's tax bill the interest expense is assumed not to be tax deductible.

_____ 4. The funds mix that will minimize the firm's composite cost of capital is said to be the firm's optimal capital structure.

_____ 5. By using more and more financial leverage the firm can increase its firm's value indefinitely.

_____ 6. Inputs to the coverage ratios generally come from the firm's balance sheet.

_____ 7. There will be some point at which the expected cost of default will outweigh the tax shield advantage of debt financing. At this point the firm will turn to other types of financing, mainly common equity.

_____ 8. Holding all other things constant, if the firm's proper financing mix is found, the firm's common stock price will be maximized.

_____ 9. Above a critical level of EBIT the firm's earnings per share will be lower if greater degrees of financial leverage are employed.

_____ 10. The mix of the long-term sources of funds used by the firm is said to be its capital structure.


MULTIPLE CHOICE

1. Which of the following assumptions does capital structure theory not include?

   a. Corporate income is not subject to any tax.
   b. Transaction costs of selling securities are prevalent.
   c. The expected values of all investors' forecasts of the future levels of EBIT for each firm are identical.
   d. The capital structures consist only of stocks and bonds.

2. The independence hypothesis suggests that the total market value of the firm's outstanding securities _____ by the manner in which the right-hand side of the balance sheet is arranged.

   a. Rises in total value.
   b. Lowers in total value.
   c. Is unaffected.
   d. First rises, but then lowers.

3. The implicit cost of debt is the change in the cost of common equity brought on by using _____.

   a. Operating leverage.
   b. Financial leverage.
   c. Trading on the equity.
   d. All of the above.

4. Possible methods to use in the approximation of an optimal capital structure include:

   a. Cash flow analysis.
   b. EBIT-EPS analysis.
   c. Comparison of selected financial ratios with those of similar firms.
   d. All of the above.

5. The firm's capital structure would consist of:

    a. Long-term debt.
    b. Common equity.
    c. Preferred equity.
    d. Only b and c.
    e. All of the above.

6. The primary weakness of EBIT-EPS analysis is that it:

    a. Disregards the implicit cost of debt financing.
    b. Puts too much emphasis on cost of debt financing.
    c. There are no weaknesses of EBIT-EPS analysis.
    d. Only uses the right-hand side of the balance sheet.

# 17

# *Dividend Policy and Internal Financing*

Orientation: In determining the firm's dividend policy, two issues are important. The dividend payout ratio (percentage of earnings paid out in dividends) must be decided as well as the manner in which dividends are to be paid out over time. These issues must be resolved in light of the objective of maximizing the value of the firm's common stock. In doing so, the financial manager should consider the investment opportunities available to the firm and any preference that the company's investors have for dividend income or capital gains. Also, stock dividends and stock splits could be used either in lieu of or to supplement cash dividends, keeping in mind the overall objective of the firm.

I. Dividend policy assuming perfect markets

    A. Perfect markets are defined as follows:

        1. There is no income tax.

        2. There is no brokerage commission when investors buy and sell stock.

        3. New securities can be issued without incurring any flotation cost.

4. Information is free and equally available to all investors.

5. No informational content is assigned to a particular policy in determinging the firm's capability to generate earnings.

6. Security prices reflect the present value of expected future cash flows accruing to their owners.

B. Under the foregoing assumptions, it may be shown that the market price of a corporation's common stock is unchanged under different dividend policies. If the firm increases the dividend to its stockholders, it has to offset this increase by issuing new common stock in order to finance the available investment opportunities. The present value of expected cash flows to be received by the current investors is independent of the dividend policy.

II. Transition from theory to practice: Under conditions of perfect markets, dividend policy has no impact on the value of the firm. However, when we recognize the following market imperfections, dividend policy may become relevant.

A. Flotation costs: Because of flotation costs firms must issue a larger amount of securities in order to receive the amount required for investments. Therefore, new equity capital will be more expensive than capital raised through retained earnings. As a result, financing investments internally (and decreasing dividends) instead of issuing new stock may be favored. Therefore, only if any internally generated funds remain after financing the equity portion of the firm's investments would a dividend be paid. This approach is often termed the residual dividend theory.

B. Personal income taxes: For most investors, the gain from the sale of stock is usually 50% of the tax for dividend income. Also, the capital gains tax is deferred until the stock is actually sold, whereas, tax on dividend income is paid when the dividend is received. Hence, the investor may prefer to have the firm retain earnings, which causes the stock price to increase, rather than pay out dividends.

C. Investors transaction costs (brokerage commissions): Whenever securities are bought or sold, brokerage fees are incurred. This fee may discourage investors from buying or selling the stock to create a desired income stream.

D. Informational content of a dividend policy: Investors may attach informational content to an unexpected change in the firm's dividend policy. They may perceive that the change reflects management's belief regarding the firm's earning capacity.

E. Conclusions: The profitability of a corporation's investment opportunities and the imperfections in the marketplace are the key determinants of a firm's dividend policy.

III. Dividend policy decisions

A. Other practical considerations

1. Legal restrictions

a. A corporation may not pay a dividend

(1) If the firm's liabilities exceed its assets.
(2) If the amount of the dividend exceeds the accumulated profits (retained earnings).
(3) If the dividend is being paid from capital invested in the firm.

b. Debtholders and preferred stockholders may impose re-strictive provisions on management, such as dividends not being paid from earnings prior to the payment of interest or preferred dividends.

2. Liquidity position: The amount of a firm's retained earn-ings and its cash position would seldom be the same. Thus, the company must have adequate cash available as well as retained earnings to pay dividends.

3. Availability of other sources of financing. All firms do not have equal accessibility to the capital markets. Con-sequently, a greater reliance has to be placed on inter-nally generated funds if the company has limited access to other financing sources.

4. Earnings predictability: A firm that has a stable trend in earnings will generally pay a larger portion of its earnings in dividends. If earnings fluctuate significant-ly, a larger amount of the profits may be retained to en-sure that enough money is available when needed.

5. Ownership control: For small firms, maintaining voting control is very important. The owners would prefer the use of debt and profits to finance new investments rather than issue new stock.

6. Inflation: Because of inflation the cost of replacing equipment has increased substantially. Depreciation funds tend to become insufficient. Hence, greater retention of profits may be required.

B. Alternative dividend policies

   1. Constant dividend payout ratio:  The percentage of earnings paid out in dividends is held constant.  Therefore, the dollar amount of the dividend fluctuates from year to year.

   2. Stable dollar dividend per share:  Relatively stable dollar dividend is maintained.  The dividend per share is increased or decreased only after careful investigation by the management.

   3. Small, low regular dividend plus a year-end extra:  Extra dividend is paid out in prosperous years.  Management's objective is to avoid the connotation of a permanent dividend increase.

C. Bases for stable dividends

   1. Investors may use the dividend policy as a surrogate for information that is not easily accessible.  The dividend policy may be thought to be useful in assessing the company's long-term earnings prospects.

   2. Many investors rely on dividends to satisfy personal needs. If dividends fluctuate from year to year, investors may have to sell or buy stock to satisfy their needs.  Such action is costly for the investor.

   3. Legal listings stipulate that certain types of financial institutions may only invest in companies that have a regular dividend payment.

   4. Conclusion:  An investor who prefers stable dividends will have a lower required rate of return for a stock paying a stable dividend, which, in turn, results in a higher market price for the stock.

D. Dividend policy:  A scenario

   1. The <u>residual dividend theory</u> is not feasible in the short term because it places undue hardship on investors who depend on dividend income.

   2. It could be useful as a long-term policy with the long-term target dividend-payout ratio being based on:

      a. The firm's expected investment opportunities during the long-term planning horizon.

    b. The company's debt-equity mix.

    c. The funds generated from operations.

IV. Dividend payment procedures

  A. Dividends are generally paid quarterly.

  B. The <u>declaration date</u> is the date on which the firm's board of directors announces the forthcoming dividends.

  C. <u>The date of record</u> designates when the stock transfer books are to be closed (who is entitled to the dividend).

  D. Brokerage firms terminate the right of ownership to the dividend 4 working days prior to the date of record. This date is called the <u>ex-dividend date</u>.

  E. The date dividend checks are mailed is the <u>payment date</u>.

V. Stock dividends and stock splits.

  A. Both a stock dividend and a stock split involve issuing new shares of stock to current shareholders.

  B. The investors' percentage ownership in the firm remains unchanged. The investor is neither better off nor worse off than before the stock split/dividend.

  C. On an economic basis there is no difference between a stock dividend and a stock split.

  D. For accounting purposes, the stock split has been defined as a stock dividend exceeding 25%.

  E. Accounting treatment

    1. In the case of a stock dividend, the dollar amount of the dividend is transferred from retained earnings to the capital accounts.

    2. In the case of a split, the dollar amounts of the accounts do not change. Only the number of shares changes and the par value of each share is decreased proportionately.

  F. Rationale for a stock dividend or split

    1. The price of stock may not fall precisely in proportion to the share increase; thus, the stockholders' value is increased.

    2. If a company is encountering cash problems, it can substi-

tute a stock dividend for a cash dividend.  Investors will probably look beyond the dividend to determine the underlying reason for the attempt to conserve cash.


Study Problems


1. The Harvestor Corporation has the following capital structure:

| | |
|---|---|
| Common stock ($5 par; 300,000 shares) | $1,500,000 |
| Paid in capital | 2,500,000 |
| Retained earnings | 4,000,000 |
| Total net worth | $8,000,000 |

(a) If the company issues a 20% stock dividend, how would the new capital structure appear?  The market price per share for the stock is $10.

(b) How would the capital accounts appear after a two-for-one split?


SOLUTION

(a)   Decrease in retained earnings

| | |
|---|---|
| ($10 x 60,000 shares) | $600,000 |
| Increase in par value of common stock | |
| ($5 X 60,000 shares) | 300,000 |
| Remainder to increase capital surplus | $300,000 |

The new capital structure after a 20% stock dividend:

| | |
|---|---|
| Common stock ($5 par; 360,000 shares) | $1,800,000 |
| Paid in capital | 2,800,000 |
| Retained earnings | 3,400,000 |
| Total net worth | $8,000,000 |

(b) The new capital structure after a two-for-one split:

| | |
|---|---|
| Common stock ($2.50 par, 600,000 shares) | $1,500,000 |
| Capital surplus | 2,500,000 |
| Retained earnings | 4,000,000 |
| Total net worth | $8,000,000 |

2. The Mansville Corporation's capital structure on June 30, 1979 is as follows:

| | |
|---|---|
| Common stock ($4 par; 5,000,000 shares outstanding) | $20,000,000 |
| Paid in capital | 1,000,000 |
| Retained earnings | 9,000,000 |
| Total net worth | $30,000,000 |

The firm's earnings after taxes for 1979 was $2 million, of which the company paid out 25% in cash dividends.  The price of the firm's common stock as of June 30, 1979 was $8.

(a) If the firm declared a 20% stock dividend on June 30, 1979, how would the capital structure appear?

(b) If the firm declared a 30% stock dividend, what would be the end result on the capital structure?  (Hint:  Stock dividends in excess of 25% should be calculated on the basis of book value less retained earnings instead of market value).

(c) If a 20% stock dividend is assumed, what would the earnings per share and dividends per share be in 1979?

SOLUTION

(a) Capital structure after a 20% stock dividend:
    Increase in the shares outstanding:

    20% X 5,000,000 shares = 1,000,000 shares

Increase in the par value:

    $4 X 1,000,000 = $4,000,000

Increase in the capital surplus account:

    ($8 - $4) X 1,000,000 = $4,000,000

Result:

| | |
|---|---|
| Common stock (6,000,000 shares) | $24,000,000 |
| Capital surplus | 5,000,000 |

| Retained earnings | 1,000,000 |
|---|---|
| Total net worth | $30,000,000 |

(b) Capital structure after a 30% stock dividend:
Increase in shares outstanding:

| 30% X 5,000,000 = | 1,500,000 shares |
|---|---|

Increase in par value:

| 1,500,000 shares X $4 par value | $6,000,000 |
|---|---|

Increase in capital surplus:

| $1,000,000 X 30% | 300,000 |
|---|---|
| Amount transferred from retained earnings: | $6,300,000 |

Revised capital structure:

| Common stock ($4 par value; 6,500,000 shares) | $26,000,000 |
|---|---|
| Paid in capital | 1,300,000 |
| Retained earnings | 2,700,000 |
| Net worth | $30,000,000 |

(c) Earnings per share after a 20% stock dividend:

$$\frac{\text{Earnings}}{\text{Number of shares}} = \frac{\$2,000,000}{6,000,000} = \$0.33$$

Dividends per share after a 20% stock dividend:

$$\frac{\text{Dividends}}{\text{Number of shares}} = \frac{\$500,000}{6,000,000} = \$0.083$$

3. Philips Limited treats dividends as a residual variable in its financial decisions (see residual dividend theory). Net income has been forecasted for the upcoming year to be $600,000, which may be used for reinvesting in the firm or for paying dividends. The firm has only equity in its capital structure and its cost of internally generated equity capital is 10%. If, however, new common stock were issued, flotation costs would raise this cost to 11%. If the firm considers the 10% cost of internal equity to be the opportunity cost of retained earnings,

(a) (1) How much in dividends should be paid if the company has $500,000 in projects with expected returns exceeding 10%?

(2) How much should the dividend be if $600,000 in investments are available having expected returns greater than 10%?

(b) How much should be paid in dividends if the firm has $1 million in projects whose expected returns exceed 11%?

(c) How would your answer change in part (b) if the firm's optimal debt-equity mix is 40% debt and 60% common and the cost of capital remains the same.

SOLUTION

(a) (1) According to the residual dividend theory, the firm should pay dividends only when it has exhausted its investments whose return exceed the firm's cost of capital. Therefore, the firm should pay $100,000 in dividends ($600,000 income available for investing less $500,000 investments).

(2) The firm should use all of the $600,000 for investing in the projects and should not pay any dividends.

(b) If the firm has investment opportunities with returns exceeding the cost of capital, the firm should undertake these investments. In this example, the cost of capital increases (to 11%) when new equity is issued. Since the returns on the available investment projects (totaling $1 million) exceed the cost of equity capital, the firm should use up its internally generated funds ($600,000) and raise the remaining $400,000 by issuing new common stock. Therefore, no dividends would be paid.

(c) We would need $400,000 in new debt; i.e., 40% of $1 million. The remaining $600,000 (which is 60% of the needed capital) will be supplied by internally generated funds. No dividend will be paid.

4. Beardsell Products and Voltas Products are identical firms in terms of (1) being in the same industry, (2) producing the same products, (3) being subject to the same risks, and (4) having equivalent earnings per share. Beardsell pays a constant cash dividend, whereas Voltas follows a constant percentage payout ratio of 50%. However, Voltas' common stock price has been lower than Beardsell's in spite of Voltas' dividend being substantially larger than Beardsell's in certain years. Given the data below:

| | Beardsell Products | | | | Voltas Products | | |
| --- | --- | --- | --- | --- | --- | --- | --- |
| Year | EPS | Dividend | Market Price | | EPS | Dividend | Market Price |
| 1974 | $2.50 | $0.65 | 9 | | $2.50 | $1.25 | 6 3/4 |
| 1975 | -0.25 | 0.65 | 8 3/4 | | -0.25 | 0 | 6 1/2 |
| 1976 | 3.00 | 0.65 | 9 1/4 | | 3.00 | 1.50 | 9 |
| 1977 | 2.00 | 0.65 | 9 | | 2.00 | 1.00 | 10 |

(a) What might account for the differences in the market prices of the two companies?

(b) What might both companies do in order to enhance the market prices of their respective shares?

SOLUTION

(a) The dissimiliarity between market prices might be a function of the different dividend policies, with a lower capitalization rate, and, accordingly, a higher price being assigned to Beardsell as a result of the stable dividend stream.

(b) It appears that neither company would appear to be growth-oriented. If both firms are valued in terms of their dividend yield, which seems to be the case, higher dividend payouts might produce higher prices.

5. The Maple Syrup Company is considering two dividend policies for the years 1979 and 1980. The firm will be liquidated in 1980. One dividend plan would pay a dividend of $2.30 in 1979 and a liquidating dividend of $37.03 in 1980. The alternative plan would pay a dividend of $6.90 in 1979 and a final dividend of $31.74 in 1980. The required rate of return for the common stockholders is 15%. If perfect capital markets are assumed, what would be the effect of each dividend policy on the price of common stock?

SOLUTION

Under perfect market conditions, the effect of each dividend policy is determined by finding the present value of the dividend stream for each dividend plan.

Plan 1:   Present value calculations

|  | Year 1979 | Year 1980 |
|---|---|---|
| Dividends | $2.30 | $37.03 |

$$\text{Present value} = \frac{\$2.30}{(1.15)} + \frac{\$37.03}{(1.15)^2} = \$30$$

Plan 2:

|  | Year 1979 | Year 1980 |
|---|---|---|
| Dividends | $6.90 | $31.74 |

$$\text{Present value} = \frac{\$6.90}{1.15} + \frac{\$31.74}{(1.15)^2} = \$30$$

We find that both plans have the same present value.   The common stockholders should be indifferent about both plans.

6. Rexall Corporation is considering five investment opportunities. The required investment outlays and expected rates of return for these investments are shown below.   The cost of capital for the firm is 13%. Investments are to be financed with 30% debt and 70% equity.   Internally generated funds available for reinvestment equal $1 million. (a) Which investments should be accepted?   (b) According to the residual dividend theory, what amount should be paid out in dividends?

| Investment | Cost | Internal Rate of Return |
|---|---|---|
| A | $200,000 | 20% |
| B | 300,000 | 15 |
| C | 900,000 | 14 |
| D | 100,000 | 10 |
| E | 400,000 | 7 |

SOLUTION

(a) The data given in the problem is shown graphically:

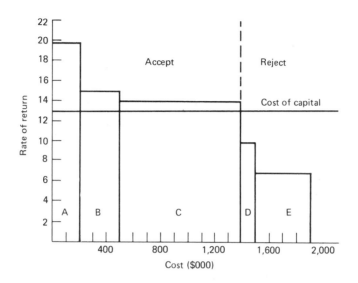

Investments A, B, C should be accepted because their expected returns exceed the firm's cost of capital.

Total cost of three projects:
$200,000 + $300,000 + $900,000          =    $1,400,000
Equity financing:   $1,400,000 x 70%     =      $980,000
Debt financing:   $1,400,000 - $980,000  =      $420,000

Internally generated funds available:    $1,000,000
Less equity necessary for projects:          980,000
Funds available for dividend payment:   $     20,000

7. International Computers, Inc., a new firm, is financed only by common stock. The firm's life is limited to 2 years (1979 and 1980), at the end of which the firm will be liquidated. At the beginning of 1979 the firm's assets are $5 million and 200,000 shares are outstanding. Cash available for reinvestment or dividend payment for 1979 is $1 million. The expected return on investment is 15%. At the end of 1979 an additional investment of $500,000 will be required. This may be financed by retaining $500,000 of the 1979 profits or issuing new stock or a combination of both. In fact, management is considering one of two plans:

Plan A:  The $500,000 investment would be financed entirely by internal financing with the investors receiving $500,000 in dividends.

Plan B:   Investors would receive $600,000 dividends, with the invest-
ment in 1979 being financed $400,000 internally and a $100,000 new
stock issue.

The proposed dividend plans for 1979 are shown below:

|                                      | Plan A       | Plan B       |
|--------------------------------------|--------------|--------------|
| Internally generated cash flow       | $1,000,000   | $1,000,000   |
| Dividend for 1979                    | 500,000      | 600,000      |
| Cash available for reinvestment      | $ 500,000    | $ 400,000    |
| Amount of investment in 1979         | 500,000      | 500,000      |
| External financing required          | $     0      | $ 100,000    |

Assume perfect markets, and demonstrate that under either dividend
plan the market price of the firm's stock remains the same, i.e.,
the dividend policy of the firm is irrelevant from the investor's
point of view.


SOLUTION

The solution to this problem is obtained by following two steps:
(1) Calculating the amount and timing of the dividend stream for
the original investors and (2) determining the present value of
the dividend stream under each plan.

For step 1, see Table 17.1.

For step 2, the present value of the dividend streams discounted
at 15% must be determined:

$$\text{Plan A:} \quad \frac{\$2.50}{(1.15)^1} + \frac{\$31.625}{(1.15)^2} = \$26.09$$

$$\text{Plan B:} \quad \frac{\$3.00}{(1.15)^1} + \frac{\$31.05}{(1.15)^2} = \$26.09$$

We see that under both plans, the market price of International
Computers is the same.

## Table 17.1

### Number of Original Shares Outstanding Equals 200,000

|  | Plan A | Plan B |
|---|---|---|
| **Year: 1979** | | |
| Dividends | $ 500,000 | $ 600,000 |
|  | ($2.50 per share) | ($3 per share) |
| **Year: 1980** | | |
| Total dividends | | |
| A. Original investment | | |
| Old investors | $5,000,000 | $5,000,000 |
| New investors | 0 | 100,000 |
| B. Retained earnings* | 500,000 | 400,000 |
| C. Profits for 1980† | 825,000 | 825,000 |
| Total dividend to all investors | $6,325,000 | $6,325,000 |
| Less dividend to new investors: | | |
| A. Original investment | 0 | (100,000) |
| B. Profits for new investors (15% of $100,000) | 0 | (15,000) |
| Dividends available to original investors | $6,325,000 | $6,210,000 |
| Amount per share | $ 31.625 | $ 31.05 |

*The portion of the 1979 profits that were reinvested in the firm at the conclusion of 1979.

†Profits for 1980 equal 15 percent of $5,500,000, the asset base in 1980.

Self-Tests

TRUE-FALSE

_____ 1. If dividend policy is treated as a passive residual, dividends are paid only if the firm has any remaining capital after financing attractive investments.

_____ 2. In practice, the firm should invest retained earnings as long as the required rate of return exceeds the expected rate of return from the investment.

_____ 3. The greater the ability of a firm to borrow, the less is its ability to pay a cash dividend.

_____ 4. If a firm has sporadic investment opportunities, it might be expected to pay out more dividends.

_____ 5. A stock dividend results in a recapitalization of returned earnings.

_____ 6. In a stock split, the only accounting change is the shifting of amounts from retained earnings to the common stock (par) account.

_____ 7. The introduction of flotation costs to the "dividend irrelevance" concept favors the retention of earnings in the firm.

_____ 8. The only wealth-creating activity under "perfect market" conditions for an all-equity firm is the management's investment decisions.

_____ 9. Dividend income and capital gains from sale of stock are taxed at the same personal income tax rate.

_____ 10. An "expected" change in the dividend policy of a firm should not affect the price of the firm's stock when the change is actually announced.


MULTIPLE CHOICE

1. Which of the following is not an assumption of the "dividend irrelevance" theory.

   a. No taxes.
   b. Efficient capital markets.

214

c. No flotation costs.
d. Costless information.

2. An argument for the relevance of dividends would be:

a. Informational content.
b. Resolution of uncertainty.
c. Preference for current income.
d. All of the above.
e. None of the above.

3. An advantage of a stock dividend is that it:

a. Helps to conserve cash.
b. Tends to increase the market price.
c. Keeps the price of the stock within a desired trading range.
d. Does both b and c.

4. When the assumption of no taxes is removed from the "dividend ir-relevance" theory:

a. There is a preference for the retention of earnings.
b. There is a preference for paying out dividends.
c. The preference depends on the individual investor's tax status, but generally there is a preference for retention of earnings.

5. The following factors may influence the dividend policy that a firm undertakes:

a. The liquidity of the firm.
b. Capital structure.
c. Legal restrictions.
d. a and c.
e. a and b.

6. A firm may not pay dividends if:

a. Its liabilities exceed its assets.
b. The dividend is being paid from capital invested in the firm.
c. Debtholders' contracts are not satisfied.
d. All of the above.
e. a and b.

7. For tax purposes, a corporation may exclude _____% of the dividend income received from another corporation?

a. 0.
b. 10.
c. 50.

  d. 85.

  e. 100.

8. When real-world considerations are taken into account, the amount
   of a firm's dividend payment depends on the following factors:

   a. Profitability of investment opportunities.
   b. Investor's preference for capital gains or dividend income.
   c. Debt to equity ratio.
   d. Trading range of the firm's stock.
   e. a and b.

9. Small-sized firms generally use retained earnings for investment
   purposes because:

   a. They do not have easy access to the capital markets.
   b. Ownership control is an important factor.
   c. Their earnings fluctuate widely.
   d. Inflation has greater impact on small companies.
   e. None of the above.
   f. a and b.

10. Which one of the following dividend policies is the most popular?

   a. Constant dividend payout ratio.
   b. Stable dividend (dollar) per share.
   c. Small, low, regular dividend plus a year-end extra.

11. The ex-dividend date is

   a. The same as the date of record.
   b. Four working days prior to date of record.
   c. Eight days prior to the payment date.
   d. Five days after the declaration date.
   e. None of the above.

# Raising Funds in the Capital Market

Orientation: This chapter considers the market environment in which long-term capital is raised. The underlying rationale for the existence of security markets is presented, investment banking services and procedures are detailed, private placements are discussed, and security market regulation is reviewed.

I. Why financial markets exist

    A. Financial markets consist of institutions and procedures that facilitate transactions in all types of financial claims.

    B. Some economic units spend more during a given period of time than they earn. Some economic units spend less than they earn. Accordingly, a mechanism is needed to facilitate the transfer of savings from those economic units that have a savings surplus to those that have a savings deficit. Financial markets provide such a mechanism.

    C. The function of financial markets, then, is to allocate savings in an economy to the ultimate demander (user) of the savings.

    D. If there were no financial markets, the wealth of an economy

would be lessened.  Savings could not be transferred to economic units, such as business firms, which are most in need
of those funds.

II. Components of the U.S. financial market system

   A. Public offerings can be distinguished from private placements.

     1. The public (financial) market is an impersonal market in
       which both individual and institutional investors have the
       opportunity to acquire securities.

       a. A public offering takes place in the public market.

       b. The security-issuing firm does not meet (face-to-face)
         the actual investors in the securities.

     2. In a private placement of securities only a limited number
       of investors have the opportunity to purchase a portion of
       the issue.

       a. The market for private placements is more personal than
         its public counterpart.

       b. The specific details of the issue may actually be devel-
         oped on a face-to-face basis among the potential inves-
         tors and the issuer.

   B. Primary markets can be distinguished from secondary markets.

     1. Securities are first offered for sale in a primary market.
       For example, the sale of a new bond issue, preferred stock
       issue, or common stock issue takes place in the primary
       market.  These transactions increase the total stock of
       financial assets in existence in the economy.

     2. Trading in currently existing securities takes place in the
       secondary market.  The total stock of financial assets is
       unaffected by such transactions.

   C. The money market can be distinguished from the capital market.

     1. The money market consists of the institutions and proce-
       dures that provide for transactions in short-term debt in-
       struments which are generally issued by borrowers who have
       very high credit ratings.

       a. "Short-term" means that the securities traded in the
         money market have maturity periods of not more than 1
         year.

      b. Equity instruments are not traded in the money market.

      c. Typical examples of money market instruments are (1) U.S. Treasury bills, (2) federal agency securities, (3) bankers' acceptances, (4) negotiable certificates of deposit, and (5) commercial paper.

  2. The capital market consists of the institutions and procedures that provide for transactions in long-term financial instruments. This market encompasses those securities that have maturity periods extending beyond 1 year.

B. <u>Organized security exchanges</u> can be distinguished from <u>over-the-counter markets</u>.

  1. Organized security exchanges are tangible entities whose activities are governed by a set of bylaws. Security exchanges physically occupy space and financial instruments are traded on such premises.

      a. Major stock exchanges must comply with a strict set of reporting requirements established by the Securities and Exchange Commission (SEC). These exchanges are said to be <u>registered</u>.

      b. The New York Stock Exchange, the American Stock Exchange, and the Midwest Stock Exchange collectively account for over 90% of the annual dollar transactions on the registered stock exchanges.

      c. Organized security exchanges provide several benefits to both corporations and investors. They (1) provide a continuous market, (2) establish and publicize fair security prices, and (3) help business raise new financial capital.

      d. A corporation must take steps to have its securities <u>listed</u> on an exchange in order to directly receive the benefits noted above. Listing criteria differ from exchange to exchange.

  2. Over-the-counter markets include all security markets <u>except</u> the organized exchanges. The money market is a prominent example. Most corporate bonds are traded over-the-counter.

III. Using an investment banker

  A. The investment banker is a financial specialist who acts as an intermediary in the selling of securities.  He or she works for an investment banking firm (house).

B. Three basic functions are provided by the investment banker:

1. He or she assumes the risk of selling a new security issue at a satisfactory (profitable) price.  This is called underwriting.  Typically, the investment banking house, along with the underwriting syndicate, actually buys the new issue from the corporation that is raising funds.  The syndicate (group of investment banking firms) then sells the issue to the investing public at a higher (hopefully) price than it paid for it.

2. He or she provides for the distribution of the securities to the investing public.

3. He or she advises firms on the details of selling securities.

C. Several distribution methods are available for placing new securities into the hands of final investors.  The investment banker's role is different in each case.

1. In a negotiated purchase the firm in need of funds contacts an investment banker and begins the sequence of steps leading to the final distribution of the securities that will be offered.  The price that the investment banker pays for the securities is "negotiated" with the issuing firm.

2. In a competitive-bid purchase the investment banker and underwriting syndicate are selected by an auction process. The syndicate willing to pay the greatest dollar amount per new security to the issuing firm wins the competitive bid. This means that it will underwrite and distribute the issue.  In this situation, the price paid to the issuer is not negotiated; instead, it is determined by a sealed-bid process much on the order of construction bids.

3. In a commission (or best-efforts) offering the investment banker does not act as an underwriter.  He or she attempts to sell the issue in return for a fixed commission on each security that is actually sold.  Unsold securities are simply returned to the firm hoping to raise funds.

4. In a privileged subscription the new issue is not offered to the investing public.  It is sold to a definite and

limited group of investors.  Current stockholders are often the privileged group.

5. In a <u>direct sale</u> the issuing firm sells the securities to the investing public without involving an investment banker in the process.  This is not a typical procedure.

D. The negotiated purchase is most likely to be the distribution method used by the private corporation.  It consists of several steps.

1. The security-issuing firm selects an investment banker.

2. A series of pre-underwriting conferences takes place.  Discussions center on (1) the amount of capital to be raised, (2) the possible receptiveness of the capital markets to a specific mode of financing, and (3) the proposed use of the new funds.  These conferences are consummated by the signing of a <u>tentative underwriting agreement</u>.  The approximate price to be paid for each security is identified in this agreement.

3. An underwriting syndicate is formed.  The syndicate is a temporary association of investment bankers formed to purchase the security issue from the corporation.  The syndicate's objective is to resell the issue at a profit.

4. Most new public issues must be registered with the SEC before they can be sold to final investors.  This involves filing a lengthy technical document called a <u>registration statement</u> with the SEC.  This document aims to disclose relevant facts about the issuing firm and the related security to potential investors.  Another document, the <u>prospectus</u>, is also filed with the SEC for examination.  It is a shortened version of the official registration statement.  Once both documents are approved, the prospectus becomes the official advertising vehicle for the security offering.

5. A selling group is formed to distribute the new securities to final investors.  Securities dealers who are part of the selling group are permitted to purchase a portion of the new issue at a price concession from the official offering price to the public.  A <u>selling group agreement</u> binds the syndicate and the members of the selling group.

6. A due diligence meeting is held to finalize all details prior to taking the offering to the public.  The price at

which the issuing firm will sell the new securities to the
syndicate is settled.  Usually, the offering is made to the
public on the day after this meeting.

7. The syndicate manager (from the investment banking house
   that generated the business) is permitted to mitigate downward price movements in the secondary market for the subject offering.  This is accomplished by the syndicate manager's placing buy orders for the security at the agreed-
   upon public offering price.

8. A contractual agreement among the syndicate members term-
   inates the syndicate.  In the most pleasant situations this
   agreement is made when the issue has been fully subscribed
   (sold).

IV. Private placements

A. Each year billions of dollars of new securities are privately
   (directly) placed with final investors.  In a private placement a small number of investors purchase the entire security
   offering.  Most private placements involve debt instruments.

B. Large financial institutions are the major investors in private placements.  These include (1) life insurance firms, (2)
   state and local retirement funds, and (3) private pension
   funds.

C. The advantages and disadvantages of private placements as opposed to public offerings must be carefully evaluated by the
   financial manager.

   1. The advantages include (1) greater speed than a public of-
      fering in actually obtaining the needed funds, (2) lower
      flotation costs than are associated with a public issue,
      and (3) increased flexibility in the financing contract.

   2. The disadvantages include (1) higher interest costs than
      are ordinarily associated with a comparable public issue,
      (2) the imposition of several restrictive covenants in the
      financing contract, and (3) the possibility that the secur-
      ity may have to be registered some time in the future at
      the lenders' option.

V. Flotation costs

A. The firm raising long-term capital typically incurs two types
   of flotation costs: (1) the underwriter's spread and (2) issuing costs.  The former is typically the larger.

1. The underwriter's spread is the difference between the gross and net proceeds from a specific security issue. This absolute dollar difference is usually expressed as a percent of the gross proceeds.

2. Many components comprise issue costs. The two most significant are (1) printing and engraving and (2) legal fees. For comparison purposes, these, too, are usually expressed as a percent of the issue's gross proceeds.

B. SEC data reveal two relationships about flotation costs.

1. Issue costs (as a percent of gross proceeds) for common stock exceed those of preferred stock, which exceed those of bonds.

2. Relative flotation costs decrease as the dollar size of the security issue increases.

VI. Regulation

A. The primary market is governed by the Securities Act of 1933.

1. The intent of this federal regulation is to provide potential investors with accurate and truthful disclosure about the firm and the new securities being sold.

2. Unless exempted, the corporation selling securities to the public must register the securities with the SEC.

3. Exemptions follow from a variety of conditions. For example, if the size of the offering is small enough (less than $500,000), the offering does not have to be registered. If the issue is already regulated or controlled by some other federal agency, registration with the SEC is not required. Railroad issues and public utility issues are examples.

4. If not exempted, a registration statement is filed with the SEC containing particulars about the security-issuing firm and the new security.

5. A copy of the prospectus, a summary registration statement, is also filed. It will not yet have the selling price of the security printed on it; it is referred to as a red herring and called that until it is approved by the SEC.

6. If the information in the registration statement and prospectus is satisfactory to the SEC, the firm can proceed to sell the new issue. If the information is not satis-

factory, a <u>stop order</u> is issued which prevents the imme-
diate sale of the issue.  Deficiencies have to be cor-
rected to the satisfaction of the SEC before the firm can
sell the securities.

7. The SEC does <u>not</u> evaluate the investment quality of any
   issue.  It is concerned, rather, with the presentation of
   complete and accurate information upon which the potential
   investor can act.

B. The secondary market is regulated by the Securities Exchange
   Act of 1934.  This federal act created the SEC.  It has many
   aspects.

   1. Major security exchanges are required to register with the
      SEC.

   2. Insider trading must be reported to the SEC.

   3. Manipulative trading that affects security prices is pro-
      hibited.

   4. Proxy procedures are controlled by the SEC.

   5. The Federal Reserve Board was given the responsibility of
      setting margin requirements.  This affects the proportion
      of a security purchase that can be made via credit.

## Self-Tests

TRUE-FALSE

_____  1. A share of IBM common stock is a real asset.

_____  2. Capital formation in underdeveloped countries might be
            assisted if those countries' financial market systems were
            more extensively developed.

_____  3. General Motors is a typical example of a financial inter-
            mediary.

_____  4. The Money Market is housed at 11 Wall Street, New York
            City.

_____  5. Common stocks are money market instruments.

_____  6. Price quotations on organized security exchanges have been
            facilitated by the existence of NASDAQ.

_____   7. The Banking Act of 1933 separated the activities of commercial banking and investment banking.

_____   8. In a negotiated purchase, the price the investment banker pays the security-issuing firm for the new issue is negotiated between these parties.

_____   9. Underwriting syndicates are prohibited by the Securities Act of 1933.

_____  10. Life insurance companies are major purchasers of privately placed securities.


MULTIPLE CHOICE

1. Which of the following is <u>not</u> a benefit provided by the existence of organized security exchanges?

   a. A continuous market.
   b. Helping business raise new capital.
   c. Keeping long-term bond prices below 8%.
   d. Establishing and publicizing fair security prices.

2. What is it called when an investment banker agrees to sell only as many securities as he or she can at an established price?

   a. A private placement.
   b. A direct placement.
   c. A privileged subscription.
   d. A best-efforts agreement.
   e. An upset agreement.

3. Which of the following security distribution methods is least profitable to the investment banker?

   a. Negotiated purchase.
   b. Competitive-bid purchase.
   c. Commission basis.
   d. Privileged subscription.
   e. Direct sale.

4. A prospectus resembles most closely:

   a. A registration statement.
   b. A red herring.
   c. A selling group agreement.
   d. A letter of credit.

5. The purpose of financial markets is to:

    a. Lower bond yields.
    b. Allocate savings efficiently.
    c. Raise stock prices.
    d. Employ stock brokers.

6. The maturity boundary dividing the U.S. money and capital markets is:

    a. An arbitrary classification system.
    b. Set by the Federal Reserve Board.
    c. Periodically reviewed and altered by the SEC.
    d. Determined by the U.S. Treasury.

7. Flotation costs are highest on:

    a. Bonds.
    b. Preferred stock.
    c. Common stock.

8. Insider trading is regulated by:

    a. The Banking Act of 1933.
    b. The Glass-Steagall Act of 1933.
    c. The Securities Act of 1933.
    d. The Securities Exchange Act of 1934.

# Term Loans
# and Leases

Orientation: The first section of this chapter provides an overview of the major sources of term loans and their characteristics. The second section of the chapter provides an overview of lease financing, including a discussion of leasing arrangements, the accounting treatment of financial leases, the lease versus purchase decision, and the potential benefits from leasing.

I. Term loans

    A. In general, term loans have maturities from 1 to 10 years and are repaid in periodic installments over the life of the loan. Term loans are usually secured by a chattel mortgage on equipment or a mortgage on real property. The principal suppliers of term credit include commercial banks, insurance companies, and to a lesser extent pension funds.

        1. The maturities of term loans are usually as follows:

            a. Commercial banks: 1 to 5 years.

            b. Insurance companies: 5 to 15 years.

            c. Pension funds: 5 to 15 years.

2. The collateral backing term loans is usually as follows:

   a. Shorter maturity loans are usually secured with a chattel mortgage on machinery and equipment or securities such as stocks and bonds.

   b. Longer maturity loans are frequently secured by mortgages on real estate.

3. In addition to collateral, the lender on a term loan agreement will very often place <u>restrictive covenants</u> which are designed to maintain the borrower's financial condition on a par with that which existed at the time the loan was made.

   a. <u>Working capital restrictions</u> involve maintaining a minimum current ratio that reflects the norm for the borrower's industry, as well as the lender's desires.

   b. <u>Additional borrowing restrictions</u> prevent the borrower from increasing the amount of debt financing outstanding without the lender's approval.

   c. A third covenant that is very popular requires that the borrower supply <u>periodic financial statements</u> to the lender.

   d. Term loan agreements often include a provision that requires that the lender approve major personnel changes and insure the lives of "key" personnel with the lender as the beneficiary.

4. Term loans are generally repaid in periodic installments in accordance with <u>repayment schedules</u> established by the lender. Each installment includes both an interest and a principal component.

II. Leasing

A. There are three major lease agreements: direct leasing, sale and leaseback, and leveraged leasing.

1. In a <u>direct lease</u> the firm acquires the services of an asset it did not previously own. Direct leasing is available through a number of financial institutions, including manufacturers, banks, finance companies, independent leasing companies, and special-purpose leasing companies. Basically, direct leasing involves the purchase of the asset

by the lessor from a vendor and leasing the asset to the lessee.

2. A sale and leaseback arrangement occurs when a firm sells land, buildings, or equipment that it already owns to a financial institution and simultaneously enters into an agreement to lease the property back for a specified period under specific terms. The lessee firm receives cash in the amount of the sales price of the asset sold and the use of the asset over the term of the lease. In return, the firm must make periodic rental payments throughout the term of lease to the lessor.

3. In a leveraged lease a third participant finances the acquisition of the asset to be leased. From the lessee's standpoint, this lease is no different from the two lease arrangements discussed above. But with a leveraged lease, specific consideration is given to the financing arrangement used by the lessor in acquiring the asset to be leased.

B. The accounting profession has recently issued new standards on accounting for leases. Specifically, Financial Accounting Statement No. 13 requires the capitalization of any lease that meets one or more of the following criteria:

1. The lease transfers ownership of the property to the lessee by the end of the lease term.

2. The lease contains a bargain repurchase option.

3. The lease term is equal to 75% or more of the estimated economic life of the leased property.

4. The present value of the minimum lease payments equals 90% of the excess of the fair value of the property over any related investment tax credit retained by the lessor.

C. The lease versus purchase decision requires a standard capital budgeting type of analysis, as well as an analysis of two alternative "packages" of financing. Two models are used to evaluate the lease versus purchase decision.

1. The first model computes the net present value of the purchase option which can be defined as follows:

$$NPV(P) = \sum_{t=1}^{n} \frac{ACF_t}{(1 + K)^t} - I_0$$

where $ACF_t$ = the annual after-tax cash flow resulting from
the purchase in period t,

$K$ = the firm's cost of capital applicable to the
project being analyzed and the particular mix
of financing used to acquire the project,

$I_0$ = the initial cash outlay required to purchase
the asset in period zero (now),

$n$ = the productive life of the project.

2. In the second model a net advantage to lease (NAL) over
purchase equation is used which indicates the more favorable (least expensive) method of financing.  The equation
used to arrive at NAL is as follows:

$$NAL = \sum_{t=1}^{n} \frac{O_t(1-T) - R_t(1-T) - TI_t - T\Delta I_t - TD_t}{(1+r)^t} - \frac{V_n}{(1+K_S)^n} + IO$$

where $O_t$ = any operating cash flows incurred in period t
which are incurred only where the asset is purchased.  Most often this consists of maintenance
expenses and insurance that would be paid by
the lessor.

$R_t$ = the annual rental for period t.

$T$ = the marginal tax rate on corporate income.

$I_t$ = the tax deductible interest expense foregone in
period t if the lease option is adopted.

$\Delta I_t$ = the interest on debt that must be repaid in the
event the asset is leased so as to maintain the
firm's desired capital structure.  That is,
since leasing involves 100% levered financing,
the firm uses up more than the leased asset's
allotment of levered financing by leasing it.
For example, if the firm's financial policy were
to finance 60% of its assets with owner funds,
by leasing the asset the firm would have to repay outstanding debt equal to 60% of the cost of
the leased asset to maintain its desired lever-

age ratio.  Thus, $\Delta I$ reflects the lost interest
tax shield from repayment of debt.

$D_t$ = depreciation expense in period t for the asset.

$V_n$ = the after-tax salvage value of the asset expected in year n.

$K_s$ = the discount rate used to find the present value
of $V_n$.  This rate should reflect the risk inherent in the estimated $V_n$.  For simplicity, the
after-tax cost of capital is often used as a
proxy for this rate.

$IO$ = the purchase price of the asset which is not
paid by the firm in the event the asset is
leased.

$r$ = the before-tax rate of interest on borrowed
funds.  This rate is used to discount the relatively certain after-tax cash flow savings accruing through leasing the asset.

If NAL were positive, there would be a positive cost advantage to lease financing.  If NAL were negative, then purchasing the asset and financing with a debt plus equity
package would be the preferred alternative.  However, we
would lease or purchase the asset in accordance with the
value of NAL in only two circumstances:

a. If NPV(P) were positive, then the asset should be acquired through the preferred financing method as indicated by NAL.

b. If NPV(P) were negative, then the asset's services
should be acquired via the lease alternative only if
NAL is positive and greater in absolute value than
NPV(P).  That is, the asset should be leased only if
the cost advantage of leasing (NAL) is great enough to
offset the negative NPV(P).  In effect, if a positive
NAL were to more than offset a negative NPV(P), then
the net present value through lease would be positive.

D. Over the years a number of potential benefits have been offered for lease financing.

1. Flexibility and convenience.  It is often argued that

lease financing is more convenient than other forms of financing because smaller amounts of funds can be raised at
lower cost.  In addition, it is often argued that lease
payment schedules can be made to coincide with cash flows
generated by the asset.  These may or may not be real advantages.  It depends on the actual circumstances faced
by the lessee firm.

2. Lack of restrictions.  It has been argued that leases require fewer restrictions on the lessee than do debt agreements.

3. Avoiding the risk of obsolescence.  This argument is generally conceded to be fallacious because the lessor includes his or her estimated cost of obsolescence in the
   lease payments.

4. Conservation of working capital.  Here it is argued that
   leasing involves no down payment.  However, the borrower
   might obtain the same effect by borrowing the down payment.

5. 100% financing.  The lease involves 100% financing but purchasing the asset would surely involve some equity.  As we
   noted above, the down payment could be borrowed to produce
   100% financing via a loan.  In addition, it is not clear
   that 100% lease financing is desirable because it represents 100% non-owner financing.

6. Tax savings.  The difference in tax shelters between leasing and other forms of financing can only be evaluated by
   using a net advantage of lease model as we discussed earlier.

7. Ease of obtaining credit.  Lease financing may be more or
   less difficult to obtain than other forms of financing.
   This advantage (or disadvantage) can only be evaluated on
   a case-by-case basis.


Study Problem


1. Palmer Industries, which has a 50% tax rate, wants to acquire a
$200,000 piece of equipment.  The equipment would be depreciated over
a 5-year life on a straight-line basis.  At the end of the 5-year
period the equipment is expected to have a zero salvage value.  Palmer

has two alternatives available to it with regard to how the equipment is to be financed. It can borrow the $200,000 at 10% interest and repay the loan in 5 equal annual installments or lease the equipment for 5 annual rental payments of $55,000 each (payable at the beginning of the year). Palmer usually finances its assets by using 40% debt and 60% equity. Maintenance services are estimated to be $4,000 under the leasing contract and net cash flows from the equipment are estimated to be $100,000 per year before depreciation and taxes. Required:

(a) Compute the annual installments, principal, interest, and remaining balance for the purchase option loan.

(b) Assuming Palmer's after-tax cost of capital is 12%, compute the net present value of the purchase alternative.

(c) Provided that Palmer has a target debt ratio of 100% for projects like this, compute the net advantage to leasing (NAL) the equipment.

(d) Which method of financing should be used by Palmer? Why?


SOLUTION:

(a)

| Year | Installment | Interest | Principal | Remaining Balance |
|------|------------|----------|-----------|-------------------|
| 0 | | | | $200,000 |
| 1 | $52,757 | $20,000 | $32,757 | 167,243 |
| 2 | 52,757 | 16,724 | 30,033 | 131,210 |
| 3 | 52,757 | 13,121 | 39,636 | 91,574 |
| 4 | 52,757 | 9,157 | 43,600 | 47,974 |
| 5 | 52,757 | 4,797 | 47,960 | 14* |

*Difference due to rounding.

(b) Initial outlay (IO) = $200,000.

Calculating annual net cash flows:

| | Book Profits | Cash Flow |
|------|--------------|-----------|
| Annual cash flow | $100,000 | $100,000 |
| Less depreciation | (40,000) | -- |
| Earnings before taxes | 60,000 | 100,000 |

|                | Book Profits | Cash Flow |
|----------------|--------------|-----------|
| Less taxes (50%) | (30,000) → | (30,000)  |
| Annual after-tax cash flow |  | $70,000 |

$$\text{Net present value} = \$70,000 \sum_{t=1}^{5} \frac{1}{(1 + 0.12)^t} - \$200,000$$

$$= \$70,000(3.605) - \$200,000$$

$$= \underline{\$52,350}$$

Thus, the equipment's purchase through normal financing is justified, as the net present value is greater than zero.

(c) The net advantage to leasing is computed as follows:

$$NAL = \sum_{t=1}^{n} \frac{O_t(1 - T) - R_t(1 - T) - TI_t - T\Delta I_t - TD_t}{(1 + r)^t} - \frac{V_n}{(1 + k_s)^n} + IO$$

Solving for NAL's component parts,

$$\sum_{t=1}^{n} \frac{O_t(1 - T)}{(1 + r)^t} = 4,000(1 - 0.50)(3.791) = \$7,582$$

$$\sum_{t=1}^{n} \frac{R_t(1 - T)}{(1 + r)^t} = 55,000(0.5)(3.791) = \$104,252.50$$

$$\sum_{t=1}^{n} T(I_t + \Delta I_t) = \frac{0.5(20,000)}{(1.10)} + \frac{0.5(16,724)}{(1.10)^2} + \frac{0.5(13,121)}{(1.10)^3}$$

$$+ \frac{0.5(9,157)}{(1.10)^4} + \frac{0.5(4,797)}{(1.10)^5}$$

$$= \$9,090.00 + 6,907.01 + 4,926.94 + 3,127.12 + 1,489.47$$

$$= \$25,540.54$$

$$\sum_{t=1}^{n} \frac{TD_t}{(1 + r)^t} = 0.5(40,000)(3.791) = 75,820.00$$

$$\frac{V_n}{(1 + k_s)^n} = 0$$

IO = \$200,000

NAL = \$7,582.00 − 104,252.50 − 25,540.54 − 75,820.00 − 0 + 200,000

= \$1,968.96

(d) The leasing alternative should be selected by Palmer since both the NAL and the NPV(P) are positive.

## Self-Tests

TRUE-FALSE

_____ 1. One of the principal economic reasons for borrowing is the inability of a firm to utilize all of the tax benefits associated with the leasing of an asset.

_____ 2. A lease payment is deductible as an expense for federal income tax purposes.

_____ 3. If leases are capitalized on the balance sheet, it will permit easier analysis of the contractual obligations of the firm and investors.

_____ 4. Over the years the accounting treatment of leases has changed toward greater disclosure.

_____ 5. Under a sale and leaseback arrangement, a company acquires the use of an asset that it did not own previously.

_____ 6. The distinguishing feature between a financial lease and an operating lease is cancellability.

_____ 7. A chattel mortgage is a lien on real property.

_____ 8. Insurance company term loans are highly competitive with bank term loans.

_____ 9. The working capital requirement is probably the most commonly used and most comprehensive provision in a loan agreement.

_____ 10. The interest rate on a term loan is higher than the rate on a short-term loan to the same borrower.

MULTIPLE CHOICE

1. Which of the following distinguishes a bank term loan from other types of business loans?

   a. A final maturity of one year or more.
   b. Credit extended under an informal loan agreement.
   c. Credit extended under a formal loan agreement.
   d. a and b only.
   e. a and c only.

2. Rarely will a bank make a term loan that has a final maturity of more than:

   a. 5 years.
   b. 10 years.
   c. 20 years.
   d. 25 years.
   e. None of the above.

3. The interest rate on a term loan is <u>not</u> set by:

   a. Periodic negotiations between the borrower and the lender.
   b. A fixed rate effective over the life of the loan.
   c. A variable rate that is adjusted in keeping with changes in the prime rate.
   d. None of the above.

4. The important protective covenants of a loan agreement may be classified as follows:

   a. General provisions.
   b. Routine provisions.
   c. Specific provisions.
   d. All of the above.
   e. a and c only.

5. The definition of a small business depends:

   a. On its sales in relation to those of the industry.
   b. On the number of employees.
   c. On its profits.
   d. On all of the above.
   e. a and b only.
   f. a and c only.

6. Which of the following is <u>not</u> a source of equipment financing?

    a. Commercial bank.
    b. Finance company.
    c. Seller of the equipment.
    d. None of the above.

# Long-Term Debt, Preferred Stock, and Common Stock

Orientation:  This chapter examines detailed variations of the three major sources of long-term and permanent funds for the firm:  long-term debt, preferred stock, and common stock.  Key terminology is introduced.  The major sources of financing are described and their usefulness to the corporation is discussed.

I.  Bonds or long-term debt

   A.  Certain terms are common to the practice of financing long-term needs through bond issues.  Some of the key definitions of these terms are noted below.

      1.  The coupon interest rate determines the fixed return on a long-term debt contract.  A coupon interest rate of 9% on a $1,000 par value bond indicates that the investment will receive $90 in interest receipts annually.

      2.  When a debt issue is offered to the public, a trustee is designated by the issuing corporation to act on behalf of the bond investors.  The formal agreement is actually between the firm and the trustee who acts for the bond-holders.  The contract between the firm and the trustee

is called the <u>bond indenture</u>.

    a. The trustee's job is to see that the terms of the indenture are actually carried out.

    b. The indenture contains the terms of the bond issue and any restrictive provisions placed on the firm.

3. Do not confuse the coupon interest rate with the <u>yield to maturity</u> on the bond. The yield to maturity is the discount rate that equates the present value of the interest and principal payments with the current market price of the bond. From our discussions of capital budgeting techniques, it is clear that this discount rate is nothing more than the internal rate of return for this bond.

B. The rate of return that investors demand on bond issues is determined by several factors, including the size of the issue, the issue's maturity, the issue's riskiness or rating, the restrictive requirements of the issue, and the current riskless interest rate.

C. There are a number of different debt instruments.

1. A <u>debenture</u> is an unsecured or general credit bond. Specific property is not pledged as collateral for these long-term promissory notes.

    a. The investor in a debenture obtains his or her protection from both the general credit worthiness of the firm and the bond indenture.

2. <u>Subordinated debentures</u> have a lower claim on assets in the event of liquidation than do other senior debtholders.

3. <u>Income bonds</u> represent a departure from the other forms of debt.

    a. Interest on these promissory notes is paid to investors only when it is earned.

    b. Although interest may be passed, it is generally allowed to accumulate for some period of time and it must be paid prior to the payment of any common stock dividends.

4. A <u>mortgage bond</u> is secured by a lien on specific assets of the firm.

    a. In the mortgage, preference in a specific asset is granted by the borrower to a class of creditors.

b. In the event of default of a provision contained in the bond indenture, the trustee can seize the pledged property, sell it, and use the proceeds to settle the lender's claim.

c. It is possible to sell more than one class of mortgage bonds using the same property as collateral. Thus, first-mortgage bonds and second-mortgage bonds could be sold pledging the same fixed asset. In the event of default, however, the holders of the first-mortgage bonds must be paid in full prior to any distribution of proceeds to the second-mortgage bondholders.

d. A mortgage may be either closed-end, open-end, or limited open-end.

e. With a closed-end mortgage, additional bonds with equal rank against the same security may not be issued.

f. With an open-end mortgage, additional bonds under an existing lien may be issued.

g. With a limited open-end mortgage, a limited amount of additional bonds may be issued with equal rank against the same security.

5. Collateral trust bonds are another form of secured, long-term financing.

a. This type of financing is secured by a pledge of stocks and/or bonds by the borrowing company to the trustee.

b. If default occurs, the securities are sold by the trustee and the proceeds are used to pay the bondholders.

6. Equipment trust certificates, which are actually a hybrid between debt and lease financing, are used extensively by railroads to acquire needed equipment.

a. According to this method, a manufacturer builds the equipment to meet the firm's specifications. The equipment is then sold to a trustee.

b. The trustee sells equipment trust certificates to pay the manufacturer. The trustee then leases the equipment to the firm.

c. The lease payments are used by the trustee to pay a fixed return to investors in the certificates. The annual installments provide for retirement of the cer-

tificates well within the economic life of the assets
being used.  When the certificates are retired, title
to the asset passes to the firm (railroad or airline).

D. Retiring debt

   1. Bonds may be retired at maturity at which time the bondholder receives the par value of the bond or the bonds can
be retired prior to maturity.

   2. A call provision entitles the corporation to repurchase or
"call" the bonds from their holders at stated prices over
specified periods.

   3. A sinking fund allows for the periodic repayment of debt,
thus reducing the total amount of debt outstanding.

E. Bond refunding

   1. It is possible to analyze the profitability of refunding a
bond issue prior to its maturity as a capital-budgeting
decision.

   2. The decision carries with it an initial cash outlay, which
is followed by interest savings in the future, if new bonds
are marketed with a lower interest rate.  A complete example will be give in the study problems.

   3. In analyzing a refunding operation, most analysts favor
discounting the projected savings not at the firm's cost
of capital, but at the after-tax cost of borrowing on the
new bonds.  This is because in a refunding decision, as
opposed to a normal investment decision, the costs and
benefits are known with complete certainty.

II. Preferred stock

A. Preferred stock is a hybrid form of financing that combines
features of debt and common stock.

   1. Preferred stockholders' claims on assets come after those
of creditors but before those of common shareholders.

   2. Although preferred stock carries a stipulated dividend,
the actual payment of a dividend is discretionary.  The
omission of a payment does not result in the default of
the obligation.

   3. Preferred stockholders are usually limited to the
specified dividend yield and do not ordinarily

share in any residual earnings.

B. Almost all preferred stocks have a cumulative feature that provides for unpaid dividends in any one year to be carried forward.

   1. The accrued preferred stock dividends must be paid before the company can meet the dividend obligation of the common shareholders.

   2. There is no guarantee or obligation that the preferred stock dividends in arrears will be paid.

      a. If the preferred stock dividends are in arrears and the company wishes to pay a common dividend, the company may choose not to clear up the arrearage but make an exchange offering to preferred stockholders instead.

C. To further provide protection for the preferred shareholder, protective provisions in addition to the cumulative feature are common to preferred stock.

   1. Many times in the event of nonpayment of dividends, the preferred stockholder will be provided with voting rights.

D. Although preferred stock does not have a set maturity associated with it, issuing firms generally provide for some method of retirement.

   1. Most preferred stock has a call provision that allows the issuing firm to replace the preferred stock if interest rates fall.

   2. Sinking fund provisions are also common to preferred stock. They allow the firm to periodically set aside an amount of money for the retirement of its preferred stock.

III. Common stock

A. The common stockholders of a corporation are its residual owners. They assume the ultimate risk associated with ownership.

   1. In the event of liquidation, these stockholders have a residual claim on the assets of the company (i.e., after the claims of all creditors and preferred stockholders are settled in full).

   2. Common stock has no maturity date. It can be liquidated by the owner's selling the stock in the secondary market.

B. Common stockholders are entitled to share in the earnings of the company only if cash dividends are paid.

1. Stockholders prosper from the market-value appreciation of their stock and the dividends paid (if the stock pays dividends).

2. Creditors can take legal action if contractual interest and principal payments are not met, but stockholders have no legal recourse if the company defaults on dividend payments.

C. The common stockholders of a company are the residual owners and thus are entitled to elect the board of directors.

1. In most large corporations the average stockholder has very little power over who manages and how the company is managed.

a. Each stockholder is entitled to one vote for each share of stock he or she owns.

b. Most stockholders vote by proxy, which is a form by which the stockholder assigns his or her rights to another person.

1. If minority stockholders can accumulate enough proxy votes, they can exercise limited control or influence over the board of directors of the company.

2. In most proxy contests the existing management wins because it has both the organization and the use of the company's financial resources to fight the unhappy stockholders.

2. Depending on the corporate charter, the board of directors is elected either under a majority voting system or under a cumulative voting system.

a. Under the majority voting system, each stockholder has one vote for each share of stock he or she owns. The stockholder must vote for each director position that is open.

b. Under the cumulative voting system, a stockholder is able to accumulate his or her votes and cast them for less than the total number of directors being elected.

c. A cumulative voting system, in contrast to the majority system, permits minority interests a possible chance to elect a certain number of directors.

D. A preemptive right entitles a common stockholder to maintain his or her proportional ownership by offering the stockholder an opportunity to purchase, on a pro rata basis, any new stock being offered or any securities being converted into common stock.

E. The rights offering

   1. An offering of securities to existing shareholders prior to selling all or part of the issue to the general public is called a <u>rights offering</u>.

   2. When a firm elects to sell new common stock by means of the privileged subscription method, each stockholder receives in the mail one <u>right</u> for each share of stock owned.

      a. The specific terms of the offering spell out the number of rights needed to buy one new share of stock, the subscription price of the stock, and the expiration date of the offering.

      b. The existing stockholder may exercise his or her rights and buy additional shares, sell his or her rights for cash, or simply do nothing.

   3. The market value of a right is determined by three major factors: (1) the current market price of the stock, (2) the subscription price of the new shares, and (3) the number of rights needed to buy one new share.

   4. To determine how many shares must be sold to raise the desired funds, the desired funds are divided by the subscription price:

$$\text{new shares to be sold} = \frac{\text{desired funds to be raised}}{\text{subscription price}}$$

   5. The number of rights needed to purchase one share of stock can be determined as follows:

$$\text{number of rights needed to purchase one Share of stock} = \frac{\text{original number of shares outstanding}}{\text{new shares to be sold}}$$

   6. When the stock is selling ex-rights, the theoretical market value of one right can be determined by using the following relationship:

$$R = \frac{P_{ex} - S}{N}$$

where   R = value of one right,
      $P_{ex}$ = the ex-rights price of the stock,
      S = the subscription price,
      N = the number of rights needed to purchase one
        share of stock.

7. Alternatively, when the stock is selling rights-on, that
is, prior to the ex-rights date, the value of a right can
be determined from the following equation:

$$R = \frac{P_{on} - S}{N + 1}$$

where $P_{on}$ = the rights-on price of the stock.


## Study Problems

1. This problem illustrates the major principles involved in determining whether or not an existing bond issue should be refunded.  First,
the financial characteristics of the existing (old) bond issue are
listed and then the financial data related to the proposed (new) issue
are presented.

Bonds currently outstanding:

| | |
|---|---:|
| Principal amount outstanding: | $20,000,000 |
| Coupon rate: | 7% |
| Years to maturity: | 15 |
| Unamortized bond discount: | $300,000 |
| Unamortized flotation costs: | $120,000 |
| Call premium: | 5% |

Proposed issue of bonds:

| | |
|---|---:|
| Principal amount outstanding: | $20,000,000 |
| Coupon rate: | 6% |
| Years to maturity: | 15 |
| Proceeds to the firm after flotation costs: | $20,000,000 |
| Issue expense: | $100,000 |
| Corporate income tax rate: | 50% |

Both issues will be outstanding simultaneously for a period of 30 days. Using the net-present-value method (on an after-tax basis), determine whether or not the firm should refund the old bond issue.

SOLUTION

Step 1:  Calculate the initial outlay.

1. Determine the difference between the inflow from the new issue and the outflow from retiring the old issue.

| | |
|---|---:|
| Cost of calling old bonds (1.05 X $20 million) | $21,000,000 |
| Proceeds, after flotation costs, from new issue | 20,000,000 |
| Difference between inflows and outflows | $ 1,000,000 |

2. Determine total issuing and overlap expenses

| | | |
|---|---:|---:|
| Issuing expense on new bonds | $100,000 | |
| Interest expense on old bonds during overlap period ($1,400,000/12) | 116,667 | $   216,667 |

3. Add:  the item above to determine the gross initial outlay

$ 1,216,667

4. Determine tax deductible expenses incurred:

| | |
|---|---:|
| Interest expenses during overlap period | $116,667 |
| Unamortized flotation costs and discount on the old bonds | 420,000 |
| Call premium (i.e., call price less par value) | 1,000,000 |
| | $1,536,667 |

5. Less: tax savings
Marginal tax rate (50% X total tax deductible expenses)

$   768,334

6. Equals:
Net initial cash flow

$   448,333

Step 2:  Calculate the annual cash benefit from eliminating the old bonds through refunding.

1. Determine annual interest expenses
   7% interest on $20,000,000                                        $ 1,400,000

2. Determine expenses incurred
   Annual interest expense                         $1,400,000
   Annual amortization of flotation
     costs and discount on old bond
     ($420,000/15)                                     28,000
   Total annual tax deductible expense              $1,428,000

3. Less:  Annual tax savings
   Marginal tax rate (50% X total annual
     tax deductible expenses)                                           714,000

4. Equals:
   Annual cash benefit from elimination
     of old bonds                                               $    686,000

Step 3:  Calculate the <u>annual cash outflow</u> from issuing the new
bonds.

1. Determine the annual interest expense
   6% on $20,000,000                                                 $ 1,200,000

2. Determine expenses incurred
   Annual interest expense                         $1,200,000
   Annual amortization of bond discount                     0
   Annual amortization of issuing ex-
     penses ($100,000/15)                              6,667
   Total annual tax deductible expenses             $1,206,667

3. Less:  annual tax savings
   Marginal tax rate (50%) total annual
     tax deductible expenses                                           603,334

4. Equals:  annual net cash outflow from
     issuing new bonds                                          $    596,666

Step 4:  Calculate the <u>annual net cash benefit</u> from the refunding
decision.

1. Add benefits:
   Annual cash benefits from eliminating the old bonds       686,000

2. Less costs:
   Annual cash outflows from issuing the new debt            596,666

3. Equals:  annual net cash benefits                         $   89,334

Step 5:  Calculate the <u>present value of the annual net cash benefits</u>.

1. Discount the 15-year $89,334 annuity back to present at the after-tax cost of borrowing on the new bonds (6%) (1 - 0.5) = 3%.

   $89,334 (11.938) =                                       $ 1,066,469

Step 6:  Calculate the <u>refunding decision's net present value</u>.

1. Present value of annual net cash benefits              $ 1,066,469

2. Less:  present value of initial outlay                    448,333

3. Equals: net present value                              $   618,136

The positive net present value of $618,136 indicates that the refunding should be undertaken.

2. Woolfolk Construction, Inc., a regional contracting firm, currently has 600,000 shares of common stock outstanding.  The company will issue another 100,000 shares through a rights offering.  The market price of the firm's common stock is $80 per share.  The subscription price to the new issue has been set at $73 per share.

(a) Compute the number of rights needed to buy one new share at the subscription price of $73.

(b) Compute the value of a right.

(c) What will be the theoretical value of one share of stock when it goes ex-rights?

(d) Prior to the rights being exercised but after the stock goes ex-rights, some adverse economic news startles the market and the price of Woolfolk stock drops to $78 per share.  Determine the price of one right under these conditions.

SOLUTION

(a) The ratio of old or existing common shares to the new shares that will be sold determines the number of rights needed to buy one new share:

$$\frac{600,000}{100,000} = 6$$

(b)

$$R = \frac{P_{on} - S}{N + 1} = \frac{80 - 73}{6 + 1} = \frac{7}{7} = \$1 \text{ (value of one right)}$$

(c) Theoretically, the value of the common stock will fall by the value of one right:

$$P_{ex} = P_{on} - R_{o} = 80 - 1 = \$79$$

(d)

$$R = \frac{P_{ex} - S}{N} = \frac{78 - 73}{6} = \$0.833$$

3. You own six shares of Woolfolk Construction common stock (see problem 2). Demonstrate that you will neither gain nor lose any monetary return if you exercise your rights and the stock sells at its theoretical value after the rights have been exercised.

SOLUTION

The value of six old shares at the current market price:                        6(80)  = $480

The cost of exercising the rights is the subscription price                                                = __73__

The value of your seven shares (what you could have received had you sold your old shares plus your out-of-pocket subscription price cost)                                                = $553

The average value of your seven shares to you, then, is $553/7 = $79 per share.  Notice that this is the theoretical value of the stock when it goes ex-rights.  This analysis, of course, ignores any transaction fees.


Self-Tests

TRUE-FALSE

_____  1. The call privilege on a bond issue will be mostly costly to the issuing firm when the general level of interest rates is low and is expected to rise.

_____  2. The generally accepted discount rate to be used in the analysis of a bond-refunding operation is the after-tax cost of borrowing on the refunded bond.

_____   3. Collateral trust bonds are actually a form of lease financing used to a large degree by the railroad industry.

_____   4. Most preferred stock issues have a noncumulative feature.

_____   5. The cumulative feature allows a preferred stockholder to accumulate his or her votes and cast them for one or more directors.

_____   6. Preferred stockholders do not ordinarily share in the residual earnings of a company.

_____   7. Sinking-fund arrangements are commonly found with preferred stock issues.

_____   8. Unlike common stock dividends, preferred stock dividends carry a legal obligation and must be paid or the company will default.

_____   9. Proxy contests usually result in the victory of the dissatisfied stockholders.

_____  10. A preemptive right entitles the common and preferred stockholders to maintain their proportional ownership in the corporation.


MULTIPLE CHOICE

1. What is the name for a bond secured by a lien on designated assets of the firm?

   a. Debenture.
   b. Income bond.
   c. Bankers' acceptance.
   d. Mortgage bond.

2. Which of the following bonds offers investors the most protection?

   a. Debentures.
   b. Subordinated debentures.
   c. Income bonds.
   d. First-mortgage bonds.
   e. Second-mortgage bonds.
   f. A second-mortgage bond in which the mortgage is open-ended.

3. A bond not secured by a mortgage will share equally in bankruptcy with:

   a. Common stock.
   b. Preferred stock.
   c. First-mortgage bonds.
   d. Unsecured general creditors.

4. A participating feature allows preferred stockholders to:

   a. Participate in the election of the corporate board of directors.
   b. Convert their preferred stock into common stock.
   c. Receive some residual earnings of the corporation.

5. In a rights offering of common stock the subscription price is:

   a. Set equal to the current market price of the stock.
   b. Set below the current market price of the stock.
   c. Set above the current market price of the stock.
   d. None of the above.

6. In calculating the value of one right when the stock is selling rights-on, the analyst needs to know the number of rights needed to buy one share of stock and:

   a. The length of the rights offering period.
   b. The transactions costs involved.
   c. The price/earnings ratio of the firm's stock.
   d. The subscription price per share to the stock issue.

# 21

# Convertibles and Warrants

Orientation: The purpose of this chapter is to explain the use of convertibles and warrants and to describe the terminology associated with them and their valuation.

I. A convertible security is a bond or preferred stock that can be exchanged for a stated number of common shares at the option of the holder.

   A. The conversion ratio is the stated number of shares that the security can be converted into.

   B. The conversion price is the face value of the security divided by the conversion ratio.

   C. The conversion value equals the conversion ratio times the market price of the stock when one converts.

   D. The bond value of a convertible is the price the convertible debenture (or preferred stock) would sell for in the absence of its conversion feature.

   E. The conversion premium is the difference between the market price of the convertible and the higher of the bond value and the conversion value.

F. The conversion parity price is the price the investor in effect buys the company's stock for.  It is the ratio of the
   market price of the convertible bond to the conversion ratio.

G. There are several reasons generally given for issuing convertibles:

   1. As a sweetening to long-term debt to make the security at-
      tractive enough to ensure a market for it.

   2. As a method of delayed common stock financing.

      a. No dilution of earnings occurs at time of issuance.

      b. Companies expect them to be converted sometime in the
         future.

      c. Less dilution of earnings occurs in the future because
         the conversion price is greater than the common stock
         price at time of issuance.

   3. Convertibles are also issued as a source of temporarily
      inexpensive funds.

   4. In addition, convertibles are also issued to financing mer-
      gers to avoid tax liabilities.

H. There are two ways in which a company can stimulate conversion:

   1. Include an acceleration clause, which periodically in-
      creases the conversion price and results in a lower con-
      version ratio over time.

   2. Force conversion by calling the convertible.

I. The value of the security is twofold.

   1. The value of the common stock when one converts is the
      first component.

   2. The value of the bond or preferred stock provides a cush-
      ion or a floor value in case the stock does not rise sig-
      nificantly (provided interest rates do not increase).

$$\text{bond value} = \sum_{t=1}^{N} \frac{\$I}{(1 + i)^t} + \frac{\$M}{(1 + i)^N}$$

   where I = annual dollar interest paid to the investor
             each year,

       i = market yield to maturity on straight bond of
          same company,

      N = number of years to maturity,

      M = maturity value or par value of the debt.

EXAMPLE:

Suppose that a company had a convertible outstanding (face $1,000)
with 20 years to maturity at an 8% rate. If the company wanted
to issue a straight bond 20 years to maturity, a 10% yield would
be required to attract investors. What is the current floor value
or market price of the bond?

$$BV = \sum_{t=1}^{20} \frac{\$80}{(1.10)^t} + \frac{\$1,000}{(1.10)^{20}}$$

$$= \$80(8.514) + \$1,000(0.149) = \$830.12$$

J. The market price of a convertible security is frequently above
its conversion value; this difference is called the premium.

K. Unless the conversion feature is considered worthless, the
security will sell for a premium-over-bond value (i.e., above
the value of the security solely as a bond).

L. In comparing the two premiums, one finds an inverse relationship between them. In the extremes, the security is selling
either as a common stock or a bond equivalent.

II. Warrants are a "sweetener" added to a bond or debt issue. Warrants entitle the holder to purchase a specified number of shares
of stock at a stated price.

A. The exercise price can be either fixed or "stepped up" over
time.

B. A warrant usually has a fixed expiration date.

C. A detachable warrant can be sold separately in the marketplace.

D. A nondetachable warrant can only be exercised by the bondholder and cannot be sold on its own.

E. Warrants are issued for two major reasons:

1. Warrants are attached to debt issues as sweeteners to in-

crease the marketability of these issues.

      2. Warrants provide an additional cash inflow when they are exercised.  Convertible securities do not.

F. The minimum price of a warrant is equal to the price of the common stock less the exercise price times the exercise ratio.

G. The premium on a warrant is the amount above the minimum price for which the warrant sells.

Study Problems

1. Corporation X is about to issue a convertible bond with face value of $1,000 for $1,000 each.  The conversion ratio is 20.  The current market price of the common stock is $35.  The coupon rate of this bond will be 10%.  If Corporation X had chosen to finance a straight bond, the effective yield to investors would have been 12%.  The number of years to maturity of the convertible is 20 years.  What is the conversion premium?

    SOLUTION

$$(20)(\$35) = \$700 \text{ conversion value}$$

$$BV = \sum_{t=1}^{20} \frac{\$100}{(1.12)^t} + \frac{\$1,000}{(1.12)^{20}}$$

$$= \$100(7.469) + \$1,000(0.104)$$

$$= \$746.90 + \$104.00 = \$850.90$$

$$\text{Conversion premium} = \binom{\text{market price of}}{\text{the convertible}} - \binom{\text{higher of the bond value}}{\text{and conversion value}}$$

$$= \$1,000 - \$850.90$$

$$= \$149.10$$

2. The L. Turner Corporation has a warrant that allows the purchase of one share of common stock at $20 per share.  The warrant is currently selling at $15, and the common stock is priced at $30 per share.  Determine the minimum price and the premium of the warrant.

SOLUTION

$$\text{minimum price} = \left(\begin{array}{c}\text{price of} \\ \text{common stock}\end{array} - \begin{array}{c}\text{exercise} \\ \text{price}\end{array}\right) \times \left(\begin{array}{c}\text{exercise} \\ \text{ratio}\end{array}\right)$$

$$= (\$30 - \$20) \times 1.0$$

$$= \$10$$

$$\text{premium} = \left(\begin{array}{c}\text{market price of} \\ \text{warrant}\end{array} - \begin{array}{c}\text{minimum price} \\ \text{of warrant}\end{array}\right)$$

$$= (\$15 - \$10)$$

$$= \$5$$

## Self-Tests

TRUE-FALSE

_____ 1. The only time a firm receives any proceeds from issuing convertibles is when the convertibles are initially issued.

_____ 2. At the time of issuance a convertible security is always priced lower than its conversion value.

_____ 3. An overhanging issue increases the firm's financing flexibility.

_____ 4. The conversion ratio is the ratio of the market price of the convertible security to the conversion price.

_____ 5. The conversion parity price is the price the investor in effect buys the company's stock for when he or she purchases the convertible.

_____ 6. Warrants usually sell for less than their minimum price.

_____ 7. The value of a convertible is determined by its value as a straight bond or preferred stock and its conversion value.

_____ 8. The exercise ratio on a warrant is the number of warrants needed to purchase one share of common stock.

_____ 9. A company can force conversion on a convertible by calling it or through the use of step-up conversion prices.

_____ 10. The stock price/exercise price ratio is one of the most important factors in determining the size of the warrant premium.

MULTIPLE CHOICE

1. Convertible bonds:

   a. Prohibit the issuance of more common stock.
   b. Can never be called.
   c. Are often an indirect way of selling common stock.
   d. Have no advantages to the investor over straight debt.

2. If a warrant carries a right to one share of common stock and is exercisable at $20 per common share while the market price of a share is $30, the minimum price of the warrant:

   a. Is $10.00.
   b. Is $5.00.
   c. Is $1.00.
   d. Cannot be determined.

3. A convertible's bond value:

   a. Will equal its face value.
   b. Changes with interest-rate movement and changes in financial risk.
   c. Will remain constant.
   d. None of the above.

4. The call price of a convertible security is:

   a. The net proceeds received by the issuing company at time of issuance.
   b. Always greater than the face of the bond.
   c. Equal to the conversion value.
   d. None of the above.

5. Nondetachable warrants:

   a. Sell for more than detachable warrants in the market.
   b. Sell for less than detachable warrants in the market.
   c. Can never be sold alone in the market.
   d. None of the above.

# Business Combinations: Mergers and Acquisitions

Orientation: There are two principal ways by which a firm may grow:
(1) internally, through the acquisition of specific assets which are
financed by the retention of earnings and/or external financing, or
(2) externally, through the acquisition of another company. We turn
now to a discussion of external growth through mergers with, and acquisition of, other firms.

I. Determining a firm's value

A. The value of a firm depends not only on its earnings capabilities but also on the operating and financial characteristics
of the acquiring firm. To determine an acceptable price of a
corporation, a number of factors must be carefully evaluated.
The final objective of this valuation process is to maximize
the stockholders' wealth (stock price) of the acquiring firm.

B. Quantitative variables to be evaluated include (1) book value,
(2) appraisal value, (3) market price of a firm's common
stock, and (4) earnings per share.

1. The book value of a firm's net worth is the depreciated
value of the company's assets less its outstanding liabilities. Book value alone is not a significant measure

of the worth of a company but should be used only as a
starting point to be compared with other analyses.

2. Appraisal value, acquired from an independent appraisal
   firm, may be considered useful in conjunction with other
   methods.  Advantages include:

   a. The reduction of accounting goodwill.

   b. A test of the reasonableness of results.

   c. The discovery of strengths and weaknesses that other-
      wise might not be recognized.

3. If a stock is listed on a major securities exchange, such
   as the New York Stock Exchange, and widely traded, an approximate value can be established on the basis of the market value.  The justification is based on the fact that the
   market quotations indicate the investors' different opin-
   ions on a firm's earnings potential and the corresponding
   risk.  The market value approach is the one most frequently
   used in valuing large corporations.  However, the value can
   change abruptly.

4. Earnings per share is important because the value of the
   prospective acquisition is frequently considered to be a
   function of the merger's impact on earnings per share.

C. Effect of earnings dilution

   1. In examining the effects of a merger on the surviving con-
      cern's earnings per share the investigation should include
      all of the variables affecting future earnings per share
      which include (1) the share exchange ratio, (2) the firms'
      relative sizes, and (3) the firms' relative expected future
      growth rates in earnings.

   2. In general, the terms of the merger must be developed in
      order to provide a mutually satisfactory earnings pattern
      for the shareholders of both firms.

II. Financing techniques in mergers

   A. Common stock financing.  Whenever common stock is used to ac-
      quire a new company, the relative price/earnings ratios of the
      two businesses are important.  A corporation that has a high
      price/earnings ratio has a distinct advantage.

   B. Debt and preferred stock financing.  The primary advantages of

convertible debt or convertible preferred stock include the
following:

1. Potential earnings dilution may be partially minimized by
   issuing a convertible security.

2. A convertible issue may allow the acquiring company to
   comply with the seller's income objectives without changing
   its own dividend policy.

3. Convertible preferred stock also represents a possible way
   of lowering the voting power of the acquired company.

4. The convertible bond or preferred stock combines senior
   security protection with a portion of the growth potential
   of common stock.

C. Earn-outs, or deferred payment plans.

   1. Benefits for the acquiring organization

      a. The earn-out provides a logical method of adjusting the
      difference between the amount of stock the purchaser is
      willing to issue and the amount the seller is agreeing
      to accept for the business.

      b. The merging company will immediately be able to report
      higher earnings per share because fewer shares of stock
      will become outstanding at the time of the acquisition.

      c. The acquiring company is provided with down-side pro-
      tection in the event that the merged business does not
      fulfill its earnings expectations.

      d. The earn-out diminishes the guesswork in establishing
      an equitable purchase price.

   2. Potential problems associated with earn-outs.

      a. The acquired corporation must be capable of being oper-
      ated as an autonomous business entity.

      b. The acquiring firm must be willing to allow the manage-
      ment of the newly acquired business freedom of oper-
      ation.

      c. The seller must be willing to contribute toward the fu-
      ture growth of the acquiring company.

D. A tender offer is a bid by an interested party, usually a corporation, to control another corporation.  The prospective

purchaser approaches the stockholders of the firm, rather than the management.

1. The management of the acquiring firm has to provide notice to the target corporation and to the Securities Exchange Commission 30 days prior to the takeover bid.

2. Managements under attack occasionally rely on state statutes to block or at least delay tender offers.

3. Disadvantages of the tender offer.

   a. If the target firm's management attempts to block an offer, the costs of executing the offer may increase significantly.

   b. The purchasing company may fail to acquire a sufficient number of shares to meet the objective of controlling the firm.

4. Advantages of the tender offer.

   a. If the offer is not strongly contested, it may possibly be less expensive than the normal route for acquiring a company.

   b. The tender offer has proven somewhat less susceptible to judicial inquiries into the fairness of the purchase price.


## Study Problems

1. The Evans Corporation has negotiated the purchase of E.D.S, Inc. The two firms have agreed that the E.D.S. shareholders are to receive common stock of Evans Corporation in exchange for their shares. The exchange is to be based on the relative earnings per share of the two firms. Evans Corporation currently has 150,000 shares of common stock outstanding with a $128 market value and earnings per share of $8. E.D.S. has issued 50,000 shares, which are selling for $57.20; earnings per share are $5.20. What will be the share exchange ratio for the merger? Will any dilution in earnings occur for either group of shareholders?

SOLUTION

$$\text{exchange ratio} = \frac{\text{EPS of E.D.S., Inc.}}{\text{EPS of Evans Corporation}}$$

$$= \frac{\$5.20}{\$8.00}$$

$$= 0.65:1$$

| Company | Original Number of Shares | Earnings per Share | Net Income |
|---------|---------------------------|--------------------|------------|
| Evans | 150,000 | $8.00 | $ 1,200,000 |
| E.D.S. | 50,000 | 5.20 | 260,000 |
| Total post-merger earnings | | | $ 1,460,000 |

Numbers of shares after the merger:
150,000 + (0.65)50,000 =        182,500

Earnings per share for Evans Corporation stockholders
after merger:
$1,460,000 ÷ 182,500 shares =       $8.00

Equivalent earnings per share for E.D.S., Inc.

(1) Prior to the merger
Earnings per share after the merger X share exchange ratio
$8.00 x 0.65 =         $5.20

(2) After the merger
Earnings per share before the merger ÷ share exchange ratio
$5.20 ÷ .65 =        $8.00

Even though E.D.S. shareholders' earnings per share have increased from $5.20 to $8.00, these stockholders only have 65% of
their original number of shares. Thus, their equivalent E.P.S.
after the merger is 65% of $8.00, or $5.20, and their effective
earnings position has not been altered by the merger.

2. Synergistics, Inc. has agreed to purchase the Berne Corporation.
Synergistics currently has $100,000 shares of common stock outstand-
ing; the market value is $122.25, and earnings per share is $8.15.
Berne's common stock has a market value of $65.25, earnings per share
are $5.65, and there are 25,000 shares outstanding. The two firms
have agreed that Berne's stockholders will receive Synergistic common
stock in exchange for their shares at a ratio of 0.5 to 1. What will be

262

the effect on the earnings position of each company's stockholders?

SOLUTION

### Merger Effect on Earnings
### (0.5:1 Exchange Ratio)

| Company | Original Number of Shares | Earnings per Share | Net Income |
|---|---|---|---|
| Synergistics | 100,000 | $8.15 | $   815,000 |
| Berne | 25,000 | 5.65 | 141,250 |
| Total post-merger earnings | | | $   956,250 |

Number of shares after the merger:
100,000 + (0.5)25,000                                                                       112,500

Earnings per share ($956,250 ÷ 112,500)                                           $8.50

Synergistics, Inc. stockholders:
Earnings per share before the merger                                                  $8.15
Earnings per share after the merger                                                      8.50

Accretion in earnings per share                                                           $ .35

Berne Corporation stockholders:
Equivalent earnings per share after the merger:
Earnings per share before the merger ÷ share exchange ratio
   ($5.65 ÷ 0.5)                                                                              $11.30
Earnings per share after the merger                                                      8.50

Dilution in earnings per share                                                          ($2.80)

---

3. Simpson Industries has negotiated an acquisition at a price of $50 million. Simpson's common stock is currently selling at $90. A convertible preferred stock could be issued to sell at $135 with a 1.3 conversion ratio. Compare the financing of the acquisition by common stock and by the convertible preferred issue. If Simpson's management wants to minimize the impact of dilution, which financing method should be chosen?

SOLUTION

If common stock financing is used, 555,556 shares would be re-

quired ($50 million ÷ $90 per share).  If the convertible preferred stock is issued, 370,370 preferred shares would be issued
($50,000,000 ÷ $135).  These shares would later be convertible
into 481,481 shares of common stock (370,370 shares of preferred
stock X 1.3 conversion ratio).  The dilution effect would be
minimized by issuing the convertible preferred stock since this
approach results in 481,481 common shares as opposed to 555,555
under the straight common issue.

4. Widgit Corporation agreed to purchase Gizmo, Inc. under a base-
period earn-out plan.  Gizmo's base-period profits were $700,000 and
its earnings subsequent to the merger are shown below, as are Widgit's common stock market value and earnings.  What would be the
total number of shares received by Gizmo's stockholders by the end of
the fifth year if the initial down payment was 400,000 shares?

SOLUTION

| Year | Gizmo's Earnings | Widgit's Stock Prices | Widget's EPS |
|------|------------------|-----------------------|--------------|
| 1 | $750,000 | $68 | $4.50 |
| 2 | 775,000 | 79 | 6.25 |
| 3 | 815,000 | 85 | 8.50 |
| 4 | 800,000 | 82 | 8.00 |
| 5 | 830,000 | 87 | 8.75 |

$$\text{Number of shares each year} = \frac{\text{excess earnings X P/E ratio}}{\text{stock market price}}$$

Year 0 Initial down payment                        400,000 shares

Year 1 $\dfrac{(\$750,000 - \$700,000) \text{ X } (\$68 \div \$4.50)}{\$68} =$   11,111

Year 2 $\dfrac{(\$775,000 - \$700,000) \text{ X } (\$79 \div \$6.25)}{\$79} =$   12,000

Year 3 $\dfrac{(\$815,000 - \$700,000) \text{ X } (\$85 \div \$8.50)}{\$85} =$   13,529

Year 4 $\dfrac{(\$800,000 - \$700,000) \text{ X } (\$82 \div \$8.00)}{\$82} =$   12,500

Year 5 $\dfrac{(\$830,000 - \$700,000) \text{ X } (\$87 \div \$8.75)}{\$87} =$   14,857

Total Shares Received by Gizmo's Shareholders        463,997

## Self-Tests

TRUE-FALSE

_____ 1. Synergism is defined as the state wherein the whole is greater than the sum of the parts.

_____ 2. The higher the P/E ratio of the acquiring company in relation to that of the company being acquired and the larger the earnings of the acquired company in relation to those of the acquiring company, the greater the increase in earnings per share of the acquiring company.

_____ 3. A higher than normal ratio of exchange is not justified, even for a stock that promises high future earnings.

_____ 4. It is wrong to examine the effect on EPS of an acquisition alone as the basis for analyzing the merger, since the effects of synergism may play an important role in determining the attractiveness of the proposed acquisition.

_____ 5. Contingent payments are most useful after new management takes over following an acquisition.

_____ 6. Goodwill is usually capitalized during the current accounting period and is not amortized because there is no way to allocate the percentage of goodwill used each period.

_____ 7. Debt, common stock, and commercial paper are all instruments used in a pooling of interest.

_____ 8. Conglomerates are the most popular form of corporate merger because of the extremely favorable accounting treatment of mergers.

_____ 9. Use of convertible preferred stock may be preferred to the use of common stock in a merger because it reduces the potential of dilution of earnings per share.

MULTIPLE CHOICE

1. The appropriate value of a firm:

   a. Depends on the firm's earnings potential.
   b. Depends on the financial characteristics of the acquiring firm.

   c. Is a range of value economically feasible to the prospective
      buyer within which a final price is negotiated.
   d. all of the above.

2. The two factors considered most important by most business people
   in estimating a factor's worth is:

    I. The book value of the firm being considered for acquisition.
   II. The appraisal value of the firm being considered for ac-
      quisition.
  III. The stock market value of the common shares of the firm being
      considered for acquisition.
   IV. The after-merger earnings per share of the. acquiring com-
      pany's stockholders.

   a. I, II.
   b. I, III.
   c. II, III.
   d. I, IV.
   e. III, IV.

3. Assume two companies with the following information:

|                                | A    | B    |
| ------------------------------ | ---- | ---- |
| Present earnings (millions)    | $25  | $ 6  |
| Shares (millions)              | 5    | 2    |
| Earnings per share             | $5   | $3   |
| Price of stock                 | $80  | $30  |
| P/E ratio                      | 13   | 10   |

   B has offered to sell its stock at a price of $33 to be paid for
   with A's stock.  What is the earnings per share after the acquisition?

   a. $4.87.
   b. $5.25.
   c. $5.32.
   d. $4.76

4. Given the information in question 3 but changing the offer of A to
   purchase B from $33 to $35, what is the effect of EPS?

   a. $5.28.
   b. $4.95.
   c. $4.83.
   d. $5.00.

# Failure and Reorganization

Orientation: Failure can be attributed to both poor internal management and uncontrollable economic conditions. This chapter examines indicators of weakness in a firm and the alternatives open to a firm that actually reaches a point of insolvency. The liquidation procedures under both voluntary and involuntary settlements, as well as possible reorganization plans, are presented.

I. What failure is

    A. <u>Economic failure</u> occurs when the company's costs exceed its revenues (internal rates of return on the company's projects are less than its cost of capital).

    B. <u>Technical insolvency</u> occurs when a firm can no longer honor its financial obligations. This happens when:

        1. A firm has insufficient liquidity to honor its debts. However, the company's net worth is positive.

        2. Liabilities actually exceed the fair market value of the company's assets; this is referred to as <u>insolvency in bankruptcy</u> (the company's net worth is negative).

II. Frequent causes of failure

A. The following key structural problems within management appear:

1. An imbalance of skills within the top echelon.

2. A chief executive who dominates a firm's operations without regard for the inputs of peers.

3. An inactive board of directors.

4. A deficient finance function within the firm's management.

5. The absence of responsibility of the chief executive officer to the stockholders.

B. The foregoing deficiencies may make the company vulnerable to several mistakes, including the following:

1. Negligence in developing an effective accounting system.

2. Lack of responsiveness to change. The firm may be unable to adjust to a general recession or unfavorable industry developments.

3. An inclination by management to undertake investment projects disproportionately larger relative to the firm's size.

4. Management relying too heavily on debt financing.

C. The primary causes of bankruptcy relate to weakness in the firm's management.

III. Symptoms of bankruptcy

A. Bankruptcy or insolvency cannot be predicted with certainty. However, several financial ratios have proven to be useful indicators of corporate failure.

1. A study by Altman developed a statistical model that found five ratios that are useful in predicting bankruptcy, weighted the ratios, and assembled them into the following equation:

Bankruptcy = $.012X_1 + .014X_2 + .033X_3 + .006X_4 + .999X_5$
Score

Where: $X_1$ = (net working capital $\div$ total assets) X 100.

$X_2$ = (retained earnings $\div$ total assets) X 100.

$X_3$ = (earnings before interest and taxes ÷ total assets) X 100.

$X_4$ = (total market value of stock ÷ book value of total debt) X 100.

$X_5$ = sales ÷ total assets.

2. We may therefore conclude that:

   a. Potentially failing corporations invest less in current assets ($X_1$).

   b. Younger companies have a greater chance of bankruptcy ($X_2$).

   c. A company approaching failure has suffered a deterioration in general earnings power ($X_3$). This variable is the best single indicator of impending bankruptcy.

   d. Potentially failing corporations often use excessive financial leverage ($X_4$).

   e. A corporation facing possible bankruptcy may be unable to generate sales from the firm's assets ($X_5$).

3. Decision criterion using Altman's model:

   a. If the bankruptcy score is above 2.99, there is little chance for bankruptcy.

   b. If the bankruptcy score is below 1.81, there is a high probability that failure will occur.

   c. If the bankruptcy score is between 1.81 and 2.99, any prediction made using the model involves considerable uncertainty. However, there will be less error if a 2.675 score is used as the cut-off point between the failure and success classifications.

   d. No prediction made using this model is 100% certain.

      (1) Unique factors may affect the eventual fate of the company.

      (2) Management may do some financial "window dressing" of the financial statements that will affect the ratios used in analyzing the firm.

      When a firm is facing severe financial problems, the following important question must be answered: "Is the firm worth more dead or alive?" In other words, is the expected value of reorganizing the firm more beneficial than the anticipated liquidation value?

IV. Voluntary remedies to insolvency

A. Prerequisites

Attainment of approval of any plan requires creditor approval, since any one creditor may legally prohibit the arrangement for the remaining creditors. Creditor approval of such a plan is usually based on:

1. The debtor's proven honesty and integrity.

2. The firm's potential for recovery.

3. The economic prospects for the industry.

B. Procedure

1. The debtor confers with the creditors to explain the plan and its benefits. This meeting is generally planned under the guidance of an adjustment bureau associated with either a local credit or trade association.

2. The creditors appoint a committee to represent both large and small claimants.

3. If a feasible plan can be developed, the committee, the firm, and the adjustment bureau construct one of the following voluntary agreements:

   a. The firm may receive an extension of the amount of time allowed for repayment of debts. In this case the debts are still payable in full. Such an agreement may contain stipulations about new purchases or the status of new liabilities incurred during the period of the contract. It may also place restrictions on the payment of dividends, require stockholders to place their shares in escrow with the creditor's committee, or stipulate that a member of the creditor's committee countersign checks.

   b. A composition actually reduces the balance the firm owes its creditors. The creditors receive a pro rata share of their claim. The creditors might opt for this method if the only alternative is bankruptcy because the costs associated with bankruptcy are so high.

C. Evaluation of voluntary remedies

1. The primary advantage of voluntary remedies is the minimization of legal, investigative, and administrative expenses and the informality of the process.

2. The major disadvantages of voluntary remedies are:

   a. A creditor may refuse to participate. In order to avoid this problem, a composition generally allows small claims to be paid in full.

   b. The debtor may maintain control of the business. This may allow the management to continue its mismanagement of the firm, resulting in further losses.

V. Reorganization

If a voluntary remedy is not workable, a company can be forced by its creditors into bankruptcy, at which point the company will either be dissolved or reorganized.

A. Chapter XI of the Bankruptcy Act

Chapter XI permits a failing company to seek an arrangement, which, in essence, is a "legal" extension or composition.

1. A court-appointed referee calls a meeting of the creditors to discuss the plan proposed by the debtor. This plan can be amended by the creditors.

2. The arrangement applies only to the unsecured creditors. The claims of the secured creditors must be met according to the terms of the obligation.

B. Chapter X of the Bankruptcy Act

Chapter X is used when the debtor and creditor cannot resolve the terms of an arrangement under Chapter XI. Creditors may request a reorganization under Chapter X in the following manner:

1. Three or more creditors having a combined claim totaling $5,000 or more may request that the court appoint a trustee to manage the company during the proceedings and to develop a reorganization plan. If the company's liabilities exceed $3 million, the trustee must also submit the plan to the Securities and Exchange Commission for advice.

2. After court approval is received, the consent of two-thirds of the creditors and a simple majority of the stockholders must be obtained. Stockholders' consent

is not necessary if the stockholders are not to participate in the reorganization.  The stockholders are involved
only if the firm's value after reorganization exceeds the
outstanding liabilities.

VI. The reorganization decision

  A. The trustee uses the following procedure in the reorgani-
     zation process:

     1. He or she must establish a going concern value for the
        firm.  This may be done by using the following equation:

        $V = E \times P/E$

        where    V = the going concern value,
                 E = the company's estimated future earnings,
               P/E = the price/earnings ratio of a similar but
                     prosperous firm (an approximation for a cap-
                     italization rate).

     2. He or she must devise a reorganization plan, including a
        way of reformulating the capital structure, to meet the
        criteria of fairness and feasibility.  The main concerns
        of the trustee in developing this plan are:

        a. Changes necessary to place the company in a more pro-
           fitable posture.

        b. Developing a capital structure that will enable the
           firm to cover fixed changes:  interest, principal re-
           payment, and preferred dividends.

  B. If the reorganization is determined to be fair and feasible
     to the respective creditors and stockholders, new securities
     are issued to reflect the revised capital structure.  This
     procedure is followed under the rule of absolute priority,
     which states that the company must completely honor senior
     claims on assets before settling junior claims.

VII. Liquidation.  If the liquidation value of the firm exceeds the
     going concern value, the firm should be dissolved.  In other
     words, if continued operation would only result in further loss,
     the business should be terminated.

  A. Liquidation by assignment

     1. This method of liquidation is done privately with a mini-
        mum amount of court involvement.  The debtor transfers

title to a third party, known as the _assignee_ or _trustee_, who is appointed by either the creditors or the court and who administers the liquidation process and sees to the distribution of the proceeds. These proceeds do not automatically discharge the debtor of the remaining balance due a creditor. The creditor may attempt to obtain the remaining balance through the court. This problem may be avoided by a prior agreement between the debtor and creditor to the effect that the liquidation procedure constitutes a complete settlement of claims.

2. The advantages of liquidation by assignment over a formal bankruptcy procedure are that:

   a. The assignment is usually quicker and less expensive and requires less legal formality.

   b. The assignee is allowed greater discretion and flexibility than a court-appointed trustee in bankruptcy because the assignee is allowed to maximize the funds received from the liquidation.

3. The disadvantages of the procedure are that:

   a. The debtor is not legally discharged from further obligation.

   b. The creditor is not protected from fraud.

B. Liquidation by bankruptcy. A petition for a company to be declared bankrupt may be filed in district court by either the debtor (voluntary) or by the creditors (involuntary).

1. Voluntary declaration of bankruptcy by the debtor is usually taken when management considers further delay to be detrimental to the stockholders' position.

2. Involuntary bankruptcy proceedings may be filed if the following three conditions are met:

   a. The firm's total debts equal or exceed $1,000.

   b. If fewer than 12 creditors are involved in the liquidation, one claimant must file the petition, provided that he or she is owed at least $500. If the total number of creditors is 12 or more, the petition must be filed by at least 3 creditors, each having a claim of at least $500.

   c. The debtor has committed an act of bankruptcy in the

past 4 months.  Any one of the following actions constitutes an act of bankruptcy:

(1) The debtor, through a written document, admits an
    inability to repay outstanding loans and a willing-
    ness to be judged bankrupt.

(2) A trustee or assignee is appointed for the benefit
    of the creditors.

(3) The debtor conceals or improperly transfers assets
    for the purpose of defrauding any or all of the
    firm's creditors.

3. The liquidation process

   a. After the filing and approval of the bankruptcy peti-
      tion,

      (1) The court adjudges the debtor bankrupt and names a
          referee in bankruptcy.

      (2) The referee then may appoint a receiver to serve as
          the interim caretaker of the company's assets until
          a trustee can be designated by the creditors.

      (3) The referee acquires a list of assets and liabili-
          ties from the debtor, along with other relevant in-
          formation.

      (4) A meeting of the creditors is called to elect a
          trustee.

   b. The trustee and creditors' committee initiates plans to
      liquidate the company's assets.

      (1) An effort is made to collect all money owed to the
          debtor.

      (2) Appraisers are selected to determine a value to be
          used as a guideline in liquidating the property.  A
          trustee may not sell an asset for less than 75% of
          its appraised value without court approval.

      (3) The assets are converted to cash through private
          sale or public auction.

      (4) All expenses incurred in the bankruptcy process are
          paid.

      (5) The remaining cash is distributed on a pro rata

basis to the creditors.

(6) The trustee provides a final accounting to the creditors and referee; the bankruptcy filing is discharged; and the debtor is relieved of all responsibility for prior debts.

4. Priority of claims. Under the rule of absolute priority, claims are honored in the following order:

a. Expenses incurred in administering the bankrupt estate.

b. Salaries and commissions not exceeding $600 per employee that were earned within the 3 months preceding the bankruptcy petition.

c. Federal, state, and local taxes.

d. Secured creditors, with the proceeds from the sale of specific property going first to these creditors. If any portion of the claim remains unpaid, the balance is treated as an unsecured loan.

e. Unsecured creditors.

f. Preferred stock.

g. Common stock.

## Study Problems

1. You are studying three companies and have decided as part of your analysis to use Altman's model to predict the probability of bankruptcy for each. The five ratios needed are given below. What are the bankruptcy scores for these companies and how are they interpreted?

| Company | Ratios | | | | |
| | $X_1$ | $X_2$ | $X_3$ | $X_4$ | $X_5$ |
|---|---|---|---|---|---|
| I | 0.17 | 0.19 | 0.40 | 3.50 | 1.80 |
| II | 0.21 | 0.24 | 0.14 | 1.20 | 0.76 |
| III | 0.10 | 0.09 | 0.11 | 0.99 | 0.45 |

SOLUTION

Bankruptcy score = $1.2(X_1) + 1.4(X_2) + 3.3(X_3) + 0.6(X_4) + 0.999(X_5)$

(Note: Rather than multiply $X_1$ through $X_4$ by 100, we have multiplied the coefficients by 100. For example, the coefficient for $X_1$ in the original equation was .012, but it has been multiplied by 100 resulting in 1.2.)

Company I
Bankruptcy
score = $1.2(0.17) + 1.4(0.19) + 3.3(0.40) + 0.6(3.50) + 0.999(1.80)$

   = 5.69

Basing your answer on the bankruptcy score, you would predict success. There is very little probability of bankruptcy in the next two years.

Company II
Bankruptcy
score = $1.2(0.21) + 1.4(0.24) + 3.3(0.14) + 0.6(1.20) + 0.999(0.76)$

   = 2.53

Any prediction based on this bankruptcy score will be questionable. However, a score this low does indicate some strong financial difficulties which may or may not be correctable.

Company III
Bankruptcy
score = $1.2(0.10) + 1.4(0.09) + 3.3(0.11) + 0.6(0.99) + 0.999(0.45)$

   = 1.653

Basing your answer on the bankruptcy scores, you would predict failure. There is a high probability of bankruptcy within the next 2 years.

2. The Over-Levered Crowbar Company is a recently formed manufacturing firm applying to your firm for credit. Your company follows a very liberal policy in extending credit to young firms. Your company operates under the assumption that as the new business grows, its business with you will increase. However, being aware that the probability of bankruptcy is highest among young firms, you do not wish to extend credit to any companies you feel will go bankrupt. Using the following financial statements and data, should you extend credit to this company?

The Over-Levered Crowbar Co.
Statement of Financial Position
December 31, 1979

_____

Assets

| | | |
|---|---:|---:|
| Cash | $  20,000 | |
| Accounts receivable | 30,000 | |
| Inventory | 50,000 | |
|    Total current assets | | $100,000 |
| Machines | $ 150,000 | |
| Building | 100,000 | |
| Land | 50,000 | |
|    Total plant and equipment | | 300,000 |
| Total assets | | $400,000 |

Liabilities and stockholders' equity

| | | |
|---|---:|---:|
| Accounts payable | $  20,000 | |
| Notes payable | 24,000 | |
|    Total current liabilities | | $ 44,000 |
| Bonds | $  56,000 | |
| Pensions | 126,000 | |
|    Total long-term liabilities | | 182,000 |
| Capital stock (10,000 shares outstanding) | $ 130,000 | |
| Retained earnings | 44,000 | |
|    Total stockholders' equity | | 174,000 |
| Total liabilities and stockholders' equity | | $400,000 |

_____

The Over-Levered Crowbar Co.
Income Statement
December 31, 1979

| | | |
|---|---|---|
| Sales | | $220,000 |
| Cost of goods sold | | 120,000 |
| Gross profits | | $100,000 |
| Other expenses | | |
| Depreciation | $ 50,000 | |
| Miscellaneous | 10,200 | 60,000 |
| Earnings before interest and taxes | | $ 40,000 |
| Interest | | 10,000 |
| Taxes | | 7,900 |
| Net Income | | $ 22,100 |

Market value per share, December 31, 1979    $10.00

SOLUTION:

Using the Altman model, you get:

$X_1$ = net working capital ÷ total assets
= (current assets - current liabilities) ÷ total assets
= ($100,000 - 44,000) ÷ $400,000
= 0.14

$X_2$ = retained earnings ÷ total assets
= $44,000 ÷ $400,000
= 0.11

$X_3$ = earnings before interest and taxes ÷ total assets
= $40,000 ÷ $400,000
= 0.10

$X_4$ = total market value of stock ÷ book value of total debt
= (market value per share X number of shares outstanding) ÷
(accounts payble + notes payable + bonds)
= ($10 X 10,000) ÷ ($20,000 + $24,000 + $56,000)
= 1.0

$X_5$ = sales ÷ total assets
= $220,000 ÷ $400,000
= 0.55

Bankruptcy
score = $1.2(X_1) + 1.4(X_2) + 3.3(X_3) + 0.6(X_4) + 0.999(X_5)$
$\quad\quad = 1.2(0.14) + 1.4(0.11) + 3.3(0.10) + 0.6(1.0) + 0.999(0.55)$
$\quad\quad = 1.80145$

This bankruptcy score is in the range in which the probability of failure is very high. Your firm would not want to extend credit to Over-Levered Crowbar Company.

3. Acme, Inc. is currently undergoing a reorganization. The trustee has estimated the firm's going concern value to be $2,480,000. Given the liabilities and equity from the balance sheet, formulate the plan for reorganization under the rule of absolute priority.

Acme, Inc.
Statement of Financial Position
December 30, 1979

| Liabilities and stockholders' equity | |
|---|---:|
| Current liabilities | |
| Accounts payable | $    350,000 |
| Notes payable | 200,000 |
| Wages payable | 465,000 |
| Total current liabilities | $ 1,015,000 |
| | |
| Long-term liabilities | |
| Mortgage bonds | $ 1,500,000 |
| Subordinated debentures* | 585,000 |
| Total long-term liabilities | $ 2,085,000 |
| Total liabilities | $ 3,100,000 |
| | |
| Equity | |
| Common stock (par $10) | $    500,000 |
| Paid in capital | $ 1,840,000 |
| Total equity | $ 2,340,000 |
| Total liabilities and equity | $ 5,440,000 |

*Subordinated to mortgage bonds.

SOLUTION

Plan for Reorganization: Acme, Inc. Because the total liabilities exceed the going concern value of the firm, the common

stockholders will receive nothing in the reorganization.  If it
is assumed that no more than $600 is owed any single employee,
the first priority will be to satisfy the employees in full.
After these liabilities have been satisfied there will be
$2,015,000 remaining for the creditors ($2,480,000 - $465,000).
The remaining creditors will therefore receive their proportion-
ate share of the $2,015,000, with the percentage received being
equal to 76.47% computed as follows:

$$\text{percentage of claim} = \frac{\text{Going-concern value - wages payable}}{\text{total liabilities - wages payable}}$$

$$= \frac{\$2,480,000 - \$465,000}{\$3,100,000 - \$465,000}$$

$$= 76.47\%$$

| Liabilities | 76.47% of Claim | New Claim After Subordination |
|---|---|---|
| Accounts receivable | $ 267,647 | $ 267,647 |
| Notes payable | 152,941 | 152,941 |
| Wages payable | 465,000* | 465,000 |
| Mortgage bonds | 1,147,059 | 1,500,000 |
| Subordinated debentures | 447,353 | 94,412 |
| Going concern value | $ 2,480,000 | $ 2,480,000 |

*100% of claim

The amount allocated to the subordinated debentures is available
first to satisfy the mortgage bonds, with the remainder going to
the holders of the subordinated debentures.

4. The trustee for the reorganization of Miller Corporation has established the going concern value at $10 million.  The creditors and
the amounts owed are given below.  As part of the reorganization
plan, the accounts payable are to be settled by renewal of $750,000
of the accounts, with a due date of 9 months.  Any remaining amount
to be received by these claimants is to be realized in the form of
long-term notes payable.  The current notes payable are to be settled by renewing $1 million of the notes payable, with the remaining
amount to be settled in preferred stock.  The mortgage bondholders
will receive one-half of their adjusted claim under the reorganization in the form of newly issued bonds, with the remainder being
common stock.  The investors who own the subordinated debentures are
to receive common stock in settlement of their claim.  What will

Warner's liabilities and equity be after reorganization?

## Miller Corporation

| Type of creditor | Amount of claim |
|---|---|
| Accounts payable | $ 2,500,000 |
| Notes payable | 1,500,000 |
| Mortgage bonds | 4,500,000 |
| Subordinated debentures* | 4,000,000 |
| Total liabilities | $12,500,000 |

*Subordinated to the mortgage bonds.

SOLUTION

Eighty percent of the claims are to be honored, representing the going concern value relative to total liabilities ($10,000,000 ÷ $12,500,000). Therefore, if the firm were to be liquidated for $10 million instead of being reorganized, the settlements would be as follows:

| | Existing Claims | 80% of Claims | Adjustment for Subordination |
|---|---|---|---|
| Accounts payable | $ 2,500,000 | $ 2,000,000 | $ 2,000,000 |
| Notes payable | 1,500,000 | 1,200,000 | 1,200,000 |
| Mortgage bonds | 4,500,000 | 3,600,000 | 4,500,000 |
| Subordinated debentures | 4,000,000 | 3,200,000 | 2,300,000* |
| Total | $12,500,000 | $10,000,000 | $10,000,000 |

*Since the debentures are subordinated to the mortgage bonds, the owners of the bonds are paid prior to the debenture holders' claims being settled.

Based upon the reorganization plan, the revisions in the capital structure would be determined as follows:

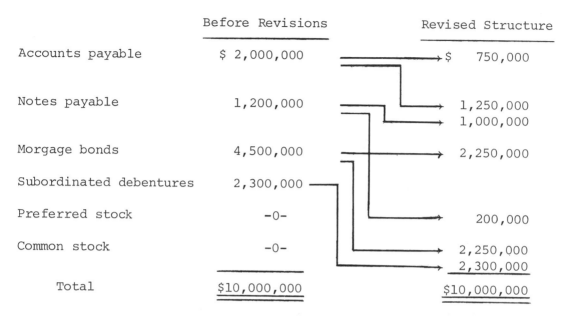

|                         | Before Revisions | Revised Structure |
|-------------------------|------------------|-------------------|
| Accounts payable        | $ 2,000,000      | $     750,000     |
| Notes payable           | 1,200,000        | 1,250,000         |
|                         |                  | 1,000,000         |
| Morgage bonds           | 4,500,000        | 2,250,000         |
| Subordinated debentures | 2,300,000        |                   |
| Preferred stock         | -0-              | 200,000           |
| Common stock            | -0-              | 2,250,000         |
|                         |                  | 2,300,000         |
| Total                   | $10,000,000      | $10,000,000       |

Consequently, the capital structure following the reorganization would appear as follows:

### Miller Corporation
### Liabilities and Equity (After Reorganization)

| | |
|---|---|
| Accounts payable | $    750,000 |
| Notes payable | 2,250,000 |
| Mortgage bonds | 2,250,000 |
| Preferred stock | 200,000 |
| Common stock | 4,550,000 |
| Total liabilities and equity | $10,000,000 |

5. August Corporation is bankrupt and being liquidated. The liabilities and equity portion of its balance sheet is given below. The book value of the assets was $90 million, but the realized value when liquidated was only $40 million, of which $9 million was from the sale of the firm's office building. Administrative expenses associated with the liquidation were $5 million. Determine the distribution of the proceeds.

## August Corporation
### Liabilities and Equities

| | | |
|---|---|---|
| Accounts payable | $ 5,000,000 | |
| Accrued wages* | 2,000,000 | |
| Notes payable | 15,000,000 | |
| Federal taxes | 2,500,000 | |
| State taxes | 500,000 | |
| Current debt | | $25,000,000 |
| First mortgage bonds† | $30,000,000 | |
| Subordinated debentures‡ | 25,000,000 | |
| Long-term debt | | 55,000,000 |
| Preferred stock | $ 2,500,000 | |
| Common stock | 7,500,000 | |
| Equity | | 10,000,000 |
| Total | | $90,000,000 |

*No single claim exceeds $600.
†Have first lien on office building.
‡Subordinated to the first mortgage bonds.

### Distribution of Proceeds

| | |
|---|---|
| Liquidation value of assets | $40,000,000 |
| Priority of claims | |
| 1. Administrative expenses | 5,000,000 |
| 2. Wages payable | 2,000,000 |
| 3. Taxes (state and federal) | 3,000,000 |
| 4. First mortgage receipts from building sale | 9,000,000 |
| Total prior claims | $19,000,000 |
| Amount available to general creditors | $21,000,000 |

## Claims of General Creditors

| Creditors | Claims | 31.82% of Claims* | Claims after Subordination |
|---|---|---|---|
| Accounts payable | $ 5,000,000 | $ 1,591,000 | $ 1,591,000 |
| Notes payable | 15,000,000 | 4,773,000 | 4,773,000 |
| Remainder of first mortgage bonds | 21,000,000 | 6,680,000 | 14,835,000 |
| Subordinated debenture | 25,000,000 | 7,955,000 | -0- |

$$*\text{Percentage of claims} = \left[\begin{array}{c}\text{Amount available}\\\text{to general creditors}\end{array}\right] \div \left[\begin{array}{c}\text{Amount of}\\\text{claims}\end{array}\right]$$

$$= \$21,000,000 \div \$66,000,000$$

$$= 31.82\%$$

## Self-Tests

TRUE-FALSE

_____ 1. A company that has a bankruptcy score above 0 will definitely be bankrupt within 6 months.

_____ 2. An extension usually results in large legal expenses and possible deterioration of assets.

_____ 3. In a composition, creditors receive a pro rata settlement in cash.

_____ 4. Creditors usually prefer a voluntary settlement instead of one brought forth by the court.

_____ 5. During a liquidation procedure the referee has the responsibility of liquidating the assets and distributing the proceeds to the creditors.

_____ 6. The company is declared a "debtor" in a reorganization as opposed to a "bankrupt" in a liquidation.

_____ 7. The absolute priority rule is fairest to the common stockholders.

_____ 8. Under Chapter XI of the Bankruptcy Act, the debtor is no longer allowed any part in the process of satisfying its creditors.

_____ 9. Under the rule of absolute priority, preferred stockholders have priority over subordinated debenture holders.

_____ 10. In a liquidation, the debtor is liable for the difference
between the liquidation value and the going concern
value.


MULTIPLE CHOICE

1. The best single indicator of bankruptcy is:

   a. Net working capital ÷ total assets.
   b. Retained earnings ÷ total assets.
   c. Earnings before interest and taxes.
   d. Total market value of stock ÷ book value of total debt.
   e. Sales ÷ total assets.

2. Under the rule of absolute priority, which of the following claims
would be the first to be honored?

   a. Secured creditors, with the proceeds from the sale of the specific property going first to these creditors.
   b. Common stock.
   c. Unsecured creditors.
   d. Federal, state, and local taxes.
   e. Preferred stock.

3. A private liquidation is preferred over a public liquidation because it usually results in which of the following?

   a. Lower legal and administrative expenses.
   b. Faster liquidation of the assets.
   c. Less deterioration of the assets' value.
   d. Less disagreement among creditors.

4. Which of the following steps is taken first in a reorganization
plan?

   a. Formulation of a new capital structure.
   b. Determination of the total valuation of the reorganized company.
   c. Determination of the total valuation of the old securities.
   d. Determination of a fair exchange of old securities and the new
securities.

5. A reorganization and a composition are similar in that:

   a. The company's assets are not liquidated and the company's oper-
      ations are continued.
   b. Creditors' claims are scaled down.
   c. Both are subject to Chapter X of the Bankruptcy Act.

6. The rule of absolute priority states that:

   a. An obligation made prior to another will be the first to be
      settled.
   b. Obligations that were absolutely essential to the operation of
      the business will be the first to be settled.
   c. The assignee has the first decision in assigning priority of
      claims.
   d. The company must completely honor senior claims on assets be-
      fore settling junior claims.

# SELF-TEACHING SUPPLEMENT: CAPITAL-BUDGETING TECHNIQUES

I. <u>Net Present Value and Profitability Index Methods</u>

In making investment decisions regarding fixed assets, the analyst compares the benefits of projects with their associated costs. Unfortunately, this comparison is complicated by the fact that the benefits and costs accruing from a given project usually do not occur in the same time period and thus are not directly comparable. This incomparability is a result of the time value of money (i.e., a dollar received today is worth more than a dollar received in the future). This comes about because a dollar today can be put into the bank and earn interest, resulting in a larger sum in the future. In economic terms we refer to the time value of money as its opportunity cost.

USING THE NET PRESENT VALUE AND PROFITABILITY INDEX

In this section we compare the present value of a project's benefits with the present value of its cost. The difference in these present values is referred to as the net present value, and the ratio of benefits to cost is called the profitability index. Definitionally, then,

$$\text{net present value} = \frac{\text{present value of future net cash flows--}}{\text{initial cash outlay}}$$

$$\text{profitability index} = \frac{\text{present value of future net cash flows}}{\text{initial cash outlay}}$$

Although both capital-budgeting techniques provide us with the same accept-reject decision, they may rank two or more projects differently.  This difference results because the net-present-value criteria measure the total dollar value of a project, while the profitability index measures its value relative to project cost.  The decision criteria used in applying these decision tools are:

|        | NPV | PI |
|--------|-----|----|
| Accept | >0  | >1 |
| Reject | <0  | <1 |

SOLVED PROBLEMS

EXERCISE 1

The initial cash outlay of a project is $100; the present value of the cash flows is $75.  Compute the project's net present value and its profitability index.  Should it be accepted?

SOLUTION

$$\text{net present value} = \frac{\text{present value of future net cash flows--}}{\text{initial cash outlay}}$$

$$= \$75 - \$100 = \$-25$$

$$\text{profitability index} = \frac{\text{present value of future net cash flows}}{\text{initial cash outlay}}$$

$$= \frac{75}{100} = 0.75$$

Thus, the project should be rejected because its net present value is negative and its profitability index is less than 1.

EXERCISE 2

The present value of a project's future net cash flow is $580 and the initial cash outlay is $500.  What is the project's net present value and what is its profitability index?  Should the project be accepted?

SOLUTION

$$NPV = \$580 - \$500 = \$80$$

$$PI = \frac{\$580}{\$500} = 1.16$$

This project should be accepted because the project's net present value is positive and its profitability index is greater than 1.0.

EXERCISE 3

A project's net present value is $300, the initial outlay is $500.  What is the present value of the project's net cash flows?

SOLUTION

NPV = PV of project's net cash flows--initial outlay

$300 = PV of project's net cash flows--$500

$800 = PV of project's net cash flows

EXERCISE 4

A project's profitability index is 1.5, and the present value of its net cash flows is $450.  What is the project's initial cash outlay?

SOLUTION

$$PI = \frac{\text{present value of future net cash flows}}{\text{initial cash outlay}}$$

$$1.5 = \frac{\$450}{x}$$

$$x = \frac{\$450}{1.5}$$

$$= \$300$$

EXERCISE 5

If either the net-present-value criteria or the profitability index gives an accept signal, will the other criteria give a similar signal?

SOLUTION

Yes. The net-present-value and profitability index will always give similar accept-reject signals. Any time the present value of future net cash flows is greater than the initial outlay, the net-present-value criteria will be positive, signaling accept; and the profitability index will be greater than 1.0, signaling accept. However, because of size differences in projects, a small project, which is relatively more profitable than a project requiring a larger initial outlay, may have a smaller net present value. In this case, unless there is a limit on the amount of funds that is allocated, the net-present-value criteria should be used.

COMPOUNDING AND DISCOUNTING: SINGLE CASH FLOWS

To determine the present value of future cash flows, it is necessary to discount those cash flows back to the present. As demonstrated in Chapter 5 of the text, discounting cash flows back to the present is merely the reverse of compounding. For example, if we put $100 (P) in the bank, earning a rate of 10% (k) annually, at the end of 1 year (n) we would have $110 ($FV_1$):

$$FV_1 = P(1 + k)^n$$

$$\$110 = \$100(1 + 0.10)$$

Correspondingly, at the end of 3 years we would have $133.10:

$$\$133.10 = \$100(1 + 0.10)^3$$

On the other hand, with an opportunity rate of 10%, the present value (P) of $110 to be received in 1 year can be found as follows:

$$\$110 = P(1 + 0.10)$$

$$P = \$110 \, \frac{1}{(1 + 0.10)}$$

$$= \$100$$

The present value of $133.10 to be received in 3 years is found similarly:

$$\$100 = \$133.10 \, \frac{1}{(1 + 0.10)^3}$$

SOLVED PROBLEMS

EXERCISE 1

What is the present value of $300 to be received in 3 years discounted at:

(a) 10% per annum?

(b)  5% per annum?

(c) 100% per annum?

SOLUTION

(a)

$$P = FV_n \, \frac{1}{(1 + k)^n}$$

$$= \$300 \, \frac{1}{(1 + 0.10)^3}$$

$$= \frac{\$300}{1.331} = \$225.39$$

(b)

$$P = \$300 \, \frac{1}{(1 + 0.05)^3}$$

$$= \frac{\$300}{1.157625} = \$259.15$$

(c)

$$P = \$300 \, \frac{1}{(1 + 1.0)^3}$$

$$= \frac{\$300}{8} = \$37.5$$

EXERCISE 2

If the appropriate discount rate is 8%, what is the present value of $300 to be received in:

(a)  5 years?

(b) 10 years?

(c) 25 years?

SOLUTION

(a)
$$P = FV_n \frac{1}{(1 + k)^n}$$

$$= \$300 \; \frac{1}{(1 + 0.08)^5}$$

$$= \$300 \frac{1}{1.4693} = \$204.18$$

(b)
$$P = \$300 \; \frac{1}{(1 + 0.08)^{10}}$$

$$= \$300 \frac{1}{2.1589}$$

$$= \$138.96$$

(c)
$$P = \$300 \; \frac{1}{(1 + 0.08)^{25}}$$

$$= \$300 \frac{1}{6.8485}$$

$$= \$43.81$$

Fortunately, it is not necessary to do the individual calculations for $1/(1 + k)^n$ because in the table in Appendix B (hereafter referred to as Table B) of the text the results of these calculations are presented for a large number of combinations of k and n. Thus, in order to determine the value of $1/(1 + 0.08)^5$ we need only look in the row of Table B corresponding to the fifth period and the 8% column to find an appropriate value of 0.681. Similarly, in Appendix A a table is provided (hereafter referred to as Table A) which gives the value of $(1 + k)^n$ for various combinations of k and n. This table can be used in compounding.

SELF-TEST 1

1. What is the present value of $250 to be received in 10 years if the appropriate discount rate is 8%?

2. How much must I put in the bank compounded annually at 6% to have $5,000 at the end of 10 years?

3. If a new machine costs $5,000 and will return $3,000 the first year, $4,000 the second year, $2,000 the third year, and my opportunity rate on money is 8%, what is the project's profitability index?

4. What is the NPV for the project in question 3? Should it be accepted?

5. If a new tractor costs $10,000 and will return $3,000 the first year, $5,000 the second year, and $4,000 the third year, calculate the net present value and profitability index using a 10% discount rate. Should the project be accepted?

6. Calculate the net present value and profitability index for the following. Assume a 12% discount rate:

| Year | Benefit (+) or Cost (−) |
|------|-------------------------|
| 0 | $-8,000 |
| 1 | +3,000 |
| 2 | +6,000 |
| 3 | +2,000 |
| 4 | +1,000 |
| 5 | -1,000 |

7. What is the net present value of a bond that pays $100 per year in interest at the end of each year for 10 years, and additionally at the end of 10 years will pay the $1,000 par value if the appropriate discount rate is 8% and the bond costs $1,093?

COMPOUNDING AND DISCOUNTING: ANNUITIES

Problem 7 of Self-Test 1 was actually an annuity problem. An annuity is simply a series of fixed payments for a specified number of years. This situation comes up frequently in finance, and in order to make the calculation of the present value of an annuity easier, you are provided with the present value of an annuity table (hereafter referred to as Table D) in Appendix D of the text, which gives present-value factors for an annuity.  In addition, a compound annuity or sum of an annuity of $1 for n periods table (hereafter referred to as Table C) is provided in Appendix C of the text.  Now, in order to determine the present value of $1,000 received at the end of each year for 5 years, discounted back to present at 7%, you have two alternatives.  You could use Table B and discount each one of the five $1,000 flows individually as follows:

$$\$1,000 \ \frac{1}{1 + 0.10} = \$1,000\,(0.935) = \$935.00$$

$$\$1,000 \ \frac{1}{1 + 0.10} = \$1,000\,(0.873) = \$873.00$$

$$\$1,000 \ \frac{1}{1 + 0.10} = \$1,000\,(0.816) = \$816.00$$

$$\$1,000 \ \frac{1}{1 + 0.10} = \$1,000\,(0.763) = \$763.00$$

$$\$1,000 \ \frac{1}{1 + 0.10} = \$1,000\,(0.713) = \underline{\$713.00}$$
$$\underline{\underline{\$4,100.00}}$$

Alternatively, you could look up the annuity discount factor in Table D.  The annuity factor for 5 years at 7% is 4.100; multiplying this times $1,000 gives $4,100.00--the same answer you got using Table B.  This is because you really only have one table, Table B, the values of which have been summed to form Table D.  Thus, the annuity discount factor for 5 years at 7% in Table D is equal to the sum of the discount factors for years 1 through 5 at 7% as found in Table B.  Therefore, the annuity table value for n years at i% is equal to

$$\begin{bmatrix} \text{Table D} \\ \text{n years} \\ \text{k\%} \end{bmatrix} = \sum_{t=1}^{n} \frac{1}{(1 + i)^t} = \sum_{t=1}^{n} \begin{bmatrix} \text{Table B} \\ \text{n years} \\ \text{k\%} \end{bmatrix}$$

SOLVED PROBLEMS

EXERCISE 1

Pick any number in Table D; note the number of years (call it n) and the discount rate (call it k).  Now look in Table B and add up the table values in the k discount-rate column for the first n years.  What do you find?

SOLUTION

The value found in Table D is equal (except perhaps for minor rounding errors) to the value found from summing the values in Table B.

EXERCISE 2

What is the present value of $50 to be received each year for 5 years if the appropriate discount rate is 8%?  Solve this problem by using Table B.

SOLUTION

Present value = $50(Table B; 1 year; 8%) + $50(Table B; 2 years; 8%) + $50(Table B; 3 years; 8%) + $50(Table B; 4 years; 8%) + $50(Table B; 5 years; 8%)

= $50(0.926) + $50(0.857) + $50(0.794) + $50(0.735) + $50(0.681)

= $46.30 + $42.85 + $39.70 + $36.75 + $34.05

= $199.65

EXERCISE 3

Solve Exercise 2 using Table D.

SOLUTION:

Present value = $50(Table D; 5 years; 8%) = $50(3.993)

= $199.65

EXERCISE 4

What is the NPV of a bond that yields $80 per year in interest at the end of each year for the next 15 years and matures in 15 years, at which time it pays an additional $1,000 if it is currently selling for $800 and your discount rate is 10%?

SOLUTION

NPV = $-800 + $80(Table D; 15 years; 10%) + $1,000(Table B; 15 years; 10%)

= $-800 + $80(7.606) + $1,000(0.239)

= $-800 + $608.48 + $239.00

= $47.48

EXERCISE 5

What is the profitability index for the bond described in Exercise 4?

SOLUTION

$$PI = \frac{\$847.48}{\$800.00} = 1.059$$

EXERCISE 6

Given the following cash flows:

| Year | Cash Flow |
| --- | --- |
| 0 | $-10,000 |
| 1 | +5,000 |
| 2 | +5,000 |
| 3 | +5,000 |
| 4 | +5,000 |
| 5 | +5,000 |
| 6 | +5,000 |
| 7 | +10,000 |

What is the NPV of this project given an appropriate discount rate of

(a)  5%?

(b)  10%?

(c)  30%?

SOLUTION

(a)    NPV = $-10,000 + $5,000(Table D; 6 years; 5%)
             + $10,000(Table B; 7 years; 5%)

           = $-10,000 + $5,000(5.076) + $10,000(0.711)

           = $-10,000 + $25,380 + $7,110

           = $22,490

(b)    NPV = $-10,000 + $5,000(Table D; 6 years; 10%)
             + $10,000(Table B; 7 years; 10%)

           = $-10,000 + $5,000(4.355) + $10,000(0.513)

           = $-10,000 + $21,775 + $5,130

           = $16,905

(c)    NPV = $-10,000 + $5,000(Table D; 6 years; 30%)
             +$10,000(Table B; 7 years; 30%)

           = $-10,000 + $5,000(2.643) + $10,000(0.159)

           = $-10,000 + $13,215 + $1,590

           = $4,805

SELF-TEST 2

1. What is the NPV of the following cash flows if the appropriate
   discount rate is 20%?

| Year | Cash Flow |
| --- | --- |
| 0 | $-15,000 |
| 1 | +2,000 |
| 2 | +2,000 |
| 3 | +4,000 |
| 4 | +5,000 |
| 5 | +6,000 |

What is the profitability index should the project be accepted?

2. For how many years must $1,000 compound at 8% to accumulate to
   $2,000?

3. At what rate must $1,000 compound to accumulate to $3,000 in 7 years?

4. How much must you put in the bank compounded annually at 8% to accumulate to $3,000 at the end of 10 years?

5. What is the present value of $100 to be received at the end of each of the next 10 years discounted back to present at

   (a)   5%?

   (b) 10%?

   (c) 20%?

   (d) 30%?

6. How much is $50 worth if it is to be received at the end of 4 years if the appropriate discount rate is

   (a) 10%?

   (b) 20%?

   (c)   0%?

   (d) 100%?

7. What is the future value of $100 if it is placed in the bank for 5 years and compounded at 16%?

   (a) Annually?

   (b) Semiannually?

   (c) Quarterly?

8. A company is examining a new machine to replace an existing machine that currently has a book value of $5,000 and can be sold for $2,000. The old machine has 5 years of expected life left, is being depreciated on a straight-line basis, and will have a salvage value of zero in 5 years. The new machine will perform the same task but more efficiently, resulting in cash benefits before depreciation and taxes of $10,000. The expected life of the new machine is 5 years; it costs $20,000 and can be sold for $5,000 at the end of the fifth year. Assuming straight-line depreciation, a 40% tax rate, and an appropriate discount rate of 14%, find the NPV and profitability index of the project.

## II. The Internal-Rate-of-Return Method

In the previous section we made capital-budgeting decisions
through the use of the profitability index and net-present-value
criteria, by comparing the present value of the benefits of the project with the present value of its costs either through division
(determining the profitability index) or subtraction (determining a
net present value).  In each case you were supplied with an appropriate discount rate or cost of capital with which to determine the
present value of future flows.  You will now examine a method of
evaluating projects that does not rely on an input discount rate but
determines the discount rate that would make the project's NPV = 0,
or, alternatively, makes its profitability index = 1.0.  With the PI
and NPV criteria we have a measure of the relative profitability and
absolute profitability of the project, with all flows adjusted for
the time value of money.  The next criterion we examine, the internal rate of return, can be thought of as a rate of return or yield on
the project.  The decision rules on this criterion can be stated as
follows: If the IRR is greater than the required rate of return or
hurdle rate, the project should be accepted; otherwise, the project
should be rejected.  Although this seems quite straightforward and
easy to understand, one finds that the solution process is often
complex and time-consuming.

### THE INTERNAL RATE OF RETURN: THE CASE OF A SINGLE CASH INFLOW

The internal rate of return is defined as that rate, IRR, which
equates the present value of a project's anticipated cash inflows
with the present value of the relevant cash outflows.  Where $ACF_t$ is
the cash flow for period t, whether it be positive (an inflow) or
negative (an outflow), and n is the last period in which any cash
flow is expected, the internal rate of return is represented by IRR
in equation (A.1):

$$\sum_{t=0}^{n} \frac{ACF_t}{(1 + IRR)^t} = 0 \tag{A.1}$$

A solution to this problem becomes quite simple in the case in which
the only outlay occurs in time period 0 (the initial outlay, IO) and
only one cash inflow occurs, say in time period t:

$$IO = \frac{ACF_t}{(1 + IRR)^t}$$

$$\frac{IO}{ACF_t} = \frac{1}{(1 + IRR)^t}$$

Since you can determine a numerical value for $IO/ACF_t$ and you know that Table B in the text gives you values for $1/(1 + IRR)^t$, we can easily solve for IRR. All we have to do is look in Table B in the nth row (corresponding to the number of years until the cash inflow) until we find the value $IO/ACF_t$; the column that gives this value indicates the appropriate value of IRR.

SOLVED PROBLEMS

EXERCISE 1

What is the internal rate of return on a project with an initial outlay of $6,000 which in the ninth year will produce one cash inflow of $18,000?

SOLUTION

$$\$6,000 = \frac{\$18,000}{(1 + IRR)^9}$$

$$\frac{\$6,000}{\$18,000} = \frac{1}{(1 + IRR)^9}$$

$$0.333 = \frac{1}{(1 + IRR)^9}$$

The value of 0.333 is found in the 9-year row of Table B in the 13% column; thus, 13% is the project's internal rate of return.

EXERCISE 2

Given the following cash flows, what is the project's internal rate of return?

| Year | Cash Flow |
| --- | --- |
| 0 | $-10,000 |
| 5 | +40,000 |

SOLUTION

$$\frac{\$10,000}{\$40,000} \qquad \frac{1}{(1 + IRR)^5}$$

$$0.25 = \frac{1}{(1 + IRR)^5}$$

Therefore, IRR = 32%

EXERCISE 3

If a project requires an initial outlay of $6,000 and will return $10,000 in year 13, what is its internal rate of return?

SOLUTION

$$\frac{\$6,000}{\$10,000} = \frac{1}{(1 + IRR)^t}$$

$$0.6 = \frac{1}{(1 + IRR)^{13}}$$

Therefore, IRR = 4%.

The accept-reject criteria for the internal-rate of-return method states that if the project's internal rate of return is greater than the required rate of return or hurdle rate, the project should be accepted; otherwise, the project should be rejected. In other words,

IRR > required rate of return     Accept

IRR < required rate of return     Reject

Thus, if the required rate of return in Exercises 1 through 3 were 10%, the projects examined in Exercises 1 and 2 would be accepted, and the project in Exercise 3 would be rejected.

THE INTERNAL RATE OF RETURN:
MULTIPLE AND EQUAL CASH INFLOWS

In the case in which there is more than one cash inflow resulting from a project's acceptance, and the cash inflows form an annuity, a similar approach to that just outlined but using Table D instead of

301

Table B will result in a correct solution.   In this case the simpli-
fication proceeds as follows:

$$IO = \sum_{t=1}^{T} \frac{ACF_t}{(1 + IRR)^t}$$

$$\frac{IO}{ACF_t} = \sum_{t=1}^{T} \frac{1}{(1 + IRR)^t}$$

If all the $ACF_t$ values are equal and occur periodically (e.g., annually), we have an annuity.  The value of the annuity discount
factor, $\sum_{t=1}^{T} 1/(1 + IRR)^t$, can be found in Table D.  Since we know
the term of the annuity, T years, when solving for IRR we need merely
look in the T-year row until we find the value $IO/ACF_t$; then looking
to the column heading yields the internal rate of return.


SOLVED PROBLEMS

    EXERCISE 1

    What is the internal rate of return on a project with an initial
    outlay of $24,000 which will produce cash inflows of $6,000 for
    each of the next 15 years?


    SOLUTION

$$\$24,000 = \sum_{t=1}^{15} \frac{\$6,000}{(1 + IRR)^t}$$

$$4.0 = \sum_{t=1}^{15} \frac{1}{(1 + IRR)^t}$$

Therefore, IRR = 24%.


    EXERCISE 2

    What is the internal rate of return on a project with an initial
    outlay of $18,000 which will produce cash inflows of $3,000 for

each year for the next 9 years?

SOLUTION

$$\$18,000 = \sum_{t=1}^{9} \frac{\$3,000}{(1 + IRR)^t}$$

$$6.0 = \sum_{t=1}^{9} \frac{1}{(1 + IRR)^t}$$

Therefore, IRR = 9%.

EXERCISE 3

Given the following cash flows, what is this project's internal rate of return?

| Year | Cash Flow |
| --- | --- |
| 0 | $20,000 |
| 1 | 5,000 |
| 2 | 5,000 |
| 3 | 5,000 |
| 4 | 5,000 |
| 5 | 5,000 |

SOLUTION

$$\$20,000 = \sum_{t=1}^{5} \frac{\$5,000}{(1 + IRR)^t}$$

$$4.0 = \sum_{t=1}^{5} \frac{1}{(1 + IRR)^t}$$

Therefore, IRR = 8%.

For Exercises 1 through 3, if the required rate of return were 10%, the project in Exercise 1 would be accepted and the projects in Exercises 2 and 3 would be rejected.

THE INTERNAL RATE OF RETURN:
MULTIPLE AND UNEQUAL CASH FLOWS

Solution using the internal-rate-of-return criteria becomes most complex when there are unequal cash inflows resulting from a project's acceptance. In this case the solution can only be found by trial and error: first, arbitrarily picking a return and solving the problem; then, depending on the result, raising or lowering that rate until the present value of the inflows equals the present value of the outflows.

SOLVED PROBLEMS

EXERCISE 1

What is the internal rate of return on a project that costs $20,000 and returns $3,000 per year for the first 4 years and $5,000 per year in years 5 through 8?

SOLUTION

$$\$20,000 = \sum_{t=1}^{4} \frac{\$3,000}{(1 + IRR)^t} + \sum_{t=5}^{8} \frac{\$5,000}{(1 + IRR)^t}$$

First, solve the problem using a discount rate picked arbitrarily. Try 20%. In this case this equation reduces to

$$\$20,000 = \$3,000(2.589) + \$7,000(3.837 - 2.589)$$
$$= \$7,767 + \$8,736$$
$$\neq \$16,503$$

Thus, 20% is not this project's internal rate of return. If it were the internal rate of return, the present value of the inflows would equal the present value of the outflows; but the present value of the inflows is much less than the present value of the outflows. Since all the inflows occur in the future, the present value of these flows will increase as the discount rate is lowered, so here you should try a lower discount rate. If you try 13%, this equation becomes

$$\$20,000 = \$3,000(2.974) + \$7,000(4.799 - 2.974)$$
$$= \$8,922 + \$12,775$$
$$\neq \$21,697$$

This time the present value of the inflows is less than the present value of the outflows. In order to raise the present value of the inflows, the discount rate must be lowered. This time try 15%.

304

$$\$20,000 = \$3,000(2.855) + \$7,000(4.487 - 2.855)$$
$$= \$8,565 + \$11,424$$
$$\cong \$19,989$$

Now the present value of the inflows is approximately equal to the present value of the outflows using a discount rate of 15%; the project's internal rate of return is very close to 15%.

EXERCISE 2

Given the following cash flows, what is the project's IRR?

| Year | Cash Flow |
|------|-----------|
| 0 | $-12,000 |
| 1 | +4,000 |
| 2 | +4,000 |
| 3 | +4,000 |
| 4 | +4,000 |
| 5 | +4,000 |
| 6 | +2,000 |

SOLUTION

First, try 30%:

$$\$12,000 = \$4,000(2.436) + \$2,000(0.207)$$
$$= \$9,744 + \$414$$
$$\neq \$10,158$$

Since the present value of the cash inflows is too low, you must lower the discount rate and try again.  This time, try 23%:

$$\$12,000 = \$4,000(2.689) + \$2,000(0.262)$$
$$= \$10,756 + \$524$$
$$\neq \$11,280$$

Again, the present value of the cash inflows is too low.  Therefore, the discount rate is lowered and the problem is tried again. Next, try 20%:

$$\$12,000 = \$4,000(2.991) + \$2,000(0.335)$$
$$= \$11,964 + \$670$$
$$\neq \$12,634$$

Since the present value of the cash inflows is too high, the discount rate must be raised.  We raised it to 23%:

$$\$12,000 = \$4,000(2.803) + \$2,000(0.289)$$
$$= \$11,212 + \$578$$
$$\neq \$11,790$$

This time the present value of the inflows is too low; thus, the discount rate is lowered. We now try 22%:

$$\$12,000 = \$4,000(2.864) + \$2,000(0.303)$$
$$= \$11,456 + \$606$$
$$\cong \$12,062$$

Thus, the IRR for this problem is between 22% and 23%, and closer to 22%.

EXERCISE 3

What is the IRR associated with this project?

| Year | Cash Flow |
| --- | --- |
| 0 | $-10,000 |
| 1 | +3,000 |
| 2 | +6,000 |
| 3 | +9,000 |

SOLUTION

Try 20%:

$$\$10,000 = \$3,000(0.833) + \$6,000(0.694) + \$9,000(0.579)$$
$$= \$2,499 + \$4,164 + \$5,211$$
$$\neq \$11,874$$

The present value of the cash inflows is too large; therefore, the discount rate must be raised. Try 30%:

$$\$10,000 = \$3,000(0.769) + \$6,000(0.592) + \$9,000(0.455)$$
$$= \$2,307 + \$3,552 + \$4,095$$
$$\neq \$9,954$$

Now it is too small; so try 29%:

$$\$10,000 = \$3,000(0.775) + \$6,000(0.601) + \$9,000(0.466)$$
$$= \$2,325 + \$3,606 + \$4,194$$
$$\neq \$10,125$$

Thus, this project's IRR is just under 30%.

As you can see by now, calculating the IRR can become quite time-consuming when a trial-and-error search is necessitated. If it is necessary, remember the following guidelines:

1. Always try a larger discount rate (or trial IRR) when the present value of the cash inflows is larger than the initial outlay.

2. Always try a smaller discount rate (or trial IRR) when the present value of the cash inflows is smaller than the initial cash outlay.


SELF-TEST 3

1. What is the internal rate of return on a project that requires an initial outlay of $10,000 and returns $14,000 at the end of the fifth year?

2. What is the internal rate of return on a project that requires an initial outlay of $700 and returns $1,857 at the end of the twentieth year?

3. What is the internal rate of return on a project that requires a $30,000 outlay and returns $6,000 at the end of each of the next 10 years?

4. What is the internal rate of return on a project that requires an initial outlay of $20,000 and returns $3,928 at the end of each year for the next 15 years?

5. Given the following cash flows, determine an internal rate of return.

| Year | Cash Flow |
|------|-----------|
| 0 | $-40,000 |
| 1 | +10,000 |
| 2 | +10,000 |
| 3 | +10,000 |
| 4 | +10,000 |
| 5 | +10,000 |
| 6 | +15,000 |

6. Given the following cash flows, determine an internal rate of return.

| Year | Cash Flow |
| --- | --- |
| 0 | $-61,630 |
| 1 | +10,000 |
| 2 | +10,000 |
| 3 | +10,000 |
| 4 | +10,000 |
| 5 | +10,000 |
| 6 | +10,000 |
| 7 | +70,000 |

7. Given the following cash flows, determine an internal rate of return

| Year | Cash Flow |
| --- | --- |
| 0 | $-2,992 |
| 1 | +700 |
| 2 | +1,400 |
| 3 | +3,000 |

8. Given the following cash flows, determine an internal rate of return.

| Year | Cash Flow |
| --- | --- |
| 0 | $5,492 |
| 1 | 2,000 |
| 2 | 2,000 |
| 3 | 4,000 |
| 4 | 3,000 |

9. What is the internal rate of return on a project that requires an initial outlay of $1,000 and returns $4,000 at the end of the second year?

Appendix A

SELF-TEST 1

1. $250(Table B; 10 years; 8%)

   $250(0.463) = $115.75

2. $P = FV_{10}$(Table B; 10 years; 6%)

   = $5,000(.558)

   = $2,790

3. $PI = \dfrac{\text{present value of future net cash flows}}{\text{initial cash outlay}}$

   Present value of future net cash flows

   = $3,000(Table B; 1 year; 8%) + $4,000(Table B; 2 years; 8%)
   + $2,000(Table B; 3 years; 8%)

   = $3,000(0.926) + $4,000(0.857) + $2,000(0.794)

   = $2,778 + $3,428 + $1,588

   = $7,794

   $PI = \dfrac{\$7,794}{\$5,000} = 1.5588$

4. NPV = PV inflows - PV outflows

   = $7,794 - $5,000

   = $2,794

   Accept the project because its NPV is positive and its PI is greater than 1.0.

5. NPV = $-10,000 + $3,000(Table B; 1 year; 10%) + $5,000(Table B; 2 years; 10%) + $4,000(Table B; 3 years; 10%)

   = $-10,000 + $3,000(0.909) + $5,000(0.826) + $4,000(0.751)

   = $-10,000 + $2,727 + $4,130 + $3,004

   = $-139

   $PI = \dfrac{\$9,861}{\$10,000} = 0.9861$

Reject the project because the NPV is negative and the PI is less than 1.0.

6. NPV = $-8,000 + $3,000(Table B; 1 year; 12%) + $6,000(Table B; 2 years; 12%) + $2,000(Table B; 3 years; 12%) + $1,000(Table B; 4 years; 12%) - $1,000(Table B; 5 years; 12%)

   = $-8,000 + $3,000(0.893) + $6,000(0.797) + $2,000(0.712) + $1,000(0.636) - $1,000(0.567)

   = $-8,000 + $2,679 + $4,782 + $1,424 + $636 - $567

   = $954

   $$PI = \frac{\$8,954}{\$8,000} = 1.1192$$

7. NPV = $-1,093.00 + $100(Table B; 1 year; 8%) + $100(Table B; 2 years; 8%) + $100(Table B; 3 years; 8%) + $100(Table B; 4 years; 8%) + $100(Table B; 5 years; 8%) + $100(Table B; 6 years; 8%) + $100(Table B; 7 years; 8%) + $100(Table B; 8 years; 8%) + $1,100(Table B; 10 years; 8%)

   NPV = $-1,093.00 + $100(0.926) + $100(0.857) + $100(0.794) + $100(0.735) + $100(0.681) + $100(0.630) + $100(0.583) + $100(0.540) + $100(0.500) + $1,100(0.463)

   = $-1,093.00 + $92.60 + $85.70 + $79.48 + $73.50 + $68.10 + $63.00 + $58.30 + $54.00 + $50.00 + $509.30

   = $40.90

## SELF-TEST 2

1. 
$$NPV = \$-15,000 + \$2,000 \begin{bmatrix} \text{Table D} \\ \text{2 years} \\ 20\% \end{bmatrix} + \$4,000 \begin{bmatrix} \text{Table B} \\ \text{3 years} \\ 20\% \end{bmatrix}$$

$$\$5,000 \begin{bmatrix} \text{Table B} \\ \text{4 years} \\ 20\% \end{bmatrix} + \$6,000 \begin{bmatrix} \text{Table B} \\ \text{5 years} \\ 20\% \end{bmatrix}$$

   = $-15,000 + $2,000(1.528) + $4,000(0.579) + $5,000(0.482) + $6,000(0.402)

$$= \$-15,000 + \$3,056 + \$2,316 + \$2,410 + \$2,412$$

$$= \$-4,806$$

$$PI = \frac{\$10,194}{\$15,000} = 0.6796$$

The project should be rejected because its NPV is negative and the PI is less than 1.0.

2.
$$\$1,000 = \$2,000 \begin{bmatrix} \text{Table B} \\ \text{? years} \\ 8\% \end{bmatrix}$$

$$0.500 = \begin{bmatrix} \text{Table B} \\ \text{? years} \\ 8\% \end{bmatrix}$$

The table value in the 8% column comes closest to 0.500 in the 9-year row. Thus, it will take 9 years for $1,000 to accumulate to $2,000 if it is compounded at 8%.

3.
$$\$1,000 = \$3,000 \begin{bmatrix} \text{Table B} \\ 7 \text{ years} \\ ?\% \end{bmatrix}$$

$$0.3333 = \begin{bmatrix} \text{Table B} \\ 7 \text{ years} \\ ?\% \end{bmatrix}$$

The table value in the 7-year row comes closest to 0.333 in the 17% column. Thus, it is necessary to compound $1,000 at 17% for 7 years in order to accumulate $3,000.

4.
$$P = \$3,000 \begin{bmatrix} \text{Table B} \\ 10 \text{ years} \\ 8\% \end{bmatrix}$$

$$= \$3,000(0.463)$$

$$= \$1,389$$

5. a.
$$P = \$100 \begin{bmatrix} \text{Table D} \\ 10 \text{ years} \\ 5\% \end{bmatrix}$$

$$= \$100(7.722)$$

$$= \$772.20$$

b.
$$P = \$100 \begin{bmatrix} \text{Table D} \\ 10 \text{ years} \\ 10\% \end{bmatrix}$$

$$= \$100(6.145)$$

$$= \$614.50$$

c.
$$P = \$100 \begin{bmatrix} \text{Table D} \\ 10 \text{ years} \\ 20\% \end{bmatrix}$$

$$= \$100(4.192)$$

$$= \$419.20$$

d.
$$P = \$100 \begin{bmatrix} \text{Table D} \\ 10 \text{ years} \\ 30\% \end{bmatrix}$$

$$= \$100(3.092)$$

$$= \$309.20$$

6. a.
$$P = \$50 \begin{bmatrix} \text{Table B} \\ 4 \text{ years} \\ 10\% \end{bmatrix}$$

$$= \$50(0.683)$$

$$= \$34.15$$

b.
$$P = \$50 \begin{bmatrix} \text{Table B} \\ 4 \text{ years} \\ 20\% \end{bmatrix}$$

$$= \$50(0.482)$$

$$= \$24.10$$

c. $P \doteq \$50 \dfrac{1}{(1 + 0)^4}$

$= \$50 \left(\dfrac{1}{1}\right)$

$= \$50$

d. $P = \$50 \dfrac{1}{(1 + 1.0)^4}$

$= \$50 \left(\dfrac{1}{16}\right)$

$= \$3.125$

7. a. $FV_5 = \$100 \begin{bmatrix} \text{Table A} \\ \text{5 years} \\ 16\% \end{bmatrix}$

$= \$100 (2.100)$

$= \$210.00$

b. $FV_{10} = \$100 \begin{bmatrix} \text{Table A} \\ \text{10 periods} \\ 8\% \end{bmatrix}$

$= \$100 (2.159)$

$= \$215.90$

c. $FV_{20} = \$100 \begin{bmatrix} \text{Table A} \\ \text{20 periods} \\ 4\% \end{bmatrix}$

$= \$100 (2.191)$

$= \$219.10$

8. a. Initial Outlay

| | |
|---|---:|
| New machine | $-20,000 |
| Sale of old machine | + 2,000 |
| Tax gain | |
| ($5,000 - $2,000)0.4 | + 1,200 |
| | $-16,800 |

b. Annual cash flows

|  | Book Method | Cash Method |
|---|---|---|
| Savings | $10,000 | $10,000 |
| Change in depreciation | (3,000 - 1,000) | |
| Taxable increase | 8,000 | |
| Taxes | 3,200 | 3,200 |
| Annual net cash flow | | $ 6,800 |

c. Terminal flow:

| Salvage value | $ 5,000 |
|---|---|
| Annual cash flow | 6,800 |
| | $11,800 |

d. Cash-flow diagram

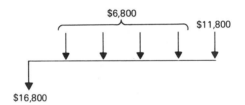

e.
$$\text{NPV} = \$-16,800 = \$6,800 \begin{bmatrix} \text{Table D} \\ \text{4 years} \\ 14\% \end{bmatrix} + \$11,800 \begin{bmatrix} \text{Table B} \\ \text{5 years} \\ 14\% \end{bmatrix}$$

$$= \$16,800 + \$6,800(2.914) + \$11,800(0.519)$$

$$= \$-16,800 + \$19,815.20 + \$6,124.20$$

$$= \$9,139.40$$

$$\text{PI} = \frac{\$25,939.40}{\$16,800} = 1.544$$

SELF-TEST 3

1. $\$10,000 = \$14,000 \dfrac{1}{(1 + \text{IRR})^5}$

$$0.714 = \frac{1}{(1 + IRR)^5}$$

Therefore, IRR = 7% because the Table B value for 5 years closest to 0.714 occurs in the 7% column (0.713).

2.  $$\$700 = \$1,857 \frac{1}{(1 + IRR)^{20}}$$

$$0.377 = \frac{1}{(1 + IRR)^{20}}$$

Therefore, IRR = 5%

3.  $$\$30,000 = \$6,000 \sum_{t=1}^{10} \frac{1}{(1 + IRR)^t}$$

$$5.0 = \sum_{t=1}^{10} \frac{1}{(1 + IRR)^t}$$

Therefore, IRR = approximately 15%.

4.  $$\$20,000 = \$3,928 \sum_{t=1}^{15} \frac{1}{(1 + IRR)^t}$$

$$5.092 = \sum_{t=1}^{15} \frac{1}{(1 + IRR)^t}$$

Therefore, IRR = 18%.

5.  $$\$40,000 = \$10,000 \sum_{t=1}^{5} \frac{1}{(1 + IRR)^t} + \$15,000 \frac{1}{(1 + IRR)^6}$$

Try 20%:

$$\$40,000 = \$10,000(2.991) + \$15,000(0.335)$$

$$= \$29,910 + \$5,025$$

$$= \$34,935$$

Try 15%:

$40,000 = $10,000(3.352) + $15,000(0.432)$

$\qquad = \$33,520 + \$6,480$

$\qquad = \$40,000$

Thus, 15% is the approximate IRR.

6.
$$\$61,615 = \$10,000 \sum_{t=1}^{6} \frac{1}{(1 + IRR)^t} + \$70,000 \frac{1}{(1 + IRR)^7}$$

Try 20%:

$61,630.0 = $10,000(3.326) + $70,000(0.279)$

$\qquad = \$33,260 + \$19,530$

$\qquad = \$52,790$

Try 15%:

$61,630.0 = $10,000(3.784) + $70,000(0.376)$

$\qquad = \$37,840 + \$26,320$

$\qquad = \$64,160$

Try 16%:

$61,630.0 = $100,000(3.685) + $70,000(0.354)$

$\qquad = \$36,850 + \$24,780$

$\qquad = \$61,630$

7.
$$\$2,992 = \$700 \frac{1}{(1 + IRR)} + \$1,400 \frac{1}{(1 + IRR)^2} + \$3,000 \frac{1}{(1 + IRR)^3}$$

Try 20%:

$2,992 = $700(0.833) + $1,400(0.694) + $3,000(0.579)$

$\qquad = \$583.10 + \$971.60 + \$1,737.00$

$\qquad = \$3,291.70$

Try 25%:

$$\$2,992 = \$700(0.800) + \$1,400(0.640) + \$3,000(0.512)$$

$$= \$560 + \$896 + \$1,536$$

$$= \$2,992$$

Thus, the IRR = 25%.

8.
$$\$5,492 = \$2,000 \sum_{t=1}^{2} \frac{1}{(1 + IRR)^t} + \$4,000 \frac{1}{(1 + IRR)^3}$$

$$+ \$3,000 \frac{1}{(1 + IRR)^4}$$

Try 20%:

$$\$5,492 = \$2,000(1.528) + \$4,000(0.579) + \$3,000(0.482)$$

$$= \$3,056 + \$2,316 + \$1,446$$

$$= \$6,818$$

Try 30%:

$$\$5,492 = \$2,000(1.361) + \$4,000(0.455) + \$3,000(0.350)$$

$$= \$2,722 + \$1,820 + \$1,050$$

$$= \$5,592$$

Try 31%:

$$\$5,492 = \$2,000(1.346) + \$4,000(0.445) + \$3,000(0.340)$$

$$= \$2,692 + \$1,780 + \$1,020$$

$$= \$5,492$$

Thus, 31% is this project's IRR.

9. $\$1,000 = \$4,000 \dfrac{1}{(1 + IRR)^2}$

$$(1 + IRR)^2 = 4.0$$

$$1 + IRR = \sqrt{4.0}$$

$$1 + IRR = 2.0$$

$$IRR = 1.0, \text{ or } IRR = 100\%$$

# COMPOUND SUM AND PRESENT-VALUE TABLES

**Appendix A** COMPOUND SUM OF $1

| n | 1% | 2% | 3% | 4% | 5% | 6% | 7% | 8% | 9% | 10% |
|---|------|------|------|------|------|------|------|------|------|------|
| 1 | 1.010 | 1.020 | 1.030 | 1.040 | 1.050 | 1.060 | 1.070 | 1.080 | 1.090 | 1.100 |
| 2 | 1.020 | 1.040 | 1.061 | 1.082 | 1.102 | 1.124 | 1.145 | 1.166 | 1.188 | 1.210 |
| 3 | 1.030 | 1.061 | 1.093 | 1.125 | 1.158 | 1.191 | 1.225 | 1.260 | 1.295 | 1.331 |
| 4 | 1.041 | 1.082 | 1.126 | 1.170 | 1.216 | 1.262 | 1.311 | 1.360 | 1.412 | 1.464 |
| 5 | 1.051 | 1.104 | 1.159 | 1.217 | 1.276 | 1.338 | 1.403 | 1.469 | 1.539 | 1.611 |
| 6 | 1.062 | 1.126 | 1.194 | 1.265 | 1.340 | 1.419 | 1.501 | 1.587 | 1.677 | 1.772 |
| 7 | 1.072 | 1.149 | 1.230 | 1.316 | 1.407 | 1.504 | 1.606 | 1.714 | 1.828 | 1.949 |
| 8 | 1.083 | 1.172 | 1.267 | 1.369 | 1.477 | 1.594 | 1.718 | 1.851 | 1.993 | 2.144 |
| 9 | 1.094 | 1.195 | 1.305 | 1.423 | 1.551 | 1.689 | 1.838 | 1.999 | 2.172 | 2.358 |
| 10 | 1.105 | 1.219 | 1.344 | 1.480 | 1.629 | 1.791 | 1.967 | 2.159 | 2.367 | 2.594 |
| 11 | 1.116 | 1.243 | 1.384 | 1.539 | 1.710 | 1.898 | 2.105 | 2.332 | 2.580 | 2.853 |
| 12 | 1.127 | 1.268 | 1.426 | 1.601 | 1.796 | 2.012 | 2.252 | 2.518 | 2.813 | 3.138 |
| 13 | 1.138 | 1.294 | 1.469 | 1.665 | 1.886 | 2.133 | 2.410 | 2.720 | 3.066 | 3.452 |
| 14 | 1.149 | 1.319 | 1.513 | 1.732 | 1.980 | 2.261 | 2.579 | 2.937 | 3.342 | 3.797 |
| 15 | 1.161 | 1.346 | 1.558 | 1.801 | 2.079 | 2.397 | 2.759 | 3.172 | 3.642 | 4.177 |
| 16 | 1.173 | 1.373 | 1.605 | 1.873 | 2.183 | 2.540 | 2.952 | 3.426 | 3.970 | 4.595 |
| 17 | 1.184 | 1.400 | 1.653 | 1.948 | 2.292 | 2.693 | 3.159 | 3.700 | 4.328 | 5.054 |
| 18 | 1.196 | 1.428 | 1.702 | 2.026 | 2.407 | 2.854 | 3.380 | 3.996 | 4.717 | 5.560 |
| 19 | 1.208 | 1.457 | 1.753 | 2.107 | 2.527 | 3.026 | 3.616 | 4.316 | 5.142 | 6.116 |
| 20 | 1.220 | 1.486 | 1.806 | 2.191 | 2.653 | 3.207 | 3.870 | 4.661 | 5.604 | 6.727 |
| 21 | 1.232 | 1.516 | 1.860 | 2.279 | 2.786 | 3.399 | 4.140 | 5.034 | 6.109 | 7.400 |
| 22 | 1.245 | 1.546 | 1.916 | 2.370 | 2.925 | 3.603 | 4.430 | 5.436 | 6.658 | 8.140 |
| 23 | 1.257 | 1.577 | 1.974 | 2.465 | 3.071 | 3.820 | 4.740 | 5.871 | 7.258 | 8.954 |
| 24 | 1.270 | 1.608 | 2.033 | 2.563 | 3.225 | 4.049 | 5.072 | 6.341 | 7.911 | 9.850 |
| 25 | 1.282 | 1.641 | 2.094 | 2.666 | 3.386 | 4.292 | 5.427 | 6.848 | 8.623 | 10.834 |
| 30 | 1.348 | 1.811 | 2.427 | 3.243 | 4.322 | 5.743 | 7.612 | 10.062 | 13.267 | 17.449 |
| 40 | 1.489 | 2.208 | 3.262 | 4.801 | 7.040 | 10.285 | 14.974 | 21.724 | 31.408 | 45.258 |
| 50 | 1.645 | 2.691 | 4.384 | 7.106 | 11.467 | 18.419 | 29.456 | 46.900 | 74.354 | 117.386 |

| n | 11% | 12% | 13% | 14% | 15% | 16% | 17% | 18% | 19% | 20% |
|---|---|---|---|---|---|---|---|---|---|---|
| 1 | 1.110 | 1.120 | 1.130 | 1.140 | 1.150 | 1.160 | 1.170 | 1.180 | 1.190 | 1.200 |
| 2 | 1.232 | 1.254 | 1.277 | 1.300 | 1.322 | 1.346 | 1.369 | 1.392 | 1.416 | 1.440 |
| 3 | 1.368 | 1.405 | 1.443 | 1.482 | 1.521 | 1.561 | 1.602 | 1.643 | 1.685 | 1.728 |
| 4 | 1.518 | 1.574 | 1.630 | 1.689 | 1.749 | 1.811 | 1.874 | 1.939 | 2.005 | 2.074 |
| 5 | 1.685 | 1.762 | 1.842 | 1.925 | 2.011 | 2.100 | 2.192 | 2.288 | 2.386 | 2.488 |
| 6 | 1.870 | 1.974 | 2.082 | 2.195 | 2.313 | 2.436 | 2.565 | 2.700 | 2.840 | 2.986 |
| 7 | 2.076 | 2.211 | 2.353 | 2.502 | 2.660 | 2.826 | 3.001 | 3.185 | 3.379 | 3.583 |
| 8 | 2.305 | 2.476 | 2.658 | 2.853 | 3.059 | 3.278 | 3.511 | 3.759 | 4.021 | 4.300 |
| 9 | 2.558 | 2.773 | 3.004 | 3.252 | 3.518 | 3.803 | 4.108 | 4.435 | 4.785 | 5.160 |
| 10 | 2.839 | 3.106 | 3.395 | 3.707 | 4.046 | 4.411 | 4.807 | 5.234 | 5.695 | 6.192 |
| 11 | 3.152 | 3.479 | 3.836 | 4.226 | 4.652 | 5.117 | 5.624 | 6.176 | 6.777 | 7.430 |
| 12 | 3.498 | 3.896 | 4.334 | 4.818 | 5.350 | 5.936 | 6.580 | 7.288 | 8.064 | 8.916 |
| 13 | 3.883 | 4.363 | 4.898 | 5.492 | 6.153 | 6.886 | 7.699 | 8.599 | 9.596 | 10.699 |
| 14 | 4.310 | 4.887 | 5.535 | 6.261 | 7.076 | 7.987 | 9.007 | 10.147 | 11.420 | 12.839 |
| 15 | 4.785 | 5.474 | 6.254 | 7.138 | 8.137 | 9.265 | 10.539 | 11.974 | 13.589 | 15.407 |
| 16 | 5.311 | 6.130 | 7.067 | 8.137 | 9.358 | 10.748 | 12.330 | 14.129 | 16.171 | 18.488 |
| 17 | 5.895 | 6.866 | 7.986 | 9.276 | 10.761 | 12.468 | 14.426 | 16.672 | 19.244 | 22.186 |
| 18 | 6.543 | 7.690 | 9.024 | 10.575 | 12.375 | 14.462 | 16.879 | 19.673 | 22.900 | 26.623 |
| 19 | 7.263 | 8.613 | 10.197 | 12.055 | 14.232 | 16.776 | 19.748 | 23.214 | 27.251 | 31.948 |
| 20 | 8.062 | 9.646 | 11.523 | 13.743 | 16.366 | 19.461 | 23.105 | 27.393 | 32.429 | 38.337 |
| 21 | 8.949 | 10.804 | 13.021 | 15.667 | 18.821 | 22.574 | 27.033 | 32.323 | 38.591 | 46.005 |
| 22 | 9.933 | 12.100 | 14.713 | 17.861 | 21.644 | 26.186 | 31.629 | 38.141 | 45.923 | 55.205 |
| 23 | 11.026 | 13.552 | 16.626 | 20.361 | 24.891 | 30.376 | 37.005 | 45.007 | 54.648 | 66.247 |
| 24 | 12.239 | 15.178 | 18.788 | 23.212 | 28.625 | 35.236 | 43.296 | 53.108 | 65.031 | 79.496 |
| 25 | 13.585 | 17.000 | 21.230 | 26.461 | 32.918 | 40.874 | 50.656 | 62.667 | 77.387 | 95.395 |
| 30 | 22.892 | 29.960 | 39.115 | 50.949 | 66.210 | 85.849 | 111.061 | 143.367 | 184.672 | 237.373 |
| 40 | 64.999 | 93.049 | 132.776 | 188.876 | 267.856 | 378.715 | 533.846 | 750.353 | 1051.642 | 1469.740 |
| 50 | 184.559 | 288.996 | 450.711 | 700.197 | 1083.619 | 1670.669 | 2566.080 | 3927.189 | 5988.730 | 9100.191 |

**Appendix A**  COMPOUND SUM OF $1 (cont.)

| n | 21% | 22% | 23% | 24% | 25% | 26% | 27% | 28% | 29% | 30% |
|---|---|---|---|---|---|---|---|---|---|---|
| 1 | 1.210 | 1.220 | 1.230 | 1.240 | 1.250 | 1.260 | 1.270 | 1.280 | 1.290 | 1.300 |
| 2 | 1.464 | 1.488 | 1.513 | 1.538 | 1.562 | 1.588 | 1.613 | 1.638 | 1.664 | 1.690 |
| 3 | 1.772 | 1.816 | 1.861 | 1.907 | 1.953 | 2.000 | 2.048 | 2.097 | 2.147 | 2.197 |
| 4 | 2.144 | 2.215 | 2.289 | 2.364 | 2.441 | 2.520 | 2.601 | 2.684 | 2.769 | 2.856 |
| 5 | 2.594 | 2.703 | 2.815 | 2.932 | 3.052 | 3.176 | 3.304 | 3.436 | 3.572 | 3.713 |
| 6 | 3.138 | 3.297 | 3.463 | 3.635 | 3.815 | 4.001 | 4.196 | 4.398 | 4.608 | 4.827 |
| 7 | 3.797 | 4.023 | 4.259 | 4.508 | 4.768 | 5.042 | 5.329 | 5.629 | 5.945 | 6.275 |
| 8 | 4.595 | 4.908 | 5.239 | 5.589 | 5.960 | 6.353 | 6.767 | 7.206 | 7.669 | 8.157 |
| 9 | 5.560 | 5.987 | 6.444 | 6.931 | 7.451 | 8.004 | 8.595 | 9.223 | 9.893 | 10.604 |
| 10 | 6.727 | 7.305 | 7.926 | 8.594 | 9.313 | 10.086 | 10.915 | 11.806 | 12.761 | 13.786 |
| 11 | 8.140 | 8.912 | 9.749 | 10.657 | 11.642 | 12.708 | 13.862 | 15.112 | 16.462 | 17.921 |
| 12 | 9.850 | 10.872 | 11.991 | 13.215 | 14.552 | 16.012 | 17.605 | 19.343 | 21.236 | 23.298 |
| 13 | 11.918 | 13.264 | 14.749 | 16.386 | 18.190 | 20.175 | 22.359 | 24.759 | 27.395 | 30.287 |
| 14 | 14.421 | 16.182 | 18.141 | 20.319 | 22.737 | 25.420 | 28.395 | 31.691 | 35.339 | 39.373 |
| 15 | 17.449 | 19.742 | 22.314 | 25.195 | 28.422 | 32.030 | 36.062 | 40.565 | 45.587 | 51.185 |
| 16 | 21.113 | 24.085 | 27.446 | 31.242 | 35.527 | 40.357 | 45.799 | 51.923 | 58.808 | 66.541 |
| 17 | 25.547 | 29.384 | 33.758 | 38.740 | 44.409 | 50.850 | 58.165 | 66.461 | 75.862 | 86.503 |
| 18 | 30.912 | 35.848 | 41.523 | 48.038 | 55.511 | 64.071 | 73.869 | 85.070 | 97.862 | 112.454 |
| 19 | 37.404 | 43.735 | 51.073 | 59.567 | 69.389 | 80.730 | 93.813 | 108.890 | 126.242 | 146.190 |
| 20 | 45.258 | 53.357 | 62.820 | 73.863 | 86.736 | 101.720 | 119.143 | 139.379 | 162.852 | 190.047 |
| 21 | 54.762 | 65.095 | 77.268 | 91.591 | 108.420 | 128.167 | 151.312 | 178.405 | 210.079 | 247.061 |
| 22 | 66.262 | 79.416 | 95.040 | 113.572 | 135.525 | 161.490 | 192.165 | 228.358 | 271.002 | 321.178 |
| 23 | 80.178 | 96.887 | 116.899 | 140.829 | 169.407 | 203.477 | 244.050 | 292.298 | 349.592 | 417.531 |
| 24 | 97.015 | 118.203 | 143.786 | 174.628 | 211.758 | 256.381 | 309.943 | 374.141 | 450.974 | 542.791 |
| 25 | 117.388 | 144.207 | 176.857 | 216.539 | 264.698 | 323.040 | 393.628 | 478.901 | 581.756 | 705.627 |
| 30 | 304.471 | 389.748 | 497.904 | 634.810 | 807.793 | 1025.904 | 1300.477 | 1645.488 | 2078.208 | 2619.936 |
| 40 | 2048.309 | 2846.941 | 3946.340 | 5455.797 | 7523.156 | 10346.879 | 14195.051 | 19426.418 | 26520.723 | 36117.754 |
| 50 | 13779.844 | 20795.680 | 31278.301 | 46889.207 | 70064.812 | 104354.562 | 154942.687 | 229345.875 | 338440.000 | 497910.125 |

**Appendix A** COMPOUND SUM OF $1 (cont.)

| n | 31% | 32% | 33% | 34% | 35% | 36% | 37% | 38% | 39% | 40% |
|---|-----|-----|-----|-----|-----|-----|-----|-----|-----|-----|
| 1 | 1.310 | 1.320 | 1.330 | 1.340 | 1.350 | 1.360 | 1.370 | 1.380 | 1.390 | 1.400 |
| 2 | 1.716 | 1.742 | 1.769 | 1.796 | 1.822 | 1.850 | 1.877 | 1.904 | 1.932 | 1.960 |
| 3 | 2.248 | 2.300 | 2.353 | 2.406 | 2.460 | 2.515 | 2.571 | 2.628 | 2.686 | 2.744 |
| 4 | 2.945 | 3.036 | 3.129 | 3.224 | 3.321 | 3.421 | 3.523 | 3.627 | 3.733 | 3.842 |
| 5 | 3.858 | 4.007 | 4.162 | 4.320 | 4.484 | 4.653 | 4.826 | 5.005 | 5.189 | 5.378 |
| 6 | 5.054 | 5.290 | 5.535 | 5.789 | 6.053 | 6.328 | 6.612 | 6.907 | 7.213 | 7.530 |
| 7 | 6.621 | 6.983 | 7.361 | 7.758 | 8.172 | 8.605 | 9.058 | 9.531 | 10.025 | 10.541 |
| 8 | 8.673 | 9.217 | 9.791 | 10.395 | 11.032 | 11.703 | 12.410 | 13.153 | 13.935 | 14.758 |
| 9 | 11.362 | 12.166 | 13.022 | 13.930 | 14.894 | 15.917 | 17.001 | 18.151 | 19.370 | 20.661 |
| 10 | 14.884 | 16.060 | 17.319 | 18.666 | 20.106 | 21.646 | 23.292 | 25.049 | 26.924 | 28.925 |
| 11 | 19.498 | 21.199 | 23.034 | 25.012 | 27.144 | 29.439 | 31.910 | 34.567 | 37.425 | 40.495 |
| 12 | 25.542 | 27.982 | 30.635 | 33.516 | 36.644 | 40.037 | 43.716 | 47.703 | 52.020 | 56.694 |
| 13 | 33.460 | 36.937 | 40.745 | 44.912 | 49.469 | 54.451 | 59.892 | 65.830 | 72.308 | 79.371 |
| 14 | 43.832 | 48.756 | 54.190 | 60.181 | 66.784 | 74.053 | 82.051 | 90.845 | 100.509 | 111.119 |
| 15 | 57.420 | 64.358 | 72.073 | 80.643 | 90.158 | 100.712 | 112.410 | 125.366 | 139.707 | 155.567 |
| 16 | 75.220 | 84.953 | 95.857 | 108.061 | 121.713 | 136.968 | 154.002 | 173.005 | 194.192 | 217.793 |
| 17 | 98.539 | 112.138 | 127.490 | 144.802 | 164.312 | 186.277 | 210.983 | 238.747 | 269.927 | 304.911 |
| 18 | 129.086 | 148.022 | 169.561 | 194.035 | 221.822 | 253.337 | 289.046 | 329.471 | 375.198 | 426.875 |
| 19 | 169.102 | 195.389 | 225.517 | 260.006 | 299.459 | 344.537 | 395.993 | 454.669 | 521.525 | 597.625 |
| 20 | 221.523 | 257.913 | 299.937 | 348.408 | 404.270 | 468.571 | 542.511 | 627.443 | 724.919 | 836.674 |
| 21 | 290.196 | 340.446 | 398.916 | 466.867 | 545.764 | 637.256 | 743.240 | 865.871 | 1007.637 | 1171.343 |
| 22 | 380.156 | 449.388 | 530.558 | 625.601 | 736.781 | 866.668 | 1018.238 | 1194.900 | 1400.615 | 1639.878 |
| 23 | 498.004 | 593.192 | 705.642 | 838.305 | 994.653 | 1178.668 | 1394.986 | 1648.961 | 1946.854 | 2295.829 |
| 24 | 652.385 | 783.013 | 938.504 | 1123.328 | 1342.781 | 1602.988 | 1911.129 | 2275.564 | 2706.125 | 3214.158 |
| 25 | 854.623 | 1033.577 | 1248.210 | 1505.258 | 1812.754 | 2180.063 | 2618.245 | 3140.275 | 3761.511 | 4499.816 |
| 30 | 3297.081 | 4142.008 | 5194.516 | 6503.285 | 8128.426 | 10142.914 | 12636.086 | 15716.703 | 19517.969 | 24201.043 |
| 40 | 49072.621 | 66519.313 | 89962.188 | 121388.437 | 163433.875 | 219558.625 | 294317.937 | 393684.687 | 525508.312 | 700022.688 |

**Appendix B** PRESENT VALUE OF $1

| n | 1% | 2% | 3% | 4% | 5% | 6% | 7% | 8% | 9% | 10% |
|---|---|---|---|---|---|---|---|---|---|---|
| 1 | .990 | .980 | .971 | .962 | .952 | .943 | .935 | .926 | .917 | .909 |
| 2 | .980 | .961 | .943 | .925 | .907 | .890 | .873 | .857 | .842 | .826 |
| 3 | .971 | .942 | .915 | .889 | .864 | .840 | .816 | .794 | .772 | .751 |
| 4 | .961 | .924 | .888 | .855 | .823 | .792 | .763 | .735 | .708 | .683 |
| 5 | .951 | .906 | .863 | .822 | .784 | .747 | .713 | .681 | .650 | .621 |
| 6 | .942 | .888 | .837 | .790 | .746 | .705 | .666 | .630 | .596 | .564 |
| 7 | .933 | .871 | .813 | .760 | .711 | .665 | .623 | .583 | .547 | .513 |
| 8 | .923 | .853 | .789 | .731 | .677 | .627 | .582 | .540 | .502 | .467 |
| 9 | .914 | .837 | .766 | .703 | .645 | .592 | .544 | .500 | .460 | .424 |
| 10 | .905 | .820 | .744 | .676 | .614 | .558 | .508 | .463 | .422 | .386 |
| 11 | .896 | .804 | .722 | .650 | .585 | .527 | .475 | .429 | .388 | .350 |
| 12 | .887 | .789 | .701 | .625 | .557 | .497 | .444 | .397 | .356 | .319 |
| 13 | .879 | .773 | .681 | .601 | .530 | .469 | .415 | .368 | .326 | .290 |
| 14 | .870 | .758 | .661 | .577 | .505 | .442 | .388 | .340 | .299 | .263 |
| 15 | .861 | .743 | .642 | .555 | .481 | .417 | .362 | .315 | .275 | .239 |
| 16 | .853 | .728 | .623 | .534 | .458 | .394 | .339 | .292 | .252 | .218 |
| 17 | .844 | .714 | .605 | .513 | .436 | .371 | .317 | .270 | .231 | .198 |
| 18 | .836 | .700 | .587 | .494 | .416 | .350 | .296 | .250 | .212 | .180 |
| 19 | .828 | .686 | .570 | .475 | .396 | .331 | .277 | .232 | .194 | .164 |
| 20 | .820 | .673 | .554 | .456 | .377 | .312 | .258 | .215 | .178 | .149 |
| 21 | .811 | .660 | .538 | .439 | .359 | .294 | .242 | .199 | .164 | .135 |
| 22 | .803 | .647 | .522 | .422 | .342 | .278 | .226 | .184 | .150 | .123 |
| 23 | .795 | .634 | .507 | .406 | .326 | .262 | .211 | .170 | .138 | .112 |
| 24 | .788 | .622 | .492 | .390 | .310 | .247 | .197 | .158 | .126 | .102 |
| 25 | .780 | .610 | .478 | .375 | .295 | .233 | .184 | .146 | .116 | .092 |
| 30 | .742 | .552 | .412 | .308 | .231 | .174 | .131 | .099 | .075 | .057 |
| 40 | .672 | .453 | .307 | .208 | .142 | .097 | .067 | .046 | .032 | .022 |
| 50 | .608 | .372 | .228 | .141 | .087 | .054 | .034 | .021 | .013 | .009 |

**Appendix B** PRESENT VALUE OF $1 (cont.)

| n | 11% | 12% | 13% | 14% | 15% | 16% | 17% | 18% | 19% | 20% |
|---|-----|-----|-----|-----|-----|-----|-----|-----|-----|-----|
| 1 | .901 | .893 | .885 | .877 | .870 | .862 | .855 | .847 | .840 | .833 |
| 2 | .812 | .797 | .783 | .769 | .756 | .743 | .731 | .718 | .706 | .694 |
| 3 | .731 | .712 | .693 | .675 | .658 | .641 | .624 | .609 | .593 | .579 |
| 4 | .659 | .636 | .613 | .592 | .572 | .552 | .534 | .516 | .499 | .482 |
| 5 | .593 | .567 | .543 | .519 | .497 | .476 | .456 | .437 | .419 | .402 |
| 6 | .535 | .507 | .480 | .456 | .432 | .410 | .390 | .370 | .352 | .335 |
| 7 | .482 | .452 | .425 | .400 | .376 | .354 | .333 | .314 | .296 | .279 |
| 8 | .434 | .404 | .376 | .351 | .327 | .305 | .285 | .266 | .249 | .233 |
| 9 | .391 | .361 | .333 | .308 | .284 | .263 | .243 | .225 | .209 | .194 |
| 10 | .352 | .322 | .295 | .270 | .247 | .227 | .208 | .191 | .176 | .162 |
| 11 | .317 | .287 | .261 | .237 | .215 | .195 | .178 | .162 | .148 | .135 |
| 12 | .286 | .257 | .231 | .208 | .187 | .168 | .152 | .137 | .124 | .112 |
| 13 | .258 | .229 | .204 | .182 | .163 | .145 | .130 | .116 | .104 | .093 |
| 14 | .232 | .205 | .181 | .160 | .141 | .125 | .111 | .099 | .088 | .078 |
| 15 | .209 | .183 | .160 | .140 | .123 | .108 | .095 | .084 | .074 | .065 |
| 16 | .188 | .163 | .141 | .123 | .107 | .093 | .081 | .071 | .062 | .054 |
| 17 | .170 | .146 | .125 | .108 | .093 | .080 | .069 | .060 | .052 | .045 |
| 18 | .153 | .130 | .111 | .095 | .081 | .069 | .059 | .051 | .044 | .038 |
| 19 | .138 | .116 | .098 | .083 | .070 | .060 | .051 | .043 | .037 | .031 |
| 20 | .124 | .104 | .087 | .073 | .061 | .051 | .043 | .037 | .031 | .026 |
| 21 | .112 | .093 | .077 | .064 | .053 | .044 | .037 | .031 | .026 | .022 |
| 22 | .101 | .083 | .068 | .056 | .046 | .038 | .032 | .026 | .022 | .018 |
| 23 | .091 | .074 | .060 | .049 | .040 | .033 | .027 | .022 | .018 | .015 |
| 24 | .082 | .066 | .053 | .043 | .035 | .028 | .023 | .019 | .015 | .013 |
| 25 | .074 | .059 | .047 | .038 | .030 | .024 | .020 | .016 | .013 | .010 |
| 30 | .044 | .033 | .026 | .020 | .015 | .012 | .009 | .007 | .005 | .004 |
| 40 | .015 | .011 | .008 | .005 | .004 | .003 | .002 | .001 | .001 | .001 |
| 50 | .005 | .003 | .002 | .001 | .001 | .001 | .000 | .000 | .000 | .000 |

**Appendix B** PRESENT VALUE OF $1 (cont.)

| n | 21% | 22% | 23% | 24% | 25% | 26% | 27% | 28% | 29% | 30% |
|---|-----|-----|-----|-----|-----|-----|-----|-----|-----|-----|
| 1 | .826 | .820 | .813 | .806 | .800 | .794 | .787 | .781 | .775 | .769 |
| 2 | .683 | .672 | .661 | .650 | .640 | .630 | .620 | .610 | .601 | .592 |
| 3 | .564 | .551 | .537 | .524 | .512 | .500 | .488 | .477 | .466 | .455 |
| 4 | .467 | .451 | .437 | .423 | .410 | .397 | .384 | .373 | .361 | .350 |
| 5 | .386 | .370 | .355 | .341 | .328 | .315 | .303 | .291 | .280 | .269 |
| 6 | .319 | .303 | .289 | .275 | .262 | .250 | .238 | .227 | .217 | .207 |
| 7 | .263 | .249 | .235 | .222 | .210 | .198 | .188 | .178 | .168 | .159 |
| 8 | .218 | .204 | .191 | .179 | .168 | .157 | .148 | .139 | .130 | .123 |
| 9 | .180 | .167 | .155 | .144 | .134 | .125 | .116 | .108 | .101 | .094 |
| 10 | .149 | .137 | .126 | .116 | .107 | .099 | .092 | .085 | .078 | .073 |
| 11 | .123 | .112 | .103 | .094 | .086 | .079 | .072 | .066 | .061 | .056 |
| 12 | .102 | .092 | .083 | .076 | .069 | .062 | .057 | .052 | .047 | .043 |
| 13 | .084 | .075 | .068 | .061 | .055 | .050 | .045 | .040 | .037 | .033 |
| 14 | .069 | .062 | .055 | .049 | .044 | .039 | .035 | .032 | .028 | .025 |
| 15 | .057 | .051 | .045 | .040 | .035 | .031 | .028 | .025 | .022 | .020 |
| 16 | .047 | .042 | .036 | .032 | .028 | .025 | .022 | .019 | .017 | .015 |
| 17 | .039 | .034 | .030 | .026 | .023 | .020 | .017 | .015 | .013 | .012 |
| 18 | .032 | .028 | .024 | .021 | .018 | .016 | .014 | .012 | .010 | .009 |
| 19 | .027 | .023 | .020 | .017 | .014 | .012 | .011 | .009 | .008 | .007 |
| 20 | .022 | .019 | .016 | .014 | .012 | .010 | .008 | .007 | .006 | .005 |
| 21 | .018 | .015 | .013 | .011 | .009 | .008 | .007 | .006 | .005 | .004 |
| 22 | .015 | .013 | .011 | .009 | .007 | .006 | .005 | .004 | .004 | .003 |
| 23 | .012 | .010 | .009 | .007 | .006 | .005 | .004 | .003 | .003 | .002 |
| 24 | .010 | .008 | .007 | .006 | .005 | .004 | .003 | .003 | .002 | .002 |
| 25 | .009 | .007 | .006 | .005 | .004 | .003 | .003 | .002 | .002 | .001 |
| 30 | .003 | .003 | .002 | .002 | .001 | .001 | .001 | .001 | .000 | .000 |
| 40 | .000 | .000 | .000 | .000 | .000 | .000 | .000 | .000 | .000 | .000 |
| 50 | .000 | .000 | .000 | .000 | .000 | .000 | .000 | .000 | .000 | .000 |

**Appendix B** PRESENT VALUE OF $1 *(cont.)*

| n | 31% | 32% | 33% | 34% | 35% | 36% | 37% | 38% | 39% | 40% |
|---|-----|-----|-----|-----|-----|-----|-----|-----|-----|-----|
| 1 | .763 | .758 | .752 | .746 | .741 | .735 | .730 | .725 | .719 | .714 |
| 2 | .583 | .574 | .565 | .557 | .549 | .541 | .533 | .525 | .518 | .510 |
| 3 | .445 | .435 | .425 | .416 | .406 | .398 | .389 | .381 | .372 | .364 |
| 4 | .340 | .329 | .320 | .310 | .301 | .292 | .284 | .276 | .268 | .260 |
| 5 | .259 | .250 | .240 | .231 | .223 | .215 | .207 | .200 | .193 | .186 |
| 6 | .198 | .189 | .181 | .173 | .165 | .158 | .151 | .145 | .139 | .133 |
| 7 | .151 | .143 | .136 | .129 | .122 | .116 | .110 | .105 | .100 | .095 |
| 8 | .115 | .108 | .102 | .096 | .091 | .085 | .081 | .076 | .072 | .068 |
| 9 | .088 | .082 | .077 | .072 | .067 | .063 | .059 | .055 | .052 | .048 |
| 10 | .067 | .062 | .058 | .054 | .050 | .046 | .043 | .040 | .037 | .035 |
| 11 | .051 | .047 | .043 | .040 | .037 | .034 | .031 | .029 | .027 | .025 |
| 12 | .039 | .036 | .033 | .030 | .027 | .025 | .023 | .021 | .019 | .018 |
| 13 | .030 | .027 | .025 | .022 | .020 | .018 | .017 | .015 | .014 | .013 |
| 14 | .023 | .021 | .018 | .017 | .015 | .014 | .012 | .011 | .010 | .009 |
| 15 | .017 | .016 | .014 | .012 | .011 | .010 | .009 | .008 | .007 | .006 |
| 16 | .013 | .012 | .010 | .009 | .008 | .007 | .006 | .006 | .005 | .005 |
| 17 | .010 | .009 | .008 | .007 | .006 | .005 | .005 | .004 | .004 | .003 |
| 18 | .008 | .007 | .006 | .005 | .005 | .004 | .003 | .003 | .003 | .002 |
| 19 | .006 | .005 | .004 | .004 | .003 | .003 | .003 | .002 | .002 | .002 |
| 20 | .005 | .004 | .003 | .003 | .002 | .002 | .002 | .002 | .001 | .001 |
| 21 | .003 | .003 | .003 | .002 | .002 | .002 | .001 | .001 | .001 | .001 |
| 22 | .003 | .002 | .002 | .002 | .001 | .001 | .001 | .001 | .001 | .001 |
| 23 | .002 | .002 | .001 | .001 | .001 | .001 | .001 | .001 | .001 | .000 |
| 24 | .002 | .001 | .001 | .001 | .001 | .001 | .001 | .000 | .000 | .000 |
| 25 | .001 | .001 | .001 | .001 | .001 | .000 | .000 | .000 | .000 | .000 |
| 30 | .000 | .000 | .000 | .000 | .000 | .000 | .000 | .000 | .000 | .000 |
| 40 | .000 | .000 | .000 | .000 | .000 | .000 | .000 | .000 | .000 | .000 |

**Appendix C**  SUM OF AN ANNUITY OF $1 FOR *n* PERIODS

| n | 1% | 2% | 3% | 4% | 5% | 6% | 7% | 8% | 9% | 10% |
|---|----|----|----|----|----|----|----|----|----|-----|
| 1 | 1.000 | 1.000 | 1.000 | 1.000 | 1.000 | 1.000 | 1.000 | 1.000 | 1.000 | 1.000 |
| 2 | 2.010 | 2.020 | 2.030 | 2.040 | 2.050 | 2.060 | 2.070 | 2.080 | 2.090 | 2.100 |
| 3 | 3.030 | 3.060 | 3.091 | 3.122 | 3.152 | 3.184 | 3.215 | 3.246 | 3.278 | 3.310 |
| 4 | 4.060 | 4.122 | 4.184 | 4.246 | 4.310 | 4.375 | 4.440 | 4.506 | 4.573 | 4.641 |
| 5 | 5.101 | 5.204 | 5.309 | 5.416 | 5.526 | 5.637 | 5.751 | 5.867 | 5.985 | 6.105 |
| 6 | 6.152 | 6.308 | 6.468 | 6.633 | 6.802 | 6.975 | 7.153 | 7.336 | 7.523 | 7.716 |
| 7 | 7.214 | 7.434 | 7.662 | 7.898 | 8.142 | 8.394 | 8.654 | 8.923 | 9.200 | 9.487 |
| 8 | 8.286 | 8.583 | 8.892 | 9.214 | 9.549 | 9.897 | 10.260 | 10.637 | 11.028 | 11.436 |
| 9 | 9.368 | 9.755 | 10.159 | 10.583 | 11.027 | 11.491 | 11.978 | 12.488 | 13.021 | 13.579 |
| 10 | 10.462 | 10.950 | 11.464 | 12.006 | 12.578 | 13.181 | 13.816 | 14.487 | 15.193 | 15.937 |
| 11 | 11.567 | 12.169 | 12.808 | 13.486 | 14.207 | 14.972 | 15.784 | 16.645 | 17.560 | 18.531 |
| 12 | 12.682 | 13.412 | 14.192 | 15.026 | 15.917 | 16.870 | 17.888 | 18.977 | 20.141 | 21.384 |
| 13 | 13.809 | 14.680 | 15.618 | 16.627 | 17.713 | 18.882 | 20.141 | 21.495 | 22.953 | 24.523 |
| 14 | 14.947 | 15.974 | 17.086 | 18.292 | 19.598 | 21.015 | 22.550 | 24.215 | 26.019 | 27.975 |
| 15 | 16.097 | 17.293 | 18.599 | 20.023 | 21.578 | 23.276 | 25.129 | 27.152 | 29.361 | 31.772 |
| 16 | 17.258 | 18.639 | 20.157 | 21.824 | 23.657 | 25.672 | 27.888 | 30.324 | 33.003 | 35.949 |
| 17 | 18.430 | 20.012 | 21.761 | 23.697 | 25.840 | 28.213 | 30.840 | 33.750 | 36.973 | 40.544 |
| 18 | 19.614 | 21.412 | 23.414 | 25.645 | 28.132 | 30.905 | 33.999 | 37.450 | 41.301 | 45.599 |
| 19 | 20.811 | 22.840 | 25.117 | 27.671 | 30.539 | 33.760 | 37.379 | 41.446 | 46.018 | 51.158 |
| 20 | 22.019 | 24.297 | 26.870 | 29.778 | 33.066 | 36.785 | 40.995 | 45.762 | 51.159 | 57.274 |
| 21 | 23.239 | 25.783 | 28.676 | 31.969 | 35.719 | 39.992 | 44.865 | 50.422 | 56.764 | 64.002 |
| 22 | 24.471 | 27.299 | 30.536 | 34.248 | 38.505 | 43.392 | 49.005 | 55.456 | 62.872 | 71.402 |
| 23 | 25.716 | 28.845 | 32.452 | 36.618 | 41.430 | 46.995 | 53.435 | 60.893 | 69.531 | 79.542 |
| 24 | 26.973 | 30.421 | 34.426 | 39.082 | 44.501 | 50.815 | 58.176 | 66.764 | 76.789 | 88.496 |
| 25 | 28.243 | 32.030 | 36.459 | 41.645 | 47.726 | 54.864 | 63.248 | 73.105 | 84.699 | 98.346 |
| 30 | 34.784 | 40.567 | 47.575 | 56.084 | 66.438 | 79.057 | 94.459 | 113.282 | 136.305 | 164.491 |
| 40 | 48.885 | 60.401 | 75.400 | 95.024 | 120.797 | 154.758 | 199.630 | 259.052 | 337.872 | 442.580 |
| 50 | 64.461 | 84.577 | 112.794 | 152.664 | 209.341 | 290.325 | 406.516 | 573.756 | 815.051 | 1163.865 |

**Appendix C SUM OF AN ANNUITY OF $1 FOR *n* PERIODS** (cont.)

| n | 11% | 12% | 13% | 14% | 15% | 16% | 17% | 18% | 19% | 20% |
|---|---|---|---|---|---|---|---|---|---|---|
| 1 | 1.000 | 1.000 | 1.000 | 1.000 | 1.000 | 1.000 | 1.000 | 1.000 | 1.000 | 1.000 |
| 2 | 2.110 | 2.120 | 2.130 | 2.140 | 2.150 | 2.160 | 2.170 | 2.180 | 2.190 | 2.200 |
| 3 | 3.342 | 3.374 | 3.407 | 3.440 | 3.472 | 3.506 | 3.539 | 3.572 | 3.606 | 3.640 |
| 4 | 4.710 | 4.779 | 4.850 | 4.921 | 4.993 | 5.066 | 5.141 | 5.215 | 5.291 | 5.368 |
| 5 | 6.228 | 6.353 | 6.480 | 6.610 | 6.742 | 6.877 | 7.014 | 7.154 | 7.297 | 7.442 |
| 6 | 7.913 | 8.115 | 8.323 | 8.535 | 8.754 | 8.977 | 9.207 | 9.442 | 9.683 | 9.930 |
| 7 | 9.783 | 10.089 | 10.405 | 10.730 | 11.067 | 11.414 | 11.772 | 12.141 | 12.523 | 12.916 |
| 8 | 11.859 | 12.300 | 12.757 | 13.233 | 13.727 | 14.240 | 14.773 | 15.327 | 15.902 | 16.499 |
| 9 | 14.164 | 14.776 | 15.416 | 16.085 | 16.786 | 17.518 | 18.285 | 19.086 | 19.923 | 20.799 |
| 10 | 16.722 | 17.549 | 18.420 | 19.337 | 20.304 | 21.321 | 22.393 | 23.521 | 24.709 | 25.959 |
| 11 | 19.561 | 20.655 | 21.814 | 23.044 | 24.349 | 25.733 | 27.200 | 28.755 | 30.403 | 32.150 |
| 12 | 22.713 | 24.133 | 25.650 | 27.271 | 29.001 | 30.850 | 32.824 | 34.931 | 37.180 | 39.580 |
| 13 | 26.211 | 28.029 | 29.984 | 32.088 | 34.352 | 36.786 | 39.404 | 42.218 | 45.244 | 48.496 |
| 14 | 30.095 | 32.392 | 34.882 | 37.581 | 40.504 | 43.672 | 47.102 | 50.818 | 54.841 | 59.196 |
| 15 | 34.405 | 37.280 | 40.417 | 43.842 | 47.580 | 51.659 | 56.109 | 60.965 | 66.260 | 72.035 |
| 16 | 39.190 | 42.753 | 46.671 | 50.980 | 55.717 | 60.925 | 66.648 | 72.938 | 79.850 | 87.442 |
| 17 | 44.500 | 48.883 | 53.738 | 59.117 | 65.075 | 71.673 | 78.978 | 87.067 | 96.021 | 105.930 |
| 18 | 50.396 | 55.749 | 61.724 | 68.393 | 75.836 | 84.140 | 93.404 | 103.739 | 115.265 | 128.116 |
| 19 | 56.939 | 63.439 | 70.748 | 78.968 | 88.211 | 98.603 | 110.283 | 123.412 | 138.165 | 154.739 |
| 20 | 64.202 | 72.052 | 80.946 | 91.024 | 102.443 | 115.379 | 130.031 | 146.626 | 165.417 | 186.687 |
| 21 | 72.264 | 81.698 | 92.468 | 104.767 | 118.809 | 134.840 | 153.136 | 174.019 | 197.846 | 225.024 |
| 22 | 81.213 | 92.502 | 105.489 | 120.434 | 137.630 | 157.414 | 180.169 | 206.342 | 236.436 | 271.028 |
| 23 | 91.147 | 104.602 | 120.203 | 138.295 | 159.274 | 183.600 | 211.798 | 244.483 | 282.359 | 326.234 |
| 24 | 102.173 | 118.154 | 136.829 | 158.656 | 184.166 | 213.976 | 248.803 | 289.490 | 337.007 | 392.480 |
| 25 | 114.412 | 133.333 | 155.616 | 181.867 | 212.790 | 249.212 | 292.099 | 342.598 | 402.038 | 471.976 |
| 30 | 199.018 | 241.330 | 293.192 | 356.778 | 434.738 | 530.306 | 647.423 | 790.932 | 966.698 | 1181.865 |
| 40 | 581.812 | 767.080 | 1013.667 | 1341.979 | 1779.048 | 2360.724 | 3134.412 | 4163.094 | 5529.711 | 7343.715 |
| 50 | 1668.723 | 2399.975 | 3459.344 | 4994.301 | 7217.488 | 10435.449 | 15088.805 | 21812.273 | 31514.492 | 45496.094 |

**Appendix C SUM OF AN ANNUITY OF $1 FOR n PERIODS (cont.)**

| n | 21% | 22% | 23% | 24% | 25% | 26% | 27% | 28% | 29% | 30% |
|---|---|---|---|---|---|---|---|---|---|---|
| 1 | 1.000 | 1.000 | 1.000 | 1.000 | 1.000 | 1.000 | 1.000 | 1.000 | 1.000 | 1.000 |
| 2 | 2.210 | 2.220 | 2.230 | 2.240 | 2.250 | 2.260 | 2.270 | 2.280 | 2.290 | 2.300 |
| 3 | 3.674 | 3.708 | 3.743 | 3.778 | 3.813 | 3.848 | 3.883 | 3.918 | 3.954 | 3.990 |
| 4 | 5.446 | 5.524 | 5.604 | 5.684 | 5.766 | 5.848 | 5.931 | 6.016 | 6.101 | 6.187 |
| 5 | 7.589 | 7.740 | 7.893 | 8.048 | 8.207 | 8.368 | 8.533 | 8.700 | 8.870 | 9.043 |
| 6 | 10.183 | 10.442 | 10.708 | 10.980 | 11.259 | 11.544 | 11.837 | 12.136 | 12.442 | 12.756 |
| 7 | 13.321 | 13.740 | 14.171 | 14.615 | 15.073 | 15.546 | 16.032 | 16.534 | 17.051 | 17.583 |
| 8 | 17.119 | 17.762 | 18.430 | 19.123 | 19.842 | 20.588 | 21.361 | 22.163 | 22.995 | 23.858 |
| 9 | 21.714 | 22.670 | 23.669 | 24.712 | 25.802 | 26.940 | 28.129 | 29.369 | 30.664 | 32.015 |
| 10 | 27.274 | 28.657 | 30.113 | 31.643 | 33.253 | 34.945 | 36.723 | 38.592 | 40.556 | 42.619 |
| 11 | 34.001 | 35.962 | 38.039 | 40.238 | 42.566 | 45.030 | 47.639 | 50.398 | 53.318 | 56.405 |
| 12 | 42.141 | 44.873 | 47.787 | 50.895 | 54.208 | 57.738 | 61.501 | 65.510 | 69.780 | 74.326 |
| 13 | 51.991 | 55.745 | 59.778 | 64.109 | 68.760 | 73.750 | 79.106 | 84.853 | 91.016 | 97.624 |
| 14 | 63.909 | 69.009 | 74.528 | 80.496 | 86.949 | 93.925 | 101.465 | 109.611 | 118.411 | 127.912 |
| 15 | 78.330 | 85.191 | 92.669 | 100.815 | 109.687 | 119.346 | 129.860 | 141.302 | 153.750 | 167.285 |
| 16 | 95.779 | 104.933 | 114.983 | 126.010 | 138.109 | 151.375 | 165.922 | 181.867 | 199.337 | 218.470 |
| 17 | 116.892 | 129.019 | 142.428 | 157.252 | 173.636 | 191.733 | 211.721 | 233.790 | 258.145 | 285.011 |
| 18 | 142.439 | 158.403 | 176.187 | 195.993 | 218.045 | 242.583 | 269.885 | 300.250 | 334.006 | 371.514 |
| 19 | 173.351 | 194.251 | 217.710 | 244.031 | 273.556 | 306.654 | 343.754 | 385.321 | 431.868 | 483.968 |
| 20 | 210.755 | 237.986 | 268.783 | 303.598 | 342.945 | 387.384 | 437.568 | 494.210 | 558.110 | 630.157 |
| 21 | 256.013 | 291.343 | 331.603 | 377.461 | 429.681 | 489.104 | 556.710 | 633.589 | 720.962 | 820.204 |
| 22 | 310.775 | 356.438 | 408.871 | 469.052 | 538.101 | 617.270 | 708.022 | 811.993 | 931.040 | 1067.265 |
| 23 | 377.038 | 435.854 | 503.911 | 582.624 | 673.626 | 778.760 | 900.187 | 1040.351 | 1202.042 | 1388.443 |
| 24 | 457.215 | 532.741 | 620.810 | 723.453 | 843.032 | 982.237 | 1144.237 | 1332.649 | 1551.634 | 1805.975 |
| 25 | 554.230 | 650.944 | 764.596 | 898.082 | 1054.791 | 1238.617 | 1454.180 | 1706.790 | 2002.608 | 2348.765 |
| 30 | 1445.111 | 1767.044 | 2160.459 | 2640.881 | 3227.172 | 3941.953 | 4812.891 | 5873.172 | 7162.785 | 8729.805 |
| 40 | 9749.141 | 12936.141 | 17153.691 | 22728.367 | 30088.621 | 39791.957 | 52570.707 | 69376.562 | 91447.375 | 120389.375 |

**Appendix C** SUM OF AN ANNUITY OF $1 FOR n PERIODS (cont.)

| n | 31% | 32% | 33% | 34% | 35% | 36% | 37% | 38% | 39% | 40% |
|---|---|---|---|---|---|---|---|---|---|---|
| 1 | 1.000 | 1.000 | 1.000 | 1.000 | 1.000 | 1.000 | 1.000 | 1.000 | 1.000 | 1.000 |
| 2 | 2.310 | 2.320 | 2.330 | 2.340 | 2.350 | 2.360 | 2.370 | 2.380 | 2.390 | 2.400 |
| 3 | 4.026 | 4.062 | 4.099 | 4.136 | 4.172 | 4.210 | 4.247 | 4.284 | 4.322 | 4.360 |
| 4 | 6.274 | 6.362 | 6.452 | 6.542 | 6.633 | 6.725 | 6.818 | 6.912 | 7.008 | 7.104 |
| 5 | 9.219 | 9.398 | 9.581 | 9.766 | 9.954 | 10.146 | 10.341 | 10.539 | 10.741 | 10.946 |
| 6 | 13.077 | 13.406 | 13.742 | 14.086 | 14.438 | 14.799 | 15.167 | 15.544 | 15.930 | 16.324 |
| 7 | 18.131 | 18.696 | 19.277 | 19.876 | 20.492 | 21.126 | 21.779 | 22.451 | 23.142 | 23.853 |
| 8 | 24.752 | 25.678 | 26.638 | 27.633 | 28.664 | 29.732 | 30.837 | 31.982 | 33.167 | 34.395 |
| 9 | 33.425 | 34.895 | 36.429 | 38.028 | 39.696 | 41.435 | 43.247 | 45.135 | 47.103 | 49.152 |
| 10 | 44.786 | 47.062 | 49.451 | 51.958 | 54.590 | 57.351 | 60.248 | 63.287 | 66.473 | 69.813 |
| 11 | 59.670 | 63.121 | 66.769 | 70.624 | 74.696 | 78.998 | 83.540 | 88.335 | 93.397 | 98.739 |
| 12 | 79.167 | 84.320 | 89.803 | 95.636 | 101.840 | 108.437 | 115.450 | 122.903 | 130.822 | 139.234 |
| 13 | 104.709 | 112.302 | 120.438 | 129.152 | 138.484 | 148.474 | 159.166 | 170.606 | 182.842 | 195.928 |
| 14 | 138.169 | 149.239 | 161.183 | 174.063 | 187.953 | 202.925 | 219.058 | 236.435 | 255.151 | 275.299 |
| 15 | 182.001 | 197.996 | 215.373 | 234.245 | 254.737 | 276.978 | 301.109 | 327.281 | 355.659 | 386.418 |
| 16 | 239.421 | 262.354 | 287.446 | 314.888 | 344.895 | 377.690 | 413.520 | 452.647 | 495.366 | 541.985 |
| 17 | 314.642 | 347.307 | 383.303 | 422.949 | 466.608 | 514.658 | 567.521 | 625.652 | 689.558 | 759.778 |
| 18 | 413.180 | 459.445 | 510.792 | 567.751 | 630.920 | 700.935 | 778.504 | 864.399 | 959.485 | 1064.689 |
| 19 | 542.266 | 607.467 | 680.354 | 761.786 | 852.741 | 954.271 | 1067.551 | 1193.870 | 1334.683 | 1491.563 |
| 20 | 711.368 | 802.856 | 905.870 | 1021.792 | 1152.200 | 1298.809 | 1463.544 | 1648.539 | 1856.208 | 2089.188 |
| 21 | 932.891 | 1060.769 | 1205.807 | 1370.201 | 1556.470 | 1767.380 | 2006.055 | 2275.982 | 2581.128 | 2925.862 |
| 22 | 1223.087 | 1401.215 | 1604.724 | 1837.068 | 2102.234 | 2404.636 | 2749.294 | 3141.852 | 3588.765 | 4097.203 |
| 23 | 1603.243 | 1850.603 | 2135.282 | 2462.669 | 2839.014 | 3271.304 | 3767.532 | 4336.750 | 4989.379 | 5737.078 |
| 24 | 2101.247 | 2443.795 | 2840.924 | 3300.974 | 3833.667 | 4449.969 | 5162.516 | 5985.711 | 6936.230 | 8032.906 |
| 25 | 2753.631 | 3226.808 | 3779.428 | 4424.301 | 5176.445 | 6052.957 | 7073.645 | 8261.273 | 9642.352 | 11247.062 |
| 30 | 10632.543 | 12940.672 | 15737.945 | 19124.434 | 23221.258 | 28172.016 | 34148.906 | 41357.227 | 50043.625 | 60500.207 |

**Appendix D** PRESENT VALUE OF AN ANNUITY OF $1 FOR $n$ PERIODS

| n | 1% | 2% | 3% | 4% | 5% | 6% | 7% | 8% | 9% | 10% |
|---|---|---|---|---|---|---|---|---|---|---|
| 1 | .990 | .980 | .971 | .962 | .952 | .943 | .935 | .926 | .917 | .909 |
| 2 | 1.970 | 1.942 | 1.913 | 1.886 | 1.859 | 1.833 | 1.808 | 1.783 | 1.759 | 1.736 |
| 3 | 2.941 | 2.884 | 2.829 | 2.775 | 2.723 | 2.673 | 2.624 | 2.577 | 2.531 | 2.487 |
| 4 | 3.902 | 3.808 | 3.717 | 3.630 | 3.546 | 3.465 | 3.387 | 3.312 | 3.240 | 3.170 |
| 5 | 4.853 | 4.713 | 4.580 | 4.452 | 4.329 | 4.212 | 4.100 | 3.993 | 3.890 | 3.791 |
| 6 | 5.795 | 5.601 | 5.417 | 5.242 | 5.076 | 4.917 | 4.767 | 4.623 | 4.486 | 4.355 |
| 7 | 6.728 | 6.472 | 6.230 | 6.002 | 5.786 | 5.582 | 5.389 | 5.206 | 5.033 | 4.868 |
| 8 | 7.652 | 7.326 | 7.020 | 6.733 | 6.463 | 6.210 | 5.971 | 5.747 | 5.535 | 5.335 |
| 9 | 8.566 | 8.162 | 7.786 | 7.435 | 7.108 | 6.802 | 6.515 | 6.247 | 5.995 | 5.759 |
| 10 | 9.471 | 8.983 | 8.530 | 8.111 | 7.722 | 7.360 | 7.024 | 6.710 | 6.418 | 6.145 |
| 11 | 10.368 | 9.787 | 9.253 | 8.760 | 8.306 | 7.887 | 7.499 | 7.139 | 6.805 | 6.495 |
| 12 | 11.255 | 10.575 | 9.954 | 9.385 | 8.863 | 8.384 | 7.943 | 7.536 | 7.161 | 6.814 |
| 13 | 12.134 | 11.348 | 10.635 | 9.986 | 9.394 | 8.853 | 8.358 | 7.904 | 7.487 | 7.103 |
| 14 | 13.004 | 12.106 | 11.296 | 10.563 | 9.899 | 9.295 | 8.746 | 8.244 | 7.786 | 7.367 |
| 15 | 13.865 | 12.849 | 11.938 | 11.118 | 10.380 | 9.712 | 9.108 | 8.560 | 8.061 | 7.606 |
| 16 | 14.718 | 13.578 | 12.561 | 11.652 | 10.838 | 10.106 | 9.447 | 8.851 | 8.313 | 7.824 |
| 17 | 15.562 | 14.292 | 13.166 | 12.166 | 11.274 | 10.477 | 9.763 | 9.122 | 8.544 | 8.022 |
| 18 | 16.398 | 14.992 | 13.754 | 12.659 | 11.690 | 10.828 | 10.059 | 9.372 | 8.756 | 8.201 |
| 19 | 17.226 | 15.679 | 14.324 | 13.134 | 12.085 | 11.158 | 10.336 | 9.604 | 8.950 | 8.365 |
| 20 | 18.046 | 16.352 | 14.878 | 13.590 | 12.462 | 11.470 | 10.594 | 9.818 | 9.129 | 8.514 |
| 21 | 18.857 | 17.011 | 15.415 | 14.029 | 12.821 | 11.764 | 10.836 | 10.017 | 9.292 | 8.649 |
| 22 | 19.661 | 17.658 | 15.937 | 14.451 | 13.163 | 12.042 | 11.061 | 10.201 | 9.442 | 8.772 |
| 23 | 20.456 | 18.292 | 16.444 | 14.857 | 13.489 | 12.303 | 11.272 | 10.371 | 9.580 | 8.883 |
| 24 | 21.244 | 18.914 | 16.936 | 15.247 | 13.799 | 12.550 | 11.469 | 10.529 | 9.707 | 8.985 |
| 25 | 22.023 | 19.524 | 17.413 | 15.622 | 14.094 | 12.783 | 11.654 | 10.675 | 9.823 | 9.077 |
| 30 | 25.808 | 22.397 | 19.601 | 17.292 | 15.373 | 13.765 | 12.409 | 11.258 | 10.274 | 9.427 |
| 40 | 32.835 | 27.356 | 23.115 | 19.793 | 17.159 | 15.046 | 13.332 | 11.925 | 10.757 | 9.779 |
| 50 | 39.197 | 31.424 | 25.730 | 21.482 | 18.256 | 15.762 | 13.801 | 12.234 | 10.962 | 9.915 |

**Appendix D** PRESENT VALUE OF ANNUITY OF $1 FOR *n* PERIODS (*cont.*)

| n | 11% | 12% | 13% | 14% | 15% | 16% | 17% | 18% | 19% | 20% |
|---|---|---|---|---|---|---|---|---|---|---|
| 1 | .901 | .893 | .885 | .877 | .870 | .862 | .855 | .847 | .840 | .833 |
| 2 | 1.713 | 1.690 | 1.668 | 1.647 | 1.626 | 1.605 | 1.585 | 1.566 | 1.547 | 1.528 |
| 3 | 2.444 | 2.402 | 2.361 | 2.322 | 2.283 | 2.246 | 2.210 | 2.174 | 2.140 | 2.106 |
| 4 | 3.102 | 3.037 | 2.974 | 2.914 | 2.855 | 2.798 | 2.743 | 2.690 | 2.639 | 2.589 |
| 5 | 3.696 | 3.605 | 3.517 | 3.433 | 3.352 | 3.274 | 3.199 | 3.127 | 3.058 | 2.991 |
| 6 | 4.231 | 4.111 | 3.998 | 3.889 | 3.784 | 3.685 | 3.589 | 3.498 | 3.410 | 3.326 |
| 7 | 4.712 | 4.564 | 4.423 | 4.288 | 4.160 | 4.039 | 3.922 | 3.812 | 3.706 | 3.605 |
| 8 | 5.146 | 4.968 | 4.799 | 4.639 | 4.487 | 4.344 | 4.207 | 4.078 | 3.954 | 3.837 |
| 9 | 5.537 | 5.328 | 5.132 | 4.946 | 4.772 | 4.607 | 4.451 | 4.303 | 4.163 | 4.031 |
| 10 | 5.889 | 5.650 | 5.426 | 5.216 | 5.019 | 4.833 | 4.659 | 4.494 | 4.339 | 4.192 |
| 11 | 6.207 | 5.938 | 5.687 | 5.453 | 5.234 | 5.029 | 4.836 | 4.656 | 4.487 | 4.327 |
| 12 | 6.492 | 6.194 | 5.918 | 5.660 | 5.421 | 5.197 | 4.988 | 4.793 | 4.611 | 4.439 |
| 13 | 6.750 | 6.424 | 6.122 | 5.842 | 5.583 | 5.342 | 5.118 | 4.910 | 4.715 | 4.533 |
| 14 | 6.982 | 6.628 | 6.303 | 6.002 | 5.724 | 5.468 | 5.229 | 5.008 | 4.802 | 4.611 |
| 15 | 7.191 | 6.811 | 6.462 | 6.142 | 5.847 | 5.575 | 5.324 | 5.092 | 4.876 | 4.675 |
| 16 | 7.379 | 6.974 | 6.604 | 6.265 | 5.954 | 5.669 | 5.405 | 5.162 | 4.938 | 4.730 |
| 17 | 7.549 | 7.120 | 6.729 | 6.373 | 6.047 | 5.749 | 5.475 | 5.222 | 4.990 | 4.775 |
| 18 | 7.702 | 7.250 | 6.840 | 6.467 | 6.128 | 5.818 | 5.534 | 5.273 | 5.033 | 4.812 |
| 19 | 7.839 | 7.366 | 6.938 | 6.550 | 6.198 | 5.877 | 5.585 | 5.316 | 5.070 | 4.843 |
| 20 | 7.963 | 7.469 | 7.025 | 6.623 | 6.259 | 5.929 | 5.628 | 5.353 | 5.101 | 4.870 |
| 21 | 8.075 | 7.562 | 7.102 | 6.687 | 6.312 | 5.973 | 5.665 | 5.384 | 5.127 | 4.891 |
| 22 | 8.176 | 7.645 | 7.170 | 6.743 | 6.359 | 6.011 | 5.696 | 5.410 | 5.149 | 4.909 |
| 23 | 8.266 | 7.718 | 7.230 | 6.792 | 6.399 | 6.044 | 5.723 | 5.432 | 5.167 | 4.925 |
| 24 | 8.348 | 7.784 | 7.283 | 6.835 | 6.434 | 6.073 | 5.747 | 5.451 | 5.182 | 4.937 |
| 25 | 8.442 | 7.843 | 7.330 | 6.873 | 6.464 | 6.097 | 5.766 | 5.467 | 5.195 | 4.948 |
| 30 | 8.694 | 8.055 | 7.496 | 7.003 | 6.566 | 6.177 | 5.829 | 5.517 | 5.235 | 4.979 |
| 40 | 8.951 | 8.244 | 7.634 | 7.105 | 6.642 | 6.233 | 5.871 | 5.548 | 5.258 | 4.997 |
| 50 | 9.042 | 8.305 | 7.675 | 7.133 | 6.661 | 6.246 | 5.880 | 5.554 | 5.262 | 4.999 |

**Appendix D**  PRESENT VALUE OF AN ANNUITY OF $1 FOR *n* PERIODS (*cont.*)

| n | 21% | 22% | 23% | 24% | 25% | 26% | 27% | 28% | 29% | 30% |
|---|-----|-----|-----|-----|-----|-----|-----|-----|-----|-----|
| 1 | .826 | .820 | .813 | .806 | .800 | .794 | .787 | .781 | .775 | .769 |
| 2 | 1.509 | 1.492 | 1.474 | 1.457 | 1.440 | 1.424 | 1.407 | 1.392 | 1.376 | 1.361 |
| 3 | 2.074 | 2.042 | 2.011 | 1.981 | 1.952 | 1.923 | 1.896 | 1.868 | 1.842 | 1.816 |
| 4 | 2.540 | 2.494 | 2.448 | 2.404 | 2.362 | 2.320 | 2.280 | 2.241 | 2.203 | 2.166 |
| 5 | 2.926 | 2.864 | 2.803 | 2.745 | 2.689 | 2.635 | 2.583 | 2.532 | 2.483 | 2.436 |
| 6 | 3.245 | 3.167 | 3.092 | 3.020 | 2.951 | 2.885 | 2.821 | 2.759 | 2.700 | 2.643 |
| 7 | 3.508 | 3.416 | 3.327 | 3.242 | 3.161 | 3.083 | 3.009 | 2.937 | 2.868 | 2.802 |
| 8 | 3.726 | 3.619 | 3.518 | 3.421 | 3.329 | 3.241 | 3.156 | 3.076 | 2.999 | 2.925 |
| 9 | 3.905 | 3.786 | 3.673 | 3.566 | 3.463 | 3.366 | 3.273 | 3.184 | 3.100 | 3.019 |
| 10 | 4.054 | 3.923 | 3.799 | 3.682 | 3.570 | 3.465 | 3.364 | 3.269 | 3.178 | 3.092 |
| 11 | 4.177 | 4.035 | 3.902 | 3.776 | 3.656 | 3.544 | 3.437 | 3.335 | 3.239 | 3.147 |
| 12 | 4.278 | 4.127 | 3.985 | 3.851 | 3.725 | 3.606 | 3.493 | 3.387 | 3.286 | 3.190 |
| 13 | 4.362 | 4.203 | 4.053 | 3.912 | 3.780 | 3.656 | 3.538 | 3.427 | 3.322 | 3.223 |
| 14 | 4.432 | 4.265 | 4.108 | 3.962 | 3.824 | 3.695 | 3.573 | 3.459 | 3.351 | 3.249 |
| 15 | 4.489 | 4.315 | 4.153 | 4.001 | 3.859 | 3.726 | 3.601 | 3.483 | 3.373 | 3.268 |
| 16 | 4.536 | 4.357 | 4.189 | 4.033 | 3.887 | 3.751 | 3.623 | 3.503 | 3.390 | 3.283 |
| 17 | 4.576 | 4.391 | 4.219 | 4.059 | 3.910 | 3.771 | 3.640 | 3.518 | 3.403 | 3.295 |
| 18 | 4.608 | 4.419 | 4.243 | 4.080 | 3.928 | 3.786 | 3.654 | 3.529 | 3.413 | 3.304 |
| 19 | 4.635 | 4.442 | 4.263 | 4.097 | 3.942 | 3.799 | 3.664 | 3.539 | 3.421 | 3.311 |
| 20 | 4.657 | 4.460 | 4.279 | 4.110 | 3.954 | 3.808 | 3.673 | 3.546 | 3.427 | 3.316 |
| 21 | 4.675 | 4.476 | 4.292 | 4.121 | 3.963 | 3.816 | 3.679 | 3.551 | 3.432 | 3.320 |
| 22 | 4.690 | 4.488 | 4.302 | 4.130 | 3.970 | 3.822 | 3.684 | 3.556 | 3.436 | 3.323 |
| 23 | 4.703 | 4.499 | 4.311 | 4.137 | 3.976 | 3.827 | 3.689 | 3.559 | 3.438 | 3.325 |
| 24 | 4.713 | 4.507 | 4.318 | 4.143 | 3.981 | 3.831 | 3.692 | 3.562 | 3.441 | 3.327 |
| 25 | 4.721 | 4.514 | 4.323 | 4.147 | 3.985 | 3.834 | 3.694 | 3.564 | 3.442 | 3.329 |
| 30 | 4.746 | 4.534 | 4.339 | 4.160 | 3.995 | 3.842 | 3.701 | 3.569 | 3.447 | 3.332 |
| 40 | 4.760 | 4.544 | 4.347 | 4.166 | 3.999 | 3.846 | 3.703 | 3.571 | 3.448 | 3.333 |
| 50 | 4.762 | 4.545 | 4.348 | 4.167 | 4.000 | 3.846 | 3.704 | 3.571 | 3.448 | 3.333 |

**Appendix D** PRESENT VALUE OF AN ANNUITY OF $1 FOR $n$ PERIODS (cont.)

| n | 31% | 32% | 33% | 34% | 35% | 36% | 37% | 38% | 39% | 40% |
|---|-----|-----|-----|-----|-----|-----|-----|-----|-----|-----|
| 1 | .763 | .758 | .752 | .746 | .741 | .735 | .730 | .725 | .719 | .714 |
| 2 | 1.346 | 1.331 | 1.317 | 1.303 | 1.289 | 1.276 | 1.263 | 1.250 | 1.237 | 1.224 |
| 3 | 1.791 | 1.766 | 1.742 | 1.719 | 1.696 | 1.673 | 1.652 | 1.630 | 1.609 | 1.589 |
| 4 | 2.130 | 2.096 | 2.062 | 2.029 | 1.997 | 1.966 | 1.935 | 1.906 | 1.877 | 1.849 |
| 5 | 2.390 | 2.345 | 2.302 | 2.260 | 2.220 | 2.181 | 2.143 | 2.106 | 2.070 | 2.035 |
| 6 | 2.588 | 2.534 | 2.483 | 2.433 | 2.385 | 2.339 | 2.294 | 2.251 | 2.209 | 2.168 |
| 7 | 2.739 | 2.677 | 2.619 | 2.562 | 2.508 | 2.455 | 2.404 | 2.355 | 2.308 | 2.263 |
| 8 | 2.854 | 2.786 | 2.721 | 2.658 | 2.598 | 2.540 | 2.485 | 2.432 | 2.380 | 2.331 |
| 9 | 2.942 | 2.868 | 2.798 | 2.730 | 2.665 | 2.603 | 2.544 | 2.487 | 2.432 | 2.379 |
| 10 | 3.009 | 2.930 | 2.855 | 2.784 | 2.715 | 2.649 | 2.587 | 2.527 | 2.469 | 2.414 |
| 11 | 3.060 | 2.978 | 2.899 | 2.824 | 2.752 | 2.683 | 2.618 | 2.555 | 2.496 | 2.438 |
| 12 | 3.100 | 3.013 | 2.931 | 2.853 | 2.779 | 2.708 | 2.641 | 2.576 | 2.515 | 2.456 |
| 13 | 3.129 | 3.040 | 2.956 | 2.876 | 2.799 | 2.727 | 2.658 | 2.592 | 2.529 | 2.469 |
| 14 | 3.152 | 3.061 | 2.974 | 2.892 | 2.814 | 2.740 | 2.670 | 2.603 | 2.539 | 2.477 |
| 15 | 3.170 | 3.076 | 2.988 | 2.905 | 2.825 | 2.750 | 2.679 | 2.611 | 2.546 | 2.484 |
| 16 | 3.183 | 3.088 | 2.999 | 2.914 | 2.834 | 2.757 | 2.685 | 2.616 | 2.551 | 2.489 |
| 17 | 3.193 | 3.097 | 3.007 | 2.921 | 2.840 | 2.763 | 2.690 | 2.621 | 2.555 | 2.492 |
| 18 | 3.201 | 3.104 | 3.012 | 2.926 | 2.844 | 2.767 | 2.693 | 2.624 | 2.557 | 2.494 |
| 19 | 3.207 | 3.109 | 3.017 | 2.930 | 2.848 | 2.770 | 2.696 | 2.626 | 2.559 | 2.496 |
| 20 | 3.211 | 3.113 | 3.020 | 2.933 | 2.850 | 2.772 | 2.698 | 2.627 | 2.561 | 2.497 |
| 21 | 3.215 | 3.116 | 3.023 | 2.935 | 2.852 | 2.773 | 2.699 | 2.629 | 2.562 | 2.498 |
| 22 | 3.217 | 3.118 | 3.025 | 2.936 | 2.853 | 2.775 | 2.700 | 2.629 | 2.562 | 2.498 |
| 23 | 3.219 | 3.120 | 3.026 | 2.938 | 2.854 | 2.775 | 2.701 | 2.630 | 2.563 | 2.499 |
| 24 | 3.221 | 3.121 | 3.027 | 2.939 | 2.855 | 2.776 | 2.701 | 2.630 | 2.563 | 2.499 |
| 25 | 3.222 | 3.122 | 3.028 | 2.939 | 2.856 | 2.776 | 2.702 | 2.631 | 2.563 | 2.499 |
| 30 | 3.225 | 3.124 | 3.030 | 2.941 | 2.857 | 2.777 | 2.702 | 2.631 | 2.564 | 2.500 |
| 40 | 3.226 | 3.125 | 3.030 | 2.941 | 2.857 | 2.778 | 2.703 | 2.632 | 2.564 | 2.500 |
| 50 | 3.226 | 3.125 | 3.030 | 2.941 | 2.857 | 2.778 | 2.703 | 2.632 | 2.564 | 2.500 |

# ANSWERS TO SELF-TESTS

| Chapter 1 | Chapter 2 | Chapter 3 | Chapter 4 |
|-----------|-----------|-----------|-----------|
| TRUE-FALSE | TRUE-FALSE | TRUE-FALSE | TRUE-FALSE |
| 1. F | 1. F | 1. F | 1. T |
| 2. T | 2. F | 2. T | 2. T |
| 3. F | 3. T | 3. F | 3. F |
| 4. T | 4. T | 4. T | 4. T |
| 5. T | 5. F | 5. T | 5. F |
| 6. F | 6. T | 6. F | 6. T |
| 7. F | 7. F | 7. T | 7. F |
| 8. T | 8. T | 8. F | 8. F |
| 9. T | 9. F | 9. T | 9. T |
| 10. F | 10. F | 10. T | 10. F |
| | 11. F | | |
| | 12. F | | |

| Chapter 1 | Chapter 2 | Chapter 3 | Chapter 4 |
|---|---|---|---|
| MULTIPLE CHOICE | MULTIPLE CHOICE | MULTIPLE CHOICE | MULTIPLE CHOICE |
| 1. d | 1. a | 1. b | 1. c |
| 2. e | 2. e | 2. e | 2. e |
| 3. e | 3. e | 3. a | 3. e |
| 4. e | 4. a | 4. d | 4. c |
| 5. d | 5. b | 5. b | 5. e |
| 6. d | 6. c | 6. b | 6. c |
| 7. c | 7. c | 7. d | |
| | 8. b | 8. d | |
| | 9. e | 9. c | |
| | 10. c | 10. b | |

| Chapter 5 | Chapter 6 | Chapter 7 | Chapter 8 |
|---|---|---|---|
| TRUE-FALSE | TRUE-FALSE | TRUE-FALSE | TRUE-FALSE |
| 1. T | 1. F | 1. F | 1. F |
| 2. T | 2. F | 2. F | 2. T |
| 3. F | 3. T | 3. T | 3. T |
| 4. T | 4. F | 4. F | 4. F |
| 5. T | 5. T | 5. T | 5. F |
| 6. T | 6. T | 6. F | 6. F |
| 7. T | 7. F | 7. T | 7. F |
| 8. F | 8. T | 8. F | 8. F |
| | 9. F | 9. F | 9. T |
| | 10. T | 10. F | 10. F |
| | | | 11. T |
| | | | 12. T |
| | | | 13. T |
| | | | 14. F |
| | | | 15. F |

| MULTIPLE CHOICE | MULTIPLE CHOICE | MULTIPLE CHOICE | MULTIPLE CHOICE |
|---|---|---|---|
| 1. a | 1. d | 1. a | 1. d |
| 2. c | 2. f | 2. d | 2. d |
| 3. d | 3. c | 3. c | 3. d |
| 4. b | 4. a | 4. a | 4. c |
| | 5. c | 5. d | 5. c |
| | 6. e | | |

| Chapter 9 | Chapter 10 | Chapter 11 | Chapter 12 |
|-----------|------------|------------|------------|
| TRUE-FALSE | TRUE-FALSE | TRUE-FALSE | TRUE-FALSE |
| 1. F | 1. F | 1. T | 1. F |
| 2. T | 2. F | 2. T | 2. T |
| 3. T | 3. T | 3. T | 3. F |
| 4. T | 4. F | 4. T | 4. T |
| 5. F | 5. F | 5. T | 5. F |
| 6. T | 6. T | 6. F | 6. F |
| 7. T | 7. F | 7. F | 7. T |
| 8. F | 8. F | 8. F | 8. T |
| 9. T | 9. T | 9. T | 9. F |
| 10. F | 10. T | 10. T | 10. T |

| MULTIPLE CHOICE | MULTIPLE CHOICE | MULTIPLE CHOICE | MULTIPLE CHOICE |
|-----------------|-----------------|-----------------|-----------------|
| 1. c | 1. c | 1. c | 1. b |
| 2. c | 2. b | 2. e | 2. c |
| 3. b | 3. a | 3. a | 3. c |
| 4. e | 4. c | 4. c | 4. b |
| 5. d | 5. b | 5. e | |
| 6. d | 6. b | | |

| Chapter 13 | Chapter 14 | Appendix 14A | Chapter 15 |
|------------|------------|--------------|------------|
| TRUE-FALSE | TRUE-FALSE | TRUE-FALSE | TRUE-FALSE |
| 1. T | 1. F | 1. T | 1. F |
| 2. T | 2. F | 2. F | 2. F |
| 3. T | 3. T | 3. F | 3. T |
| 4. F | 4. F | 4. T | 4. F |
| 5. F | 5. F | 5. F | 5. F |
| 6. F | 6. T | | 6. T |
| 7. T | 7. F | | 7. T |
| 8. T | 8. T | | 8. T |
| 9. T | 9. T | | 9. F |
| 10. T | 10. T | | 10. T |
| 11. T | | | |
| 12. F | | | |

| Chapter 13 | Chapter 14 | Appendix 14A | Chapter 15 |
|---|---|---|---|
| MULTIPLE CHOICE | MULTIPLE CHOICE | MULTIPLE CHOICE | MULTIPLE CHOICE |
| 1. a | 1. f | 1. b | 1. c |
| 2. a | 2. d | 2. c | 2. c |
| b. b | 3. b | 3. b | 3. a |
| 4. e | 4. d | 4. b | 4. a & b |
| 5. a | 5. b | | 5. d |
| 6. d | | | 6. b |
| 7. c | | | 7. b |
| 8. b | | | 8. b |

| Chapter 16 | Chapter 17 | Chapter 18 | Chapter 19 |
|---|---|---|---|
| TRUE-FALSE | TRUE-FALSE | TRUE-FALSE | TRUE-FALSE |
| 1. T | 1. T | 1. F | 1. F |
| 2. T | 2. F | 2. T | 2. T |
| 3. F | 3. F | 3. F | 3. T |
| 4. T | 4. F | 4. F | 4. T |
| 5. F | 5. T | 5. F | 5. F |
| 6. F | 6. F | 6. F | 6. T |
| 7. T | 7. T | 7. T | 7. T |
| 8. T | 8. T | 8. T | 8. F |
| 9. F | 9. F | 9. F | 9. T |
| 10. T | 10. T | 10. T | 10. T |
| MULTIPLE CHOICE | MULTIPLE CHOICE | MULTIPLE CHOICE | MULTIPLE CHOICE |
| 1. b | 1. b | 1. c | 1. a |
| 2. c | 2. d | 2. d | 2. a |
| 3. b | 3. d | 3. e | 3. a |
| 4. d | 4. c | 4. b | 4. e |
| 5. e | 5. d | 5. b | 5. f |
| 6. a | 6. d | 6. a | |
| | 7. d | 7. c | |
| | 8. e | 8. d | |
| | 9. f | | |
| | 10. b | | |
| | 11. b | | |

| Chapter 20 | Chapter 21 | Chapter 22 | Chapter 23 |
|------------|------------|------------|------------|
| TRUE-FALSE | TRUE-FALSE | TRUE-FALSE | TRUE-FALSE |

| Chapter 20 | Chapter 21 | Chapter 22 | Chapter 23 |
|------------|------------|------------|------------|
| 1. F | 1. T | 1. T | 1. F |
| 2. F | 2. F | 2. T | 2. F |
| 3. F | 3. F | 3. F | 3. F |
| 4. F | 4. F | 4. T | 4. T |
| 5. F | 5. T | 5. F | 5. F |
| 6. T | 6. F | 6. F | 6. T |
| 7. T | 7. T | 7. F | 7. F |
| 8. F | 8. F | 8. F | 8. F |
| 9. F | 9. T | 9. T | 9. F |
| 10. F | 10. T | | 10. T |

| MULTIPLE CHOICE | MULTIPLE CHOICE | MULTIPLE CHOICE | MULTIPLE CHOICE |
|------------|------------|------------|------------|
| 1. d | 1. c | 1. d | 1. c |
| 2. d | 2. a | 2. e | 2. d |
| 3. d | 3. b | 3. c | 3. a |
| 4. c | 4. b | 4. a | 4. b |
| 5. b | 5. c | | 5. b |
| 6. d | | | 6. d |